# Women and Gender in the Qur'an

# Women and Gender in the Qur'an

CELENE IBRAHIM

OXFORD
UNIVERSITY PRESS

OXFORD
UNIVERSITY PRESS

Oxford University Press is a department of the University of Oxford. It furthers the University's objective of excellence in research, scholarship, and education by publishing worldwide. Oxford is a registered trade mark of Oxford University Press in the UK and certain other countries.

Published in the United States of America by Oxford University Press
198 Madison Avenue, New York, NY 10016, United States of America.



Library of Congress Cataloging-in-Publication Data
Names: Ibrahim, Celene, author.
Title: Women and gender in the Qur'an / Celene Ibrahim.
Description: New York : Oxford University Press, 2020. |
Includes bibliographical references and index.
Identifiers: LCCN 2020010449 (print) | LCCN 2020010450 (ebook) |
ISBN 9780190063818 (hardback) | ISBN 9780190063832 (epub) |
ISBN 9780190063825 (updf) | ISBN 9780190063849 (digital online)
Subjects: LCSH: Women in the Qur'an. | Qur'an—Criticism, interpretation, etc. | Women in Islam.
Classification: LCC BP134.W6 I27 2020 (print) |
LCC BP134.W6 (ebook) | DDC 297.1/2283054—dc23
LC record available at https://lccn.loc.gov/2020010449
LC ebook record available at https://lccn.loc.gov/2020010450

7 9 8 6

Printed by Sheridan Books, Inc., United States of America

*To my daughter, Rahma Ibrahim, with admiration for her delightful audacity, wit, and fierce willpower.*

# Contents

# Preface

The Qur'an is a source of moral and ethical guidance for more than a billion people in the contemporary world; it is esteemed by many as the unadulterated Word of God. Exegesis of the Qur'an, especially with regard to themes as primal and contentious as sex and gender, can sway opinions, influence subcultures, and inspire minds. In this book, I analyze Qur'anic depictions of women's political agency, public voice, and other such themes, with sensitivity to the importance of these topics in devotional contexts. The work contributes to the dynamic field of Qur'anic studies—in both its secular and confessional modalities.

In a recent work, Aysha Hidayatullah argues that sexual difference, as depicted in the Qur'an, is "based not on fixed binaries but rather on constructive, interdependent relationality" wherein "difference does not derive from one's self-generated 'uniqueness' but rather from a dynamic and relative contrast with the other."[1] Drawing inspiration from the writing of other contemporary feminists, Hidayatullah pushes back against a trend in exegesis whereby the male human being is depicted as the normative prototype and the female is portrayed as a necessary—but less interesting, and potentially inferior—permutation of the normative masculine ideal. Hidayatullah argues against reifying "essential, fixed, self-same differences between men and women," but she recognizes that there are certain "material, embodied differences" between genders.[2] Does the Qur'an, we might ask, depict women and girls as less interesting or inferior permutations of a normative masculine ideal? How does the Qur'an depict embodied women in the context of its stories and parables? What is the extent of female agency, faith, wisdom, knowledge, and proximity to God? Do Qur'anic depictions of women's faith, wisdom, and knowledge differ in any substantial way from qualities with which men are endowed?

Before we engage much further in debates about sex, sexuality, and gender in the Qur'an, a few preliminary observations will allow me to better situate this work. Indisputably, exegesis by women scholars has lagged in Islamic intellectual history, a trend that is also reflected in other domains of knowledge production. Asma Sayeed, for one, traces in detail the "fluctuating fortunes" of early Muslim women religious scholars and finds that "women's initial participation—a largely ad hoc, unregulated enterprise—was sharply curtailed by the professionalization of this field in the early second/eighth century" but was "somewhat resuscitated" in the mid-fourth/tenth century.[3] Sayeed draws a key distinction between the initial generation of women authorities who were companions of the Prophet Muḥammad (d. 11/632) and who are credited with generating new Islamic knowledge in matters of law, ritual, and creed, and the later women scholars who were "honored primarily as faithful reproducers" of key texts, but who did not author their own works.[4]

Likewise, in her study of gender in early exegetical works, Aisha Geissinger notes the social contexts that resulted in a dearth of women's "authorial ingenuity"; a work by Nānā Asmāʾu (d. 1280/1864), the daughter of Shehu Usmān dan Fodio of the West African Sokoto caliphate, is, according to Geissinger, "the only example of a text pertaining to the Quran written by a woman prior to the late nineteenth century CE."[5] As Geissinger observes, this work, "while indicative of the breadth of Nana Asmāʾu's knowledge and stature," is not primarily an original work of exegesis.[6] Geissinger further observes that the "limited involvement" for a "small number of women from scholarly families" rendered women scholars somewhat "marginal and subsidiary within transhistorical exegetical communities."[7]

Similarly, Ahmed El Shamsy summarizes the social contexts in which premodern orthodoxy took shape and the factors that resulted in the "conspicuous absence" of women scholars at the upper echelons of most fields of Islamic knowledge:

> Given that the process of transmitting knowledge was based on an intimate relationship between student and teacher, the socially prescribed distance between the sexes severely curtailed women's opportunities to become apprentices to famous scholars. In effect, such apprenticeships were possible only in the rare instances when the senior scholar was female or the student's close relative. This is not to deny that women attended the public lectures of jurists, traditionists,[8] theologians, Sufis and other scholars. However, women were rarely among the closest or most advanced students of the teacher. In general, although there are countless examples of highly educated women in the medieval Islamic world, they are conspicuously absent in the production of scholarly literature and do not feature in the top echelons of any field of study. The

> only real exception to this trend is represented by the study of prophetic traditions [hadith].[9]

In so acknowledging that women scholars played a relatively marginal role, historically speaking, in the development of Qur'anic exegesis, we might ask: Are the factors that led to a relative dearth of women's voices among the ranks of influential authors and exegetes in any way rooted in, or explained by, Qur'anic depictions of women's spiritual or intellectual aptitude? If the answer is a resounding "no"—that rather, the relative marginalization of women scholars is attributable to social factors, and is *not* intrinsically related to women's capacity for insight—then we might elicit works of exegesis from women scholars. Hence, in this book I am something akin to a female exegete (*mufassira*), and I engage the work of my colleagues who are also leveraging means of production and networks made possible by the secular academy. At the same time, I do not engage directly with the Qur'an's claim of providential origin so as to ensure that this work is accessible to audiences of varying theological commitments; I intentionally avoid the issue of authorship by using phrases such as "the Qur'an says..." or "the Qur'an contains...."

Why are insights from another *mufassira*-type warranted? Fatima Seedat summarizes the potential for women's scholarship on the Qur'an not only to ameliorate a historic lacuna but also to provide perspective: "the recognition of women scholars of *tafsir* [Qur'anic exegesis] is more than a simple historical correction to their absence but a necessary realignment of the trajectory between the Creator, the text, and the addressee that identifies women as learned scholars and readers of the text."[10] The "realignment" that Seedat describes entails deconstructing assumptions and correcting some derogatory assertions about women that have unfortunately been grounded within a devotional episteme.[11] On the constructive side, my research has identified multiple aspects of the Qur'an that can be seen as "female-affirming," aspects that have not yet been fully appreciated in existing literature.[12]

Such an open acknowledgment of the need for reappraisal and for an expansion does not delegitimize or derail the entire exegetical edifice and heritage, as those situated within this episteme may fear. Rather, to abandon deconstructive critique in a contemporary political climate exacerbated by bombastic neo-colonial rhetoric and flagrant anti-Muslim bias is to risk surrendering the enterprise of Islamic knowledge production to those with potentially less benevolent objectives. Constructive critique, then, is necessary for the continued salience and vibrancy of the intellectual tradition for new generations of Muslims.

Structural barriers and challenges to the full participation of women exegetes and minoritized persons remain; at the same time, one can hope for a continuing expansion of the boundaries of Qur'anic studies in the academy.[13] In particular, I hope that this book encourages more "believing women" with academic rigor to pursue Qur'anic scholarship so as to keep alive the heritage of our foremothers who helped found and sustain a scholarly tradition. Their legacies reassure me that new generations of exegetes will—despite the headwinds—continue striving to influence and inspire, to acquire knowledge, and to do this, *in shāʾ Allāh,* with a spirit of humility and resolve.

Celene Ibrahim
27 Ramadan 1440
June 1, 2019

## Notes

1. Aysha A. Hidayatullah, *Feminist Edges of the Qur'an* (New York: Oxford University Press, 2014), 189. See also Sachiko Murata, *The Tao of Islam: A Sourcebook on Gender Relationships in Islamic Thought* (Albany: State University of New York Press, 1992).
2. Hidayatullah, *Feminist Edges*, 189–90. See related discussions in Fatima Seedat, "On Spiritual Subjects: Negotiations in Muslim Female Spirituality," *Journal of Gender and Religion in Africa* 22, no. 1 (2006): 27–30. Similarly, in her recent exploration of Qur'anic women figures, Georgina L. Jardim laments that the "liberative import" of female figures in the Qur'an is too frequently overlooked and that treatment of these figures in devotional contexts is often curtailed to discussions of "qualities to imitate or to avoid." See Jardim, *Recovering the Female Voice in Islamic Scripture: Women and Silence* (New York: Routledge, 2016), 7–8.
3. Asma Sayeed, *Women and the Transmission of Religious Knowledge in Islam* (New York: Cambridge University Press, 2013), 2–3. Aisha Geissinger offers a few examples of women scholars from scholarly families who were "on what could be termed the fringes of quranic exegesis"; see Aisha Geissinger, *Gender and Muslim Constructions of Exegetical Authority: A Rereading of the Classical Genre of Qurʾān Commentary* (Leiden: Brill, 2015), 269. For an analysis of women's epistemic authority in comparison to that of men, see Ahmed Ragab, "Epistemic Authority of Women in the Medieval Middle East," *Hawwa: Journal of Women of the Middle East and the Islamic World* 8, no. 2 (2010): 190–214.

4. Sayeed, *Women and the Transmission.*
5. See Geissinger, *Gender and Muslim Constructions*, 272.
6. Ibid.
7. Ibid., 274. Geissinger speculates: "if any pre-modern woman (or women) wrote an exegetical work which remains to be discovered, it would likely have similar characteristics [to the text by Nana Asmāʾu], in being more akin to transmission than authorial creation" (273).
8. This term refers to hadith scholars. Hadith are a vast corpus of the purported sayings, teachings, and actions of the Prophet Muḥammad and consist of reports from his companions and their successors; they began predominantly as an oral tradition and were later compiled in compendia.
9. See Ahmed El Shamsy, "The Social Construction of Orthodoxy," in *The Cambridge Companion to Classical Islamic Theology*, ed. Tim Winter (Cambridge: Cambridge University Press, 2008), 102. For a thorough analysis of the roles and contributions of women scholars, particularly in the domain of hadith transmission from the earliest Muslim generations through the 1500s, see Mohammad Akram Nadwi, *Al-Muḥaddithāt: The Women Scholars in Islam* (Oxford: Interface Publications, 2013). For an analysis of this topic from the third/ninth century through the modern period, see Ruth Roded, *Women in Islamic Bibliographical Collections, from Ibn Saʿd to Who's Who* (Boulder, CO: Lynne Rienner, 1994).
10. See Fatima Seedat, "On the Convergence of Islam, Feminism, and Qur'anic Interpretation: A Critical Review of Aysha Hidayatullah's *Feminist Edges of the Qur'an*," *Journal of the Society for Contemporary Thought and the Islamicate World* (March 24, 2016), 6. For an overview of contentious theological issues and the approaches of Muslim feminist thinkers, see Ndeye Adújar, "Feminist Readings of the Qur'an: Social, Political, and Religious Implications," in *Muslima Theology: The Voices of Muslim Women Theologians*, ed. Elif Medeni, Ednan Aslan, and Marcia Hermansen (Frankfurt am Main: Peter Lang Verlag, 2013). For a summary of the work of Muslim women scholar-activists from the mid-twentieth century to the contemporary period, see Roxanne D. Marcotte, "Muslim Women's Scholarship and the New Gender Jihad," in *Women and Islam*, ed. Zayn R. Kassam (Santa Barbara, CA: Praeger, 2010).
11. This is not to claim that all authors exhibited derogatory tendencies; rather, such tendencies are noticeable. See Ayesha S. Chaudhry, *Domestic Violence and the Islamic Tradition: Ethics, Law and the Muslim Discourse on Gender* (New York: Oxford University Press, 2013).
12. For reflections on the concept of "believing women" as it relates to exegesis, see Asma Barlas, *"Believing Women" in Islam: Unreading Patriarchal Interpretations of the Qur'an* (Austin: University of Texas Press, 2002), 19–20.
13. For instance, in a deeply personal reckoning with Qur'anic ethics and his own position as a colored South African, a Muslim, and a liberation theologian, Farid Esack spoke poignantly of the "tests and constant battles against systems that want to either destroy us totally or make us 'good Muslims' who are Westoxicated, battling to fit in and find a seat at the side table of the Master." Farid Esack, "Lot and His Offer: 2016 IQSA Presidential Address," *Journal of the International Quranic Studies Association* 2 (2017): 31–32.

# Acknowledgments

Many mentors, colleagues, foundations, and family members have supported this endeavor. Carl Sharif El-Tobgui offered much thoughtful critique from the project's inception to its completion. Theo Calderara at Oxford University Press saw the project through from proposal to book. Valerie Joy Turner brought her extensive expertise to editing and indexing the book, and Dorothy Bauhoff provided indispensable editorial guidance. I owe special thanks to Jennifer Banks at Yale University Press for being the first to recognize the value of the project. My anonymous reviewers at Oxford, Yale, and Cambridge University Presses gave helpful feedback.

Marion Holmes Katz, Jonathan Decter, Suleyman Dost, ChaeRan Freeze, Marlyn Miller, Gregory Freeze, Sara Shostak, Joan Listernick, Shenila Khoja-Moolji, Janan Delgado, Bruce Lawrence, Nora Zaki, Tasneem Zawahreh, Umar Shareef, and Monica Poole gave feedback on my work in progress. I received research funding from the Andrew W. Mellon Foundation. The Dillon Fund at Groton School contributed toward the book's indexing. Parts of this work were presented at numerous universities and venues, including Zaytuna College and the International Institute for Islamic Thought. My gratitude goes to all the individuals who engaged with the work in progress and whose suggestions, insights, and wisdom I sought to reflect in the final work.

I am grateful for Seema Duhan and team at Zaytuna College, Or Rose and team at the Miller Center for Interreligious Learning and Leadership at Hebrew College, Suheil Laher, my colleagues and students at the Boston Islamic Seminary and at Hartford Seminary, and for my many dear former colleagues and students at Tufts University. In particular, the Reverend Gregory McGonigle and Michael Baenen worked closely with me during critical junctures to ensure that I had bandwidth to work on this project alongside my university commitments. Kecia Ali, Ousmane Kane, Marc Brettler, Bernadette Brooten, Jennifer Howe Peace, and Joseph Lumbard have been cherished mentors. I am much indebted to the inspired teaching of Leila Ahmed, Baber Johansen, Jane I. Smith, Ahmed Ragab, Elisabeth Schüssler Fiorenza, Ann Braude, Susan Abraham, and William A. Graham at Harvard University, as well as my early mentors Hossein Modarressi, Barbara

Romaine, Hisham Mahmoud, Abdellah Hammoudi, and Muhammad Qasim Zaman at Princeton University.

My life and work have been greatly enriched by the companionship and encouragement of Nayma Tasnim Islam, Seema Ahmed, Salma Kazmi, Mariam Sheibani, Cassie Webb, Carol Zahra Lee, Palak Khanna, Megan Fairweather, and the Morrissey and Sperling families. I am indebted to Cynthia Lizzio Wetzel, Salvatore Lizzio, Awatif Abu-Shaddy, Mahmud Mostafa, the Horton, Ingram, Brennecke, and Esposito families, and most immediately, Ahmed and Rahma Ibrahim.

*Wa-l-ḥamdu li-llāhi rabb al-ʿālamīn.*

# Notes on Transliteration and Translation

I have employed the Arabic transliteration system as outlined in the *International Journal of Middle East Studies* (*IJMES*). I have not transliterated terms that are increasingly common in English dictionaries, such as Qur'an, hadith, and surah. For Qur'anic names with common Anglicized forms, I give the Arabic on the first occurrence and thereafter use the English name. For figures and dates in early Islamic history, I give the Hijra date (AH, *anno hegirae*) followed by the Common Era (CE) date.

Citations from the Qur'an refer to the 1924 Cairo edition and are abbreviated by the letter Q, followed by the surah and verse number. Qur'an quotations in English are adopted from *The Study Quran,* with slight modifications. For instance, I substitute more gender-neutral terms such as "humankind" for "mankind" and employ "the human being" when translating the Arabic word *insān* ("person") and similar terms. In cases where a non-gender-specific human pronoun is implied, such as when an Arabic word signifying "person" (such as *insān*) appears with a corresponding pronoun, I gloss the term in order to differentiate, as best as can be discerned, between verses that speak to or about men or boys and verses that speak to or about human beings in a general sense. I also use simpler and more modern English expressions than the more archaic expressions in *The Study Quran* (e.g., "thee," "thou," and so forth).

In a few places where *The Study Quran* uses different terms for the same Arabic word (such as "save" in Q 28:21 and "deliver" in Q 66:11 for *najji*), I have amended translations in order to better highlight stylistic elements and intra-textual repetitions. The inverse is also true; in places where *The Study Quran* uses the same word in English to translate different terms in Arabic, I modify the translation in places to highlight nuances in the Arabic terminology (such as *nisāʾ al-nabī* versus *azwāj al-nabī*). I also depart from the system of capitalization in *The Study Quran* and instead employ guidelines from the *Chicago Manual of Style* (17th ed.).

English lacks a non-gendered pronoun to refer to God. In the Qur'an, the pronoun regularly used to refer to God (*huwa*) has a wider semantic range than the pronoun "He" does in current gender-conscious English usage. Muslim theologians do not understand God to have an ontological gender,[1] and the use of an English pronoun denoting a specific ontological gender in contemporary English parlance is not ideal. Moreover, English does not typically assign gender to entities that do not possess an ontological gender, so using a gendered pronoun for God in English is more conspicuous than it is in Arabic, a language in which all entities (both animate and inanimate) are grammatically gendered. As such, when masculine pronouns are used to signify God, readers who may be more familiar with theological paradigms wherein God is conceived of as "Father" or "Son" may need to pause to recognize that "He" does not signify a male god. Readers who are not accustomed to Qur'anic discourse may also be surprised by the alternating use of a variety of pronouns for God, including "We" (as the *pluralis majestatis*).[2]

For pronoun references to the human soul (*nafs*), which is grammatically feminine in Arabic but ostensibly not ontologically female, I employ a feminine pronoun. Many English translations employ the pronoun "it"; however, given that the human soul can be considered a higher-order entity with some rational capacity, "it" arguably falls short as a signifier.

In this work, I employ the noun "female" as a category that includes women and girls, certain non-human entities, and potentially also, as we will see, beings in paradise. When I use the term "women," it refers to a subset of human beings only. I am aware of the vast literature that gives nuance to categories of sex and gender by arguing that these categories are fluid and non-binary. In the Qur'anic discourse, however, sex-based categories of male and female are most commonly presented in a clear-cut binary way. Sex-based categories (female/male) also seem to map onto gender categories (woman/man) in a fairly straightforward way; however, there are some interesting nuances that we will examine.

Finally, I am aware that several individuals who are mentioned in this book prefer that their names appear in lowercase, including miriam cooke, bell hooks, and amina wadud. In conformity with standard style guidelines, their names are capitalized in this work.

## Notes

1. For extensive discussion of this point in relation to contemporary feminist discourses, see Abdal Hakim Murad, "Islam, Irigaray, and the Retrieval of Gender," April 1999, at http://masud.co.uk/ISLAM/ahm/gender.htm (accessed January 15, 2018). See also Barlas, *Believing Women*, 15, 94–98, 105–6.
2. For a study of pronominal shifts, see Neal Robinson, *Discovering the Qur'an: A Contemporary Approach to a Veiled Text* (Washington, DC: Georgetown University Press, 2004), 224–55.

# Abbreviations

| | |
|---|---|
| *AED* | *Arabic-English Dictionary*, Francis Joseph Steingass |
| *AEDQ* | *Arabic-English Dictionary of Qur'anic Usage*, Elsaid M. Badawi and Muhammad Abdel Haleem |
| *AEL* | *Arabic-English Lexicon*, Edward William Lane |
| *CSQ* | *Concordance of the Sublime Quran*, Laleh Bakhtiar |
| *EQ* | *Encyclopaedia of the Qurʾān*, Jane Dammen McAuliffe, ed. |
| *LA* | *Lisān al-ʿArab*, Muḥammad b. Mukarram b. Manẓūr |
| *SQ* | *The Study Quran: A New Translation and Commentary*, Seyyed Hossein Nasr et al., eds. |

# Women and Gender in the Qur'an

# Introduction

## Bearing Revelation

On the occasion of the birth of Mary (Maryam), her "Lord accepted her with a beautiful acceptance" and then "made her grow in a beautiful way" (Q 3:37). Mary is "purified by her Lord" and "chosen" for the unique task of giving birth to a "Word from Him [God]" (Q 3:42, 45). The Qur'an emphasizes the source and purpose of this revelatory impregnation: "We [God] breathed into her of Our Spirit (*rūḥ*), and We made her and her son a sign (*āya*) for the worlds" (Q 21:91). The resulting child is "a sign for humankind, and a mercy from Us [God]" (Q 19:21). To be sure, other individuals in the Qur'an are given the task of delivering God's revelatory "Word" (*kalima*) in the form of scripture, but Mary delivers God's Word in bodily form.[1]

In the surah of the Qur'an known as "The Prophets" (*al-Anbiyāʾ*), Mary features as the final individual in a long series of righteous figures, some of whom are described as "guiding imams," others as recipients of divine mercy, as possessing "judgment and knowledge," and as having been granted gifts and powers by God's leave (Q 21:71–91). The Qur'an mentions over a dozen figures as receiving divine grace and benefit in these verses. Alongside many male figures, one family and two women are featured in this particular listing: Noah (Nūḥ) and his family are saved "from great distress," and Zachariah's (Zakariyyā's) wife is "set aright for him," that is, she becomes fertile in response to Zachariah's prayer for an heir. Finally, we find "she who preserved her chastity," who then becomes, with her son, "a sign for the worlds" (Q 21:91).[2]

A "hermeneutic of suspicion" might muse about why significantly fewer women are listed in this particular litany of righteous men. Are women and girls obscured "in the narrative of Islamic prophethood, and consequently in the world of the Qur'an"?[3] Why are the women who are mentioned both described relationally—that is, through men? Why are the women depicted in the context of becoming impregnated? What do such representations imply about sex and gender in the Qur'an? And if litanies of righteous women

*Women and Gender in the Qur'an.* Celene Ibrahim, Oxford University Press (2020). © Oxford University Press.
DOI: 10.1093/oso/9780190063818.001.0001.

do not appear in quite the same way as litanies of men, where *is* the female presence?

These questions were the genesis of this project. I set out to map all the women figures in the Qur'an and to probe themes related to biological sex and female sexuality, voices, and identity. In so doing, I note the interplay between Qur'anic prophets and their mothers, wives, daughters, female supporters, and even, occasionally, adversaries. I examine how sex, as a feature of embodiment and as an act of intimacy, factors into Qur'anic depictions of human origins, sexual desires, and social behaviors. I also highlight depictions of female character, wit, and spiritual excellence and how the needs and desires of female figures often become the abiding concern of the Qur'an. I track how female figures—women, girls, old, young, barren, fertile, chaste, profligate, reproachable, and saintly—advance the Qur'an's stated didactic aims.

## Women and Girls in Qur'anic Narratives

Stories animate the Qur'an. From aristocrats to the beleaguered, from ingrates to paragons of virtue, from the actions of young women to miracles for barren matriarchs, Qur'anic narratives regularly feature women. They appear in the accounts of human origins, the stories of the founding and destruction of nations, and in narratives of conquest, family, romance, and more. The Qur'an's women figures are pious and impious, insightful and ignorant, commanding and timid, old and young, famous and obscure, married and single, ruling and ruled over, fertile and childless, and so forth. These figures are notable for their diversity of character; there is not one standard archetypal woman or girl. The Qur'an extols certain female figures and rebukes others for their moral comportment; it regularly depicts women and girls with agency and power, even when some women act immorally and to their own detriment. In their breaches and virtues, numerous women serve as exemplars for developing moral character and navigating human struggles.

Themes related to women and girls generally—in the context of family or social relations, for instance—are the subject of hundreds of Qur'anic verses. Qur'anic stories and parables mention or allude to several dozen female figures, and by my count, the Qur'an contains approximately three hundred verses that directly involve these women or girls. This work considers all the major and minor female figures referenced in the Qur'an, including those who appear in the context of narratives of sacred history, in verses that directly allude to events contemporaneous with the Qur'an, in parables, and in descriptions of the eternal abode; some appear in single verses or in the context of narratives about particular families. Only one—Mary—is referred to by first name; all others are referred to by titles (e.g., the Queen of Sheba), by their roles in the story (e.g., the women of the city), or by their familial affiliations (e.g., the wife of so-and-so).

At the outset, I offer a list of female figures in the Qur'an that aims to be comprehensive.[4] On the first usage, I employ Qur'anic appellations transliterated from Arabic, but subsequently, I use a literal translation into English. For example, I refer to *imraʾat al-ʿazīz* as "the wife of the viceroy" or "the viceroy's wife" in keeping with the Qur'an itself. Likewise, the spouse of Adam (*zawj Ādam*) is widely known as Ḥawwāʾ in Arabic (Eve in English), but I refer to her as "the wife of Adam" or "Adam's wife" in keeping as closely as possible with the Qur'anic representation.

## From Adam's Spouse (Ḥawwāʾ) to Heavenly Companions (*Ḥūrīs*)

The Qur'an includes references to the following individual women, girls, female family members, and female groups, listed according to the approximate arc of sacred history, from the primordial couple to those females in the Arabian milieu of the Prophet Muḥammad, to the beings of paradise: the spouse of Adam (*zawj Ādam*); the parents of Noah (*wālidā Nūḥ*), the family of Noah (*ahl Nūḥ*), and the wife of Noah (*imraʾat Nūḥ*); the family of Job (*ahl Ayyūb*); the family (*ahl*) of the Arabian prophet Ṣāliḥ; the parents of Abraham (*wālidā Ibrāhīm*), the family (*ahl*) and House (*āl*) of Abraham generally, and the wife of Abraham (*imraʾat Ibrāhīm*), who is the mother of their son Isaac (*Isḥāq*) and who is known in extra-Qur'anic sources as Sarah (Sāra). The list also includes the wife of Lot (*imraʾat Lūṭ*), Lot's daughters (*banāt Lūṭ*), Lot's family (*ahl*), and the House of Lot (*āl Lūṭ*) more generally.

I discuss at length the wife of the Egyptian viceroy (*imraʾat ʿazīz Miṣr*), who is widely known in extra-Qur'anic sources as Zulaykha (Zulaykhā). Figures from this narrative also include the companions of the viceroy's wife, who are referred to as "women of the town" (*niswatun fī l-madīna*), the parents of Joseph (*abawā Yūsuf*), their family (*ahl*), as well as the House of Jacob (*āl Yaʿqūb*) generally. I discuss the family and House of Moses (*āl Mūsā*), including his mother and sister, his foster mother, who is the wife of Pharaoh (*imraʾat Firʿawn*), as well as his future wife and her sister from Midian (Madyan). Narratives of the life of Moses also include the parents of a boy (*abawā ghulām*) that Moses witnesses being slain, Moses's unsuccessful wet nurses (*al-marāḍiʿ*), references to "the women of the Children of Israel" (*nisāʾ Banī Isrāʾīl*) who are oppressed by the House of Pharaoh (*āl Firʿawn*), and a reference to the House of Aaron (*āl Hārūn*), the brother of Moses.

I analyze a reference to the House of David (*āl Dāwūd*) and a reference to the parents of the prophet Solomon (*wālidā Sulaymān*). I discuss at length the Queen of Sheba (*malikat Sabaʾ*), who is widely known in extra-Qur'anic sources as Bilqīs. Attention is given to the wife of Zachariah (*imraʾat Zakariyyā*), the wife of ʿImrān (*imraʾat ʿImrān*), and Mary the mother of Jesus (ʿĪsā).

Additionally, I analyze groups of women from the Prophet Muḥammad's immediate family and other close female relations, including those referred to as "people of the house" (*ahl al-bayt*), as the "women of the prophet" (*nisāʾ al-nabī*), as the "mothers" (*ummahāt*) of the "believers" (*al-muʾminīn*), as "spouses of the Prophet" (*azwāj al-nabī*), and as "spouses" (*azwāj*) of the "Messenger of God" (*rasūl Allāh*). The Prophet Muḥammad's daughters (*banāt*) and a host of other female relations are also mentioned.

I examine other Meccan women mentioned in the Qur'an: one who is described as "the disputer" (*al-mujādila*); one referred to as "she who is examined" (*al-mumtaḥana*); and one known as the wife of Abū Lahab (*imraʾat Abī Lahab*), a vehement critic of the early Muslims who is insulted in the Qur'an with her husband and who is derided as a firewood carrier (*ḥammālat al-ḥaṭab*) in hell. A woman is mentioned briefly in the context of a parable as "she who unravels her yarn" (*allatī naqaḍat ghazlahā*), and sorceresses are referred to on one occasion as "the blowers on knots" (*al-naffāthāti fī l-ʿuqad*). There is a singular mention of an unidentified pregnant woman who, with her husband, beseeches God for a righteous child.

Multiple Qur'anic depictions of the inhabitants of paradise include beings described with grammatically feminine adjectives and pronouns. This includes terms such as the "wide-eyed" (*ḥūr ʿīn*, Anglicized as "houris"), the "good and beautiful" (*khayrātun ḥisān*), "those of restrained glances" (*qāṣirāt al-ṭarf*), the "amorous peers" (*ʿuruban atrāban*), the "adolescent-like peers" (*kawāʿiba atrāban*), the "pure spouses" (*azwāj muṭahhara*), and virgins (*abkār*).[5] We explore these categories of beings in relation to earthly women as well as other inhabitants of paradise.

## Women Personalities in Islamic Sacred History

Many women who are important in Muslim sacred history or the establishment of Islam do not appear frequently—or at all—in Qur'anic narratives. For instance, the prophet Abraham's consort (Hājar/Hagar) is not named explicitly in the Qur'anic narrative beyond general references to the household of Abraham (Ibrāhīm); yet, she is of central importance to rituals related to God's "sacred house" (*al-bayt al-ḥarām*) in Mecca.[6] As another example, the Prophet Muḥammad's first wife, Khadīja bt. Khuwaylid (d. 619 CE), made major political, financial, and other contributions to the establishment of Islam in Mecca, yet she is referred to only implicitly in the Qur'an.[7] The same can be said for many figures—both male and female—who played pivotal roles in the establishment of Islam in Arabia.

In general, the Qur'an does not refer to names of the companions of the Prophet Muḥammad, female or male; Zayd b. Ḥāritha (d. 8/629) is the only companion mentioned by name. His name appears in an episode concerning the divorce of his wife, a woman who subsequently married the Prophet Muḥammad.[8] The only other figure contemporary to the Prophet Muḥammad who is mentioned explicitly is a man known to be a paternal uncle of the Prophet; he is referred to ironically as Abū Lahab ("father of the flame"). He is rebuffed for haughtiness, and his aristocratic wife is castigated with the disparaging title "firewood carrier" (*ḥammālat al-ḥaṭab*); with her firewood, she feeds the flame (*lahab*) of hell.[9]

The Qur'an contains multiple explicit references to women who are also referenced in the Hebrew Bible or in the Christian Gospels; other potential references are less than explicit. For instance, the scandal and intrigue associated with Bathsheba in biblical literature does not play an overt role in the Qur'an; however, the figure of Bathsheba may indeed be alluded to when David mediates between two men who scale the walls of his palace to seek judgment regarding the distribution of their ewes (Q 38:21–26), as in the biblical account. After providing judgment, David repents as he realizes that judging between the men with their ewes was a trial from God (Q 38:24). God accepts David's repentance (Q 38:25) and then, in a verse addressed to David, warns (among other reminders) against following "caprice" (*hawā*) (Q 38:26). This word, *hawā*, can mean sexual desire, but it can also signify whims more generally. On account of the narrative parallels, some commentators link this reference in the Qur'an to the encounter between David and Bathsheba as narrated in the Hebrew Bible.[10] In this book,

I emphasize narratives that refer to women figures more explicitly, but I do mention more ambiguous references as well.

The Qur'an, of course, also contains many references to events that transpired during the Prophet Muḥammad's lifetime. Notable girls and women from among the companions of the Prophet, including the woman remembered as the first martyr, for instance, are not referenced explicitly in the Qur'an beyond a general address to the companions of the Prophet Muḥammad.[11] I note a few figures in the early Muslim polity who are mentioned in early biographical reports as being rather unambiguously linked to particular verses. On nearly a dozen occasions, the direct cause (*sabab*) of particular Qur'anic verses is an action, request, or specific need of a woman; several of these "occasions of revelation" (*asbāb al-nuzūl*) have axiomatic bearing on subsequent communal and ethical norms. I occasionally mention well-known events narrated in early biographies of the Prophet Muḥammad, such as the episode involving the slanderer Ḥamna bt. Jaḥsh, who is said to have been among "those who brought forth the lie" (Q 24:11). I do not address women who are related to the "cause" of a verse but who are not, to the best of my discernment, alluded to directly.[12]

## Deciphering Qur'anic Narratives

The Qur'an is—surprisingly for many who encounter its prose for the first time—not primarily invested in recounting history in a chronological order. It frequently relates narratives about the trials of Semitic prophets and their families, and it regularly alludes to events during the lifetime of the Prophet Muḥammad, but these chronologies are not, in fact, the meta-narrative at the core of the Qur'an. Taken in its entirety, the Qur'an is primarily concerned with the genesis and fate of human beings. Thus, Qur'anic discussions of events in the past—what I refer to here as sacred history—are interwoven with discussions of biodiversity on earth, the moral constitution of human beings, and the nature of other phenomenal realms, to name a few central themes. These subjects are addressed throughout the Qur'an in service of the Qur'anic aims of inculcating monotheism, promoting piety, and preparing human beings for their death and judgment in the final abode.

As is clear even to a neophyte reader or listener, the Qur'an frequently addresses the struggles unfolding in the Prophet Muḥammad's intimate family and geopolitical community, and such communal events and struggles are the immediate and often explicit context for many verses of the Qur'an. I focus on Qur'anic female figures who are mentioned explicitly, but also analyze some passages that allude to specific female personalities whose life stories unfold concurrently with the advent of new Qur'anic verses. My central focus is on the Qur'an itself; however, I occasionally refer to widely mentioned events in the biography of the Prophet Muḥammad in order to probe the relationship between the expanding corpus of the Qur'an and events that are said to have transpired during his lifetime.

Given the unique composition of the Qur'an—the result of what is widely understood to be a gradual process in Arabia in the early seventh century of the Common Era—I approach the Qur'an as an aural phenomenon, a self-proclaimed scripture, and a literary work that promulgated the religion of Islam. As a literary phenomenon, the Qur'an has distinct characteristics, including self-reflexive statements, the brief and unconventional ordering of stories, routine references to scriptural antecedents, allusions to concurrent and future events, and the prevailing presence of God as narrator. I study these literary features as they relate to Qur'anic depictions of women and femininity more broadly. My notes provide more in-depth philological observations and reference to secondary literature on linguistic and structural aspects of Qur'anic prose.[13]

The Qur'an does not retell sacred history in a linear way, and a reading or recitation of the Qur'an from cover to cover does not reveal a chronological narrative of sacred history; as such, verses involving women figures are interspersed throughout the Qur'an without an apparent chronological order. Qur'anic topography is limited, and indicators of setting and epoch are terse, in keeping with the Qur'an's overarching style. In researching this work, I examined how each female figure is situated along an arc from the genesis of humanity, through ancient peoples and their prophets, to the advent of the Qur'an in Arabia. To reconstruct such an arc of sacred history, I studied scriptural antecedents and their commentary traditions in order to better situate Qur'anic timelines and topographies. Yet, even as I trace the footsteps of female figures across the arc of sacred history, my project is not to provide a definitive rendering of events. Instead, I reflect upon the ways in which retelling the sacred past through a specific theological and ethical paradigm generates a new sacred present that is affective and didactic.[14]

Qur'anic stories at times explicitly confirm details found in biblical and extra-biblical accounts, and at other times contradict such details. The biblical and Qur'anic commentary traditions are thoroughly intertwined in a manner that cannot be easily disentangled, and often the broad contours of narratives run parallel, even if important details differ. On the whole, shared figures—including female figures—reinforce the fact that the Qur'an is engaged in dialogue with biblical and post-biblical ideas, as were some early Muslims. The dialogue continues as scholars and exegetes interact with this voluminous material in new ways. Ultimately, the intertextuality of Islamic, Jewish, and Christian exegesis is beyond the scope of the present work. I have had the good fortune of sustained conversations with scholars of early Christianity and Judaism, as well as Christian and Jewish theologians. In this sense, my engagement with pre-Qur'anic exegetical traditions is not dissimilar to the way earlier generations of Muslim exegetes may have experienced Qur'anic storytelling, that is, in part through their encounters—deliberate or fortuitous—with the stories and scriptures of other Semitic monotheisms.[15]

## The Tentative *Mufassira*

In recent decades, Muslim women exegetes have published an unprecedented number of works as a result of the political, social, and technological forces that have enabled a changing intelligentsia.[16] This most recent wave of women's writing on the Qur'an has been enabled by increased attention to gender, racial diversity, identity, and representation in Western academic institutions. Yet, even with the opportunities such institutions offer, disciplinary norms and cultures still promulgate constraints on scholars with respect to how they orient their scholarship, perform their femininity, embody their womanhood, and express their Muslim identity in the context of a historically male-dominated, Euro-American-centric, secular academic milieu.[17]

I have asked myself some key questions in writing this book: To what extent do I wish to engage existential themes while performing objectivity? Am I at liberty to intervene in the field in such a way that devotional writings are not merely the object of study, but such that their concerns become my subject? Who will police the boundaries and for what ends?[18] To what extent must this study, situated as it is in part within a secularized academy, be subject to the presumptions of a discourse that is—by virtue of its insistence on secularity—antithetical to the underlying premises of the Qur'an? Because I have reflected on such questions throughout the project, in many ways, this study has been, for me, as much an exploration of the state of Qur'anic studies and its limits as it has been an exploration of the female figures in the Qur'an. The two lines of questioning are perhaps related; both involve the re-examination of historically dominant frames of reference in intellectual climates that may not be entirely hospitable to a reappraisal.

## Power and Privilege in "Qur'anic Studies"

Qur'anic studies in the Euro-American academy arose as a subcategory of "oriental" studies. The field is a veritable methodological mélange; scholars in the field now range in ideological orientation from those whose research agenda is to affirm the Qur'an's uniqueness and sacred origins to those whose driving objective is to discredit religious claims of Qur'anic originality or conceptual coherence. Given these widely diverging motivations for engaging in the study of the Qur'an—motivations that are grounded in vastly different starting points with respect to Qur'anic origins and worth—I prefer to be clear about how my own work is embedded within the "apparatus" of a secularized episteme that is inherently skeptical of (or even openly hostile to) Muslim modes of engaging the Qur'an.[19] How much room among the ranks of academics is there for someone who is invested in Qur'anic interpretation as a source of moral guidance and sacred truth?

Well established standards in the academy often value "objective distance" and moral neutrality; this is regularly taken to be an indicator of the quality of scholarship.[20] This dynamic undermines the fact that Qur'an interpreters, even those based in the secularized academy, often *do* have personal interests in the results of their interpretations. In my case, to feign detached distance from the subject matter in this context is antithetical to the project's original impetus: if I were not invested in the outcomes and implications of the study—beyond mere curiosity or the quest for highbrow prestige—what motivation would remain? Thus, I openly concede—at the risk of being dismissed as somehow less competent—that my work is grounded in an awareness that no small number of human beings orient themselves, their actions, their understandings of their world, and their most intimate selves vis-à-vis the Qur'an.

In the larger arena of Qur'anic interpretation, and in the often ideologically driven field of Qur'anic studies, where scholars from different persuasions have disparate stakes, what can I hope to contribute in *this* study, methodologically and conceptually, to the intellectual fray? Beyond its topical scope, in what ways is this project positioned to make a distinct hermeneutic contribution? What conceptual constraints or methodological limits does this project present? What promise does it offer for understanding depictions of sex and gender in the Qur'an? To begin answering these questions, we must look to the emerging field of "Muslima theology."

## Muslima Theology and Feminist Qur'anic Exegesis

As prior scholarship in the field has shown in detail, the Qur'an affirms the presence and importance of "females" as a sex-based category.[21] The Qur'an also gives clear endorsement of male–female parity on a number of issues; but it also articulates different prescriptions for women and men, particularly in areas having to do with marriage and reproduction.[22] For some scholars, the specific rulings that are gender-differentiated are historically dependent and potentially malleable. Nimat Hafez Barazangi, for instance, advances an argument that Qur'anic principles should set in motion a "gender revolution" whereby "the entire view of male-female structure changes" such that "no limitation or advance privilege is ascribed to any group under any circumstances."[23] Aysha Hidayatullah delineates shared aims of the broad genre of Muslim feminist exegesis, among them "advocating the full personhood and moral agency of Muslim women within the parameters of the Qur'an."[24]

Questions related to sexual differences, gender, and women's religious authority are now also being approached under the rubric of "Muslima theology."[25] The present work could be included in the genre of Muslima theology, and it might even be considered a feminist *tafsīr*, as I critique in places certain interpretations that have facilitated women's domination or exclusion. I, however, prefer "female-centric" to the adjective "feminist" for this book because of the history of disputation over what constitutes "feminism" and who can be rightfully regarded as a "feminist." The descriptor "female-centric" describes this study's focus without ascribing to it a set of motives that could cloud its reception for some readers in my target audience.[26]

This work also contributes toward understanding structural elements of surah composition and aspects of overarching Qur'anic coherence. I detail instances of coherence in the macro- and micro-organization of surahs, I highlight thematic connections, and I point out provocative juxtapositions between Qur'anic figures, the situations they navigate, and the moral valences of their actions. Numerous works—classical, modern, and contemporary—address aspects of Qur'anic coherence, but none has done it through a focus on Qur'anic narratives involving female figures. Similarly, no work that is primarily interested in Qur'anic female figures takes as comprehensive an approach to matters of intra-textual coherence as I do here.[27]

What virtues, vices, and personality traits do female figures display in the Qur'an? How is female worldly agency informed by faith and by knowledge? Why, for instance, does the Qur'an not explicitly name any female figure as a prophet (*nabī*) or messenger (*rasūl*), while two dozen or more male figures are called to such lofty stations? What does the Qur'an's presentation of female agents—and their interactions with the men and boys in their midst—suggest overall about Qur'anic depictions of female biological sex, sexuality, and the feminine gender? Beyond undeniably unique reproductive capacities, what qualities differentiate the sexes in Qur'anic descriptions? These questions may be idiosyncratic to a twenty-first-century Western audience. But they may also be honest inquiries that women, in particular, have long brought to their engagement with the Qur'an.

## Notes

1. See Q 3:45 and 4:171 for additional references to Mary's child (Jesus) as God's "word." Q 21:91 and 19:21 are topically related verses that address Mary and her child being "signs"; a related verse, Q 23:50, mentions both figures, this time with the mention of the child preceding that of the mother: "And We made the son of Mary and his mother a sign. . . ." See also Q 66:12 for the blowing of the spirit into Mary and her "confirmation of the words of her Lord." As Kecia Ali notes, "In narrating Mary's pregnancy, labor, and delivery, qurʾānic discourse affirms the sacredness and power of biologically female and specifically maternal experiences; it invests childbearing with value in a way that places it parallel to, though distinct from, prophecy." See Ali, "Destabilizing Gender, Reproducing Maternity: Mary in the Qurʾān," *Journal of the International Qur'anic Studies Association* 2 (2017): 163–74; 90. See also Aisha Geissinger, "Mary in the Qur'an: Rereading Subversive Births," in *Sacred Tropes: Tanakh, New Testament, and Qur'an*, ed. Roberta Sterman Sabbath, 379–92 (Leiden: Brill, 2009), and Daniel A. Madigan, "Mary and Muhammad: Bearers of the Word," *Australasian Catholic Record* 80 (2003), 417–27. On the genealogy of Mary, see Suleiman A. Mourad, "Mary in the Qurʾān: A Reexamination of Her Presentation," in *The Qurʾān in Its Historical Context*, ed. Gabriel Said Reynolds, 163–74 (London: Routledge, 2007); for discussion of the figure of Mary in comparison to individuals who are explicitly named as prophets, see Loren Lybarger, "Gender and Prophetic Authority in

the Qur'anic Story of Maryam: A Literary Approach," *Journal of Religion* 80, no. 2 (2000): 240–70; and for a discussion of historical debates on women as prophets in Islam with discussion of the case of Mary, see Maribel Fierro, "Women as Prophets in Islam," in *Writing the Feminine: Women in Arab Sources*, ed. Manuela Marin and Randi Deguilhem, 183–98 (New York: I. B. Tauris, 2002).

2. For detailed analysis of this and other Qur'anic litanies of righteous individuals and prophets, see A. H. Johns, "Narrative, Intertext and Allusion in the Qurʾānic Presentation of Job," *Journal of Qurʾanic Studies* 1 (1999): esp. 10–14.
3. Georgina L. Jardim, *Recovering the Female Voice in Islamic Scripture: Women and Silence* (New York: Routledge, 2016), 65. See also Barlas, *Believing Women*, 22, and Jerusha Tanner Lamptey [Rhodes], *Divine Words, Female Voices: Muslima Explorations in Comparative Feminist Theology* (New York: Oxford University Press, 2018), 121–55. "Hermeneutics of suspicion" has become popular in feminist theological studies; following closely the works of Catholic theologian Elisabeth Schüssler Fiorenza, the *New Catholic Encyclopedia* defines hermeneutics of suspicion as "concerned not only with critical engagement about what is said about women that may diminish their full human dignity, but also with the silences that presume women's secondary status by ignoring their experiences of the divine." See A. Clifford, "Feminist Hermeneutics," in *New Catholic Encyclopedia*, ed. Catholic University of America (Detroit, MI: Thompson/Gale Group, 2003), 674.
4. Appendix A provides brief synopses of different personalities, including entries for girls, women, or groups of women. Appendix B provides a list of key terms or phrases organized along the arc of sacred history from the female progenitor to paradisal beings. Appendix C provides data on the location, content, context, and other qualities of the speech of women in the Qur'an, as well as a list of divine and angelic speech to female figures. Appendix D includes references to female figures, families, and households according to the approximate order of the advent of the surahs; this provides a quick reference to the approximate sequence of relevant verses over the revelatory period. Finally, there is a select list of individuals from among the Prophet Muḥammad's close female kin.
5. For an alternate list that is organized categorically but does not include references to families, see Amina Wadud, *Qur'an and Woman: Rereading the Sacred Text from a Woman's Perspective* (New York: Oxford University Press, 1999), 106–8. For a critique of Wadud's list, see Jardim, *Recovering the Female Voice*, 66–67. Other major works that focus on different groups of Qur'anic female figures include Barbara Freyer Stowasser, *Women in the Qur'an, Traditions, and Interpretation* (New York: Oxford University Press, 1994), and Rawand Osman, *Female Personalities in the Qur'an and Sunna: Examining the Major Sources of Shi'i Islam* (New York: Routledge, 2014). Stowasser focuses primarily on the history of early Sunni exegesis, and Osman studies Shīʿī hadith, exegesis, and biographical sources. Asma Lamrabet also offers psychoanalytic analysis of many female figures in the Qur'an and hadith. See Lamrabet, *Women in the Qur'an: An Emancipatory Reading*, trans. Myriam François-Cerrah (New York: Kube, 2016), and Lamrabet, *Women and*

*Men in the Qur'ān*, trans. Muneera Salem-Murdock (Cham, Switzerland: Palgrave Macmillan, 2018).

6. See Q 2:158 for mention of a ritual involving the two hills of al-Ṣafā and al-Marwa (which is a re-enactment of Hagar's struggles to find sustenance in an uncultivated valley). According to sacred history, that valley is where Abraham and Ishmael "raise the foundations of the house" (Q 2:127), the Kaʿba. See also Q 14:37. For reflections on Hagar as a model for female agency, see Lamptey, *Divine Words*, 184–89, and Hibba Abugideiri, "Hagar: A Historical Model for 'Gender Jihad,'" in *Daughters of Abraham: Feminist Thought in Judaism, Christianity, and Islam*, ed. John Esposito and Yvonne Haddad (Gainsville: University Press of Florida, 2001), 87–107. For analysis of Hagar as a concubine and mother, see Elizabeth Urban, "Hagar and Mariya: Early Islamic Models of Slave Motherhood," in *Concubines and Courtesans: Women and Slavery in Islamic History*, ed. Matthew Gordon and Kathryn Hain (New York: Oxford University Press, 2017), 225–43.
7. Verses that address the Prophet Muḥammad's wives generally are subsequent to the death of Khadīja in the year 619 CE. See discussions of Khadīja as a model of righteousness in Jardim, *Recovering the Female Voice*, 49–51. For a critical discussion of biographies of Khadīja throughout Muslim intellectual history, see Kecia Ali, *The Lives of Muhammad* (Cambridge, MA: Harvard University Press, 2014), 114–54.
8. See Q 33:37, as discussed in subsequent chapters. The commentary tradition identifies the woman as Zaynab bt. Jaḥsh (d. 20/641), a paternal cousin of the Prophet Muḥammad. See *SQ*, 1030–31 n. 37. For analysis of the figure of Zayd, see David S. Powers, *Zayd* (Philadelphia: University of Pennsylvania Press, 2014). Ultimately, I do not find the revisionist claim that Powers makes persuasive (that Zayd and his consorts are later literary constructions modeled on biblical figures); however, the work is a foray into texts and traditions surrounding this significant early Muslim figure.
9. See Q 111:1; see also *SQ*, 1575–76. She is identified in biographical traditions as Umm Jamīl and by the name Arwā bt. Ḥarb. Abū Lahab means "father of the flame," on account of the man's striking hair color, according to some bibliographies. He is said to be ʿAbd al-ʿUzzā b. ʿAbd al-Muṭṭalib (d. ca. 2/624), a paternal uncle of the Prophet Muḥammad. See Mona Zaki, "The Depiction of Hell in Medieval Islamic Thought" (PhD diss., Princeton University, 2015), 324–25. As we will see, the pair represent the only irretrievably corrupt husband and wife duo mentioned in Qur'anic vignettes. Another morally questionable husband and wife duo are reproached in a parable (Q 7:189–91), but this couple is not subjected to malediction of the same degree as Abū Lahab and his wife.
10. See Carol M. Walker, "David and the Single Ewe Lamb: Tracking Conversation between Two Texts (2 Samuel 12:3 and Q38:23) When They Are Read in Their Canonical Contexts," in *Reading the Bible in Islamic Context: Qur'anic Conversations*, ed. Daniel J. Crowther et al. (New York: Routledge, 2018), 77–87; Khaleel Mohammed, *David in the Muslim Tradition: The Bathsheba Affair* (Lanham, MD: Lexington Books, 2014); and Peter Matthews Wright, "The Qur'anic David," in *Constructs of Prophecy in the Former and Latter Prophets and in Other Texts*, ed. Lester L. Grabbe and Martii Nissinen (Atlanta: Society of Biblical Literature, 2011), 187–96. The corpus on

biblical and Qur'anic intertextuality is burgeoning, but Jane Dammen McAuliffe aptly summarizes the historically dominant Muslim exegetical outlook: "Previous revelations and scriptures do not authenticate the Qurʾān. Rather, the Qurʾān mandates how they are to be read and received, thereby providing what partial authorization or authentication it chooses to bestow." See McAuliffe, "Text and Textuality: Q. 3:7 as a Point of Intersection," in *Literary Structures of Religious Meaning in the Qurʾān*, ed. Issa J. Boullata (New York: Routledge, 2009), 66.

11. The first martyr is remembered in biographical literature as a woman of Ethiopian origins, Sumayya bt. Khayyāṭ (d. ca. 615 CE). For analysis, see David Cook, *Martyrdom in Islam* (New York: Cambridge University Press, 2012), 14. The main source for prophetic biography is a detailed work by Ibn Hishām (d. ca. 218/833–34), which is a redacted version of an earlier work by Ibn Isḥāq (d. ca. 150/767–68) that is no longer extant. Another early, influential biographical work, the *Ṭabaqāt* (Generations) of Ibn Saʿd (d. 230/845), includes extensive entries on the Prophet Muḥammad's contemporaries. Kecia Ali surveys scholarly and popular biographies of the Prophet Muḥammad in *The Lives of Muhammad* (Cambridge, MA: Harvard University Press, 2014).
12. This work is not an exploration of the hadith corpus or the role of hadith in premodern exegesis; for an excellent volume on this subject, including discussions of early women contributors, see Geissinger, *Gender and Muslim Constructions*. See also Jardim, *Recovering the Female Voice*, 73–74. For discussion of hadith and the biography of the Prophet Muḥammad more generally as a source of Islamic knowledge, see Lamptey, *Divine Words*, 104–14. See also Jonathan A. C. Brown, *Misquoting Muhammad: The Challenge and Choices of Interpreting the Prophet's Legacy* (London: Oneworld, 2014), esp. 141–47 on the Prophet Muḥammad's marriages.
13. For a reflection on the study of the Qur'an in the Western academy and efforts to approach the Qur'an as literature, see Travis Zadeh, "Quranic Studies and the Literary Turn," *Journal of the American Oriental Society* 135, no. 2 (2015): 329–42. For a concise discussion of the challenges and benefits of treating the Qur'an as a literary artifact, see Carl W. Ernst, *How to Read the Qur'an: A New Guide with Select Translations* (Chapel Hill: University of North Carolina Press, 2011), 205–12. For an extensive overview of Arabian society and the legacy of the Qur'an and Islam more broadly therein, see Aziz al-Azmeh, *The Emergence of Islam in Late Antiquity* (Cambridge, MA: Harvard University Press, 2017). Qur'anic verses themselves refer to a gradual revelatory process, addressing detractors and supplying reasons for the graduation; see, for instance, Q 17:106 and 25:32. For other instances of self-referential verses, see Q 29:45, 27:91–92, and 73:2.
14. As Gabriel Said Reynolds observes, "the Qurʾān, much like a homilist, reports certain elements of the narratives, alludes to others, and skips over others, since narrative is not the goal but only the means"; Reynolds, *The Qurʾān and Its Biblical Subtext* (New York: Routledge, 2010), 233. I differ with Reynolds in some of the particulars, but he rightfully depicts the homiletic quality of Qur'anic narrative. For further discussion, see Barbara Freyer Stowasser, "The Qur'an and History," in *Beyond the Exotic: Women's Histories in Islamic Societies*, ed. Amira El-Azhary Sonbol (Syracuse,

NY: Syracuse University Press, 2005), 15–18. See also Angelika Neuwirth, *Scripture, Poetry, and the Making of a Community* (New York: Oxford University Press, 2015).

15. An excellent resource with a comparative scope on Jewish, Christian, and Muslim depictions of shared figures is Robert C. Gregg, *Shared Stories, Rival Tellings: Early Encounters of Jews, Christians, and Muslims* (New York: Oxford University Press, 2015). Another helpful volume by John Kaltner and Younus Y. Mirza contains synopses of many different Qur'anic figures and their biblical counterparts, including many female figures. See *The Bible and the Qur'an: Biblical Figures in the Islamic Tradition* (London: Bloomsbury T&T Clark, 2018). In contrast, Travis Zadeh criticizes a trend in Qur'anic studies that aims to depict the "derivative and fragmentary nature of the Quran" and that seeks to "expose the Quran's imperfect understanding" of biblical sources. See Zadeh, "Quranic Studies," 338. Zadeh is correct: to dismiss the Qur'an as an inferior epigone willfully ignores the unique aspects of these narratives in Qur'anic discourse, in the formative Islamic milieu, and in Muslim affective encounters with the Qur'an. For similar criticisms, see Angelika Neuwirth, "Qurʾānic Studies and Philology: Qurʾānic Textual Politics of Staging, Penetrating, and Finally Eclipsing Biblical Tradition," in *Qur'ānic Studies Today*, ed. Angelika Neuwirth and Michael A. Sells (New York: Routledge, 2016), 178–83.
16. Ayesha Chaudhry, for one, gives the examples of "the printing press, increased literacy, and the internet" as giving women increased access to religious knowledge production. See Chaudhry, "Islamic Legal Studies: A Critical Historiography," in *The Oxford Handbook of Islamic Law*, ed. Anver M. Emon and Rumee Ahmed (Oxford Handbooks Online, Oxford University Press, 2017), 20, online at: http://www.oxfordhandbooks.com/view/10.1093/oxfordhb/9780199679010.001.0001/oxfordhb-9780199679010-e-1. Egyptian exegete ʿĀʾisha ʿAbd al-Raḥmān (d. 1998), who is known by her pen name Bint al-Shāṭiʾ, was "ambitious" and was "carefully invading a traditionally male domain," 57; see Ruth Roded, "Bint al-Shati's Wives of the Prophet: Feminist or Feminine?" *British Journal of Middle Eastern Studies* 33, no. 1 (2006). Notably, Shuruq Naguib observes how "women's exegetical agency" was "constrained, particularly in its written articulation" (60), but that ʿAbd al-Raḥmān strove to overcome sexism and strike a balance between continuity and reevaluation; see Naguib, "Bint al-Shāṭiʾ's Approach to *tafsīr*: An Egyptian Exegete's Journey from Hermeneutics to Humanity," *Journal of Qur'anic Studies* 17, no. 1 (2015): 45–84. Amina Wadud's topical exegesis on women and gender in the Qur'an (first published in 1992 in Kuala Lumpur) broke ground for women's exegesis in English and was followed by the work of Asma Barlas. Laleh Bakhtiar is one of the first women to produce a critical translation of the Qur'an in English (*The Sublime Quran* [Chicago: Kazi Publications, 2007]); she has since published other companion resources. Maria Massi Dakake has also made significant contributions to *The Study Quran* project as one of the main contributing editors. For an analysis of contemporary American Muslim women's exegesis, see Juliane Hammer, *American Muslim Women, Religious Authority, and Activism: More than a Prayer* (Austin: University of Texas Press, 2013), 56–76.
17. Ayesha Chaudhry reflects on the field of Islamic studies and on the compound marginalization of Muslims in this field, who are racialized and subjected to the

prevailing white supremacist tropes in the Euro-American academy and the broader societal dispositions that have shaped and epitomized it. Chaudhry elaborates how this discourse marginalizes, in compound fashion, the voices and interests of contemporary Muslim women, who are subjected not only to social dynamics that normalize sexism, but to the legacies of colonizing discourses as well. See Chaudhry, "Islamic Legal Studies," 5–6. Kecia Ali discusses these dynamics in a lecture entitled "Muslim Scholars, Islamic Studies, and the Gendered Academy" for the Annual al-Faruqi Memorial Lecture at the American Academy of Religion Annual Meeting (November 19, 2017), online at: https://www.youtube.com/watch?v=ai5XF-bP3KE (accessed April 10, 2018).

18. Similarly, Angelika Neuwirth observes, "those very 'inspectors' of scholarly borderlines who still loom large in our approaches have imposed their rules—or defined their objectives—not without ideological bias, but, as we shall see, with a sizable interest in their own identity politics." See Angelika Neuwirth, "Orientalism in Oriental Studies? Qur'anic Studies as a Case in Point," *Journal of Qur'anic Studies* 9, no. 2 (2011): 115–27, and Zadeh, "Quranic Studies," 334–35 and 339. Joseph Lumbard outlines this dynamic as well in his remarks entitled "Decolonizing Qur'anic Studies," presented at the School of Oriental and African Studies at the University of London (November 11, 2016). As a corrective to epistemic biases found in Euro-American Qur'anic studies, Lumbard argues for a "transmodern" approach that enables "discourse across methodological and epistemological divides" in order to "decolonize" the field of Qur'anic studies. See also Miranda Fricker's description of "hermeneutical marginalization" in *Epistemic Injustice: Power and the Ethics of Knowing* (New York: Oxford University Press, 2007), 153–55.
19. For example, speaking in 1982, Andrew Rippin outlined his reservations for studying the Qur'an as literature, including the peril of the "committed critic." See Andrew Rippin, "The Qur'an as Literature: Perils, Pitfalls and Prospects," *British Society of Middle Eastern Studies Bulletin* 10, no. 1 (1983): 38–47.
20. For a critique of the necessity of suspending moral judgment in Islamic studies, see Chaudhry, "Islamic Legal Studies," 10–11.
21. The Qur'an regularly depicts the interconnectivity of all human beings (beyond sex or gender), but it does seem to depict gender dimorphisms as rooted directly in biological sex. Normative rules for relations between wives and husbands, for instance, are one example of a collapse of biological sex and gender roles. Here, I disagree with Asma Barlas, who argues that "the Qur'ān does not locate gender dimorphisms in sex"; *Believing Women,* 166. Similarly, Amina Wadud argues that "femininity and masculinity are not created characteristics imprinted into the very primordial nature of female and male persons" or even concepts to which the Qur'an refers. They are rather "culturally determined factors of how each gender should function" that have factored into exegesis. See Wadud, *Qur'an and Woman,* 22. For a discussion of the extent to which a distinct Qur'anic concept of "femininity" can be delineated, see Osman, *Female Personalities,* 6–7.
22. Kecia Ali warns against simplistic arguments that the Qur'an is egalitarian with respect to men and women: "Progressive approaches to the Qur'anic text cannot be

limited to selective presentation of egalitarian verses in isolation from their broader scriptural context. Such an approach is both fundamentally dishonest and ultimately futile; arguments about male–female equality built on the systematic avoidance of inconvenient verses will flounder at the first confrontation with something that endorses the hierarchical and gender differentiated regulations for males and females that so many reformers would like to wish away." See Kecia Ali, *Sexual Ethics and Islam: Feminist Reflections on Qur'an, Hadith, and Jurisprudence*, rev. ed. (Oxford: Oneworld, 2016), 196. Similarly, Raja Rhouni posits that "Islamic feminist theory based on the postulate of the normativity of gender equality in the Qur'an has reached a theoretical dead end." Raja Rhouni, *Secular and Islamic Feminist Critiques in the Work of Fatima Mernissi* (Boston: Brill, 2010), 251, as also quoted in Hidayatullah, *Feminist Edges*, viii.

23. See Nimat Hafez Barazangi, *Women's Identity and the Qur'an: A New Reading* (Gainesville: University Press of Florida, 2004), 77. "If the Qur'anic social revolution involving gender is to be practiced," writes Barazangi, "the Qur'anic assertion that the female is an autonomous moral being who has a direct relationship with God as her only Guardian may not be compromised. Rather, it should be asserted, even if it results in a controversy" (ibid., 78).
24. Hidayatullah, *Feminist Edges*, 4; see the full volume for reflections on the genesis of "feminist *tafsīr*," including reflections on the advantages and drawbacks of the use of the term "feminist." Well before the flourishing of contemporary Muslim women's theological writings, but communicating a strikingly similar spirit, the Egyptian exegete Maḥmūd Shaltūt authored a short but provocative treatise reflecting on a number of female figures in the Qur'an. See *The Quran and Woman: Annotated English Version with Arabic Text* (*al-Qurʾān wa-l-marʾa*), trans. Wajihuddin Ahmed and Abdel Malik Dardir (Cairo: International Islamic Center for Population Studies and Research, 1986), esp. 5–8. For poignant observations regarding gender in Islamic ontology, anthropology, and cosmology, see Saʿdiyya Shaikh, *Sufi Narratives of Intimacy: Ibn ʿArabī, Gender, and Sexuality* (Chapel Hill: University of North Carolina Press, 2012).
25. As I have defined it elsewhere, "*Muslima* theology is a branch of theological studies that is conversant with other confessional and/or regionally situated feminist discourses and that offers an intellectual platform to advance female-centric contemplations of piety, female-centric modes of leadership, and female-centric epistemological authority." This emphasis does not signal female superiority to the exclusion or at the expense of male engagement; however, it does prioritize the generation of physical and intellectual spaces wherein "the contributions and perspectives of women in the sphere of religion are valued and actively solicited," not merely within the sphere of exclusively "women's issues," but across a spectrum of theological, judicial, and social matters. See Celene Ibrahim-Lizzio, "'The Garment of Piety Is Best': Islamic Legal and Exegetical Works on Bodily Covering," *Claremont Journal of Religion* 4, no. 1 (2015), 21. For a recent collection of essays on this theme, see *Muslim Women and Gender Justice: Concepts, Sources, and Histories*, ed. Dina El Omari, Juliane Hammer, and Mouhanad Khorchide (New York: Routledge, 2019). For themes related to manhood and masculinity in Islam—including Qur'anic

depictions of men—see Amanullah De Sondy, *The Crisis of Islamic Masculinities* (New York: Bloomsbury, 2013).

26. The concept of "feminism" has rhetorical and political power, but feminist advocacy has historically been detrimental, in certain respects, to colonized peoples, women of color, and immigrants. See Lila Abu Lughod, *Do Muslim Women Need Saving?* (Cambridge, MA: Harvard University Press, 2013), and Sara Farris, *In the Name of Women's Rights: The Rise of Femonationalism* (Durham, NC: Duke University Press, 2017). For a genealogical survey of modern and contemporary feminist political activism, see Margot Badran, *Feminism in Islam: Secular and Religious Convergences* (Oxford: Oneworld, 2009). For a discussion of the term "feminism" and its use by Muslim exegetes in the North American context, see Juliane Hammer, *American Muslim Women*, 57–59. See also Lamptey, *Divine Words*, 6–11.
27. For instance, for insights on the importance of repetition (*takrār*) and coherence in Qur'anic narratives, see Faraan Alamgir Sayed, "Repetition in Qur'ānic *Qaṣaṣ*: With Reference to Thematic and Literary Coherence in the Story of Moses," *Journal of Islamic and Muslim Studies* 2, no. 2 (2017): 70–71; for a recent book on this theme, see Raymond Farrin, *Structure and Qur'anic Interpretation: A Study of Symmetry and Coherence in Islam's Holy Text* (Ashland, OR: White Cloud Press, 2014).

# 1
# Female Sex and Sexuality

Sex—as a feature of embodiment and as the act of intercourse—is a central facet of human experience; from a person's origination from a sex act, to awareness of the sexed body, desires, and inclinations, to sexual encounters, and even (potentially) to otherworldly sexual experiences, many aspects of sex and sexuality enter into the Qur'anic discourse. The Qur'an deals with issues of human reproduction, uses terms that refer to sexual anatomy and intercourse, and presents stories of sexual desire and of licit versus illicit sex. Qur'anic narratives address sex and sexuality in the cosmological, biological, and social realms. The imperative to regulate sexuality is, in fact, one of the Qur'an's most accentuated narrative tropes.

What, according to the Qur'an, is the divine design behind biological sex and human sexuality? How and when do figures in the Qur'an engage in sexual relations? In such encounters, what constitutes an illicit sexual partner as compared to a virtuous one? How does the Qur'an describe female beauty and depict sexual desire toward women? Is there sex in paradise? With consideration to such questions, I here approach themes of sex and sexuality from the vantage point of Qur'anic narratives. Reading intra-textually, I consider sexual intercourse in and beyond the confines of marriage as well as in, and beyond, the earthly realm.[1]

Much of the Qur'anic discourse on sexual relations, broadly speaking, defines what constitutes licit versus illicit relations. Accordingly, many Qur'anic narratives touch on fundamental questions relevant to establishing this distinction: With whom is sex licit? In what contexts? According to what prearranged terms? And how should breaches of proper sexual etiquette (and other such breakdowns in sexual partnerships) be handled on a communal level? I assess the relevant episodes here, and then in subsequent chapters I continue to address these narratives from different angles. I also interrogate the potential for sexual differentiation and sexual intimacy in the otherworldly realm, according to Qur'anic characterizations. But before we delve into narratives and into otherworldly realms, we must survey key concepts related to sex and sexuality.

*Women and Gender in the Qur'an*. Celene Ibrahim, Oxford University Press (2020). © Oxford University Press.
DOI: 10.1093/oso/9780190063818.001.0001.

## Sex and Telos

In the Qur'anic cosmic schema, God is singular and creates at will; God created "all things" as pairs (Q 51:49); hence, human beings have a derivative capacity to engender new life only in consort with a mate (*zawj*, pl. *azwāj*).[2] This dyad, composed of the female (*unthā*) and the male (*dhakar*), enables the "spread abroad [of] a multitude of men and women" (Q 4:1) by God's leave.[3] The genesis of human beings from a pair and the subsequent pairing of human mates are oft-repeating Qur'anic themes.[4] The sexual bifurcation of species mirrors other aspects of cosmic duality: "And of all things We created pairs (*zawjayn*), that perchance you may remember" (Q 51:49).[5]

The duality in creation stands in contrast to God's unicity. In another contrast, human beings are made from a soul (*nafs*) and her mate (*zawj*) and then formed in a womb, "creation after creation, in threefold darkness" (Q 39:6); by contrast, God alone has no partner (*kufu'*)[6] and is "the Light of the heavens and the earth" (Q 24:35). Moreover, God is "beyond need" for human beings, as the Qur'an asserts in an uncompromising manner when describing the human's place in cosmic creation:

> He created the heavens and the earth in truth. He rolls the night up into the day and rolls the day up into the night, and He made the sun and the moon subservient, each running for a term appointed. Is He not the Mighty, the Forgiving?
>
> He created you from a single soul, then made from her [the soul] her mate, and sent down for you of cattle eight pairs. He creates you in your mothers' wombs, creation after creation, in threefold darkness. He is God, your Lord; to Him belongs sovereignty. There is no god but He. How, then, are you turned away?
>
> If you do not believe, surely God is beyond need of you. (Q 39:5–7)[7]

Like the sun and the moon mentioned in the preceding verse, human beings also run for an appointed term as material bodies and are then extinguished, unlike the Everlasting, who remains forever.[8] The origins of the human being as a humble clinging clot (Q 96:2), generation upon generation, contrasts with the primal unicity of God.

One verse describes this procreative aspect of human design in relation to God's creative power as follows: "God has made mates (*azwāj*) for you from among yourselves (*min anfusikum*), and from your mates He has made for you children and grandchildren" (Q 16:72). Notably, the Qur'an does not make procreation obligatory as a dimension of pious obedience to God. Procreation—about which the Qur'an speaks at length—is not a divine command, and moreover, the act of procreation does not carry an inherent moral reward in the Qur'anic discourse. The moral rewards with respect to sex, procreation, and kinship lie in treating relatives justly and mercifully by minding the bonds of "the wombs" (e.g., Q 4:1).[9]

The creation of human beings "from a male and a female" is highlighted alongside ethnic diversity and kinship lineages as a sign of God's purposeful creation: "O humankind! Truly We [God] created you from a male and a female, and We made you peoples and tribes that you may come to know one another. Surely the most noble of you before God are the most reverent of you (*inna akramakum ʿinda Allāhi atqākum*). Truly God is Knowing, Aware" (Q 49:13).[10] This verse situates biological reproduction in a theological telos: human beings are distinguished in matters of nobility and reverence for God. When the matter is placed on the divine scales, piety, not biological sex or ethnic origin, is the criterion for human differentiation.[11]

Further observations can be made on the bifurcation of the human species into sexed dyads as it relates to other phenomena in God's creation. For instance, in the following segment of a verse, consider the mention of water: "And He it is who created from water a human being (*bashar*), and made him lineage (*nasab*) and kinship [through marriage] (*ṣihr*). And your Lord is Powerful" (Q 25:54).[12] The water evokes the "fluid" that is mentioned in many verses on human conception and embryonic development: "Truly We created the human being (*al-insān*) from a drop of mixed fluid that We may test him, and We endowed him with hearing, seeing" (Q 76:2).[13] The water from which human beings are made, in a literal and a metaphorical sense, links humans inextricably with other cosmic phenomena, as in the fuller context of the verse just quoted:

> And He it is who mixed the two seas, one sweet, satisfying, the other salty, bitter, and set between them a divide and a barrier, forbidden.
>
> And He it is who created from water a human being, and made him lineage and kinship [through marriage]. And your Lord is Powerful. (Q 25:53–54)[14]

The division of the waters of the seas is similar, figuratively, to the sexual fluids of the female and the male in sexual union: like the fertile estuaries where the fresh and salt waters meet in currents, the sexual waters mix and on occasion fuse to create new life, extending lineages. The verse also emphasizes the common material origin of all human beings; they are created from the same sources, by the same processes, by leave of the same God.

Another verse evokes water in relation to the original unity of the heavens and the earth, a unity that, like the pattern of human creation, also moves—fundamentally—from unity toward duality: "Have those who disbelieved not considered that the heavens and the earth were sewn together (*kānatā ratqan*) and We rent them asunder (*fa-fataqnāhumā*)? And We made every living thing from water. Will they not then believe?" (Q 21:30).[15] How does the metaphorical tearing apart of the heavens and the earth relate to the creation of "every living thing from water"? Aside from being two examples of the creative power of God, a contemporary reader might note that the sewing and tearing of the cosmos in its bifurcation process bear a metaphorical similarity to the lengthwise splitting of the strands of chromosomes in the nucleoplasm of cells in the process of reproduction. The Qur'an explicitly uses cosmic scale in another verse discussing the signs of God's majesty, as manifested for human beings: "We shall show them Our signs upon the horizons and within themselves till it becomes clear to them that it is the truth. Does it not suffice that your Lord is Witness over all things?" (Q 41:53).

Discussions of human production and reproduction are not limited to material forms alone. Like the fusion of the heavens and earth before their bifurcation, the Qur'an describes "one soul" (*nafs wāḥida*)[16] as the origin of the human being, a single soul from which God forms a mate:

> O humankind! Reverence your Lord, who created you from a single soul and from her created her mate, and from the two has spread abroad a multitude of men and women. Reverence God, through whom you demand [your rights of one another], and [reverence] the wombs (*wa-l-arḥām*).[17] Truly God is a Watcher over you. (Q 4:1)

From one soul, God made two; the process is an inverse of human reproduction, whereby two human beings engender (typically) one new life. This verse does not explicitly identify this original single soul as belonging to a male human being. It is quite the opposite; the verse reinforces an overarching theme in Qur'anic discourse, namely, the solemn and "total negation" of biologically based hierarchies, "be [they] racial, ethnic, sexual, or otherwise."[18]

In the Qur'anic descriptions, bifurcation from a single soul into a pair does not ascribe a differing value, worth, or capacity to either entity. Just as the night is not worthier than the day, nor the day more valuable than the night, nor the heavens more remarkable than the earth, nor the earth more wondrous than the heavens, the original human unicity in the primordial realm engenders a type of equivalency that, in turn, engenders a relational difference. The creation of human beings as sexed dyads follows the pattern of duality in other aspects of creation (such as the heavens and earth, or the day and night) that mutually interpose and interpenetrate.[19]

One verse describes a purpose for this bifurcation: "It is He who created you [pl.] from a single soul (*nafs wāḥida*), and made from her [the soul] her spouse (*zawjahā*), that he might find rest in her (*li-yaskuna ilayhā*)" (Q 7:189). This passage seemingly intertwines the metaphysical and the corporeal and grounds sexual intimacy in a metaphysical and ontological reality. The soul entity (which is grammatically gendered feminine) is bifurcated, and then the soul dyads become partners. Another verse echoes the theme of spousal enjoyment: "And among His signs is that He created spouses (*azwāj*) for you (*lakum*) from among yourselves (*anfusikum*), that you might find rest (*li-taskunū*) in them (*ilayhā*), and He established between you (*baynakum*) affection and mercy. Truly in that are signs for a people who reflect" (Q 30:21).[20] The construction "in them" arguably refers back to the "spouses" (pl., *azwāj*), or even possibly to the selves (pl., *anfus*).

The *nafs* is grammatically feminine but is not ontologically female (unless it explicitly references the self or life of a female being, a point that becomes relevant in later discussions of spouses in paradise). The word *nafs*, in its predominant usage in nearly three hundred instances in the Qur'an, is most commonly used to refer to an individual human (irrespective of sex). For instance, the axiomatic verse in the preceding surah (*al-ʿAnkabūt*), "Every soul (f., *nafs*) will taste death. Then to Us you will be returned" (Q 29:57), does not literally mean that only female human beings will "taste death"; it refers to a collective experience of death. Similarly, Q 36:36 professes glory to God who "created the pairs (*azwāj*), all of them (f., *kullahā*), from what the earth makes grow, and from themselves (*anfusihim*), and from what they know not."[21] Here, the emphasis on "the pairs, all of them" (vegetable, human, and otherwise) clearly illustrates that it is not exclusively female human beings that are being referenced with such grammatically feminine phrasing.

An interpretation or translation of verse Q 30:21 as "He created *wives* for you [men] . . . so that you [men] can find rest in them [your wives]" amounts to imposing an androcentric bias about who is entitled to find rest in whom. Such a gender exclusive reading would require that the word *azwāj* be narrowly defined as "female spouse" (without any contextual signal that it should be restricted), and it also requires that women be explicitly excluded from the pronoun "yourselves" (*anfusikum*) and the verb "find rest" (*li-taskunū*). There is no compelling reason to restrict the meaning of this verse such that it is husbands exclusively finding rest in wives, rather than a situation of reciprocity. Instead, these terms should be read (and translated) as a reference to spouses generally.[22] This latter reading is supported by the relational aspect of "affection and mercy" being established "between you" (*baynakum*). Moreover, the preceding verses of this surah (and the concluding verses of the previous surah, including verse Q 29:57 cited earlier) all pertain to the experience of human collectivities. Take the immediately preceding verse, Q 30:20, in which God's "signs" include that God "created you (m. pl., *-kum*) from dust" as humans (*bashar*) "ranging far and wide" (*tantashirūn*). Again, this verse is in a grammatical form that is occasionally restricted to males or men only, but the verse clearly (contextually and intertextually) refers to the collective human experience.

Another verse expresses the ideal of spousal reciprocity with respect to the enjoyment of intercourse. In this case, the verse explicitly and emphatically addresses men *about* women, and the verse uses the pronoun *hunna*, which is exclusive to women: "They [f., *hunna*] are a garment for you [m., *lakum*], and you [m., *antum*] are a garment for them [f., *lahunna*]" (Q 2:187). This metaphor of garments evokes an intimate, protective relationship, one that is fundamentally characterized by reciprocity, as is conveyed emphatically in the parallel sentence structure. The verse is addressed to men *about* women and reiterates—specifically for a male audience—the reciprocity entailed in sexual intimacy. Rather than draw the conclusion that the Qur'an is androcentric because it addresses men *about* the sexuality of women, we can observe instead that the Qur'an affirms female sexuality and encourages men to value women's experiences of intimacy.[23]

Taking this point further, verses about sexual restraint and "guarding" the private parts (as discussed later) are addressed to both men and women (for instance, Q 24:30–31); however, instructions limiting when, where, and how sexual relations occur, also discussed later, are frequently addressed explicitly to men. This may suggest that in the Qur'anic worldview, on balance, men need more frequent instruction and reminders. In Q 24:30–31, verses that command lowering the gaze and guarding the private parts for both men and women, the Qur'an addresses men and women separately, with men first. The practice of addressing one gender first does not necessarily signify preference—it could, for instance, imply that one gender needs more urgent guidance. From this vantage point, the requirements for women to conceal "their adornments" (*zīnatahunna*) in the second of this pair of verses—requirements that are *not* mentioned for men—can be seen as a contingency measure, a form of protection against men who do not heed the direct command to "lower their eyes and guard their private parts," something which is described as "purer for them" (*azkā lahum*) (Q 24:30).

## Recognizing Anatomical Difference

Among the first narratives in the Qur'an is that of a couple who seem to become aware of their sexed anatomy for the first time.[24] When Adam and his spouse (*zawj*) are expelled from the garden after "tast[ing] of the tree," they become aware of their nakedness: "And when they tasted of the tree, their nakedness (*saw'ātuhumā*) was exposed to them, and they began to sew together the leaves of the garden to cover themselves" (Q 7:22).[25] Satan had succeeded in "expos[ing] to them that which was hidden from them of their nakedness" (Q 7:20). Their "tast[ing] of the tree" (Q 7:22) caused their expulsion from their garden home and introduced a new type of socialization in which nakedness (specifically, it seems, exposure of the pudenda) produces shame. That Adam and his spouse ate from a specific tree and then became aware of their nakedness suggests that some characteristic of the fruit of the tree itself, or their transgression, brought about the need for new decorum.[26]

The expulsion from the garden in Qur'anic sacred history may be the actual or metaphorical point at which human beings became aware of somatic sexual difference or became aware of its function and creative potency. This realization may be akin to the socialization of a child who, at a certain age, discerns that public nudity is a social taboo and (eventually) that reproductive organs have previously unexplored capabilities. This awakening of body-consciousness often happens in parallel to a child's development of moral consciousness; through socialization, the child assembles a particular understanding of morality and, in an idealized theological framework, begins to understand the state and station of the human being's creative potential in relation to God's ultimate creativity and life-giving force. Here and elsewhere, nakedness in the physical world relates to spiritual deprivation; the human being can elect to cover with the "raiment of reverence" that is "sent down" by God to the "Children of Adam" (Q 7:26) or can refuse that garment.

Notably, the couple eat from a tree, the edible parts of which are generally the reproductive structure of the organism. This imagery evokes a contrast between the human and vegetal worlds: in the vegetal world, the reproductive organ is often eye-catching and on vibrant display; yet, in the kind of socialization mandated by the Qur'an, human reproductive organs must be concealed. The pudenda of the body correspond most directly to human sexuality, to the reproductive bifurcation of the human species, and thus also to the entity of the soul itself at the primal/cosmic moment of human creation. Thus, the procreative capacity is much more than a biological process for humankind; it is situated in a particular cosmology and teleology. In this cosmology, the human reproductive capacity is an indirect reflection of the creative, generative, sustaining, life-giving attributes of God. From this vantage point, sexual organs are covered because they contain a sacred potency. In turn, spiritual deprivation is equated with nakedness because flaunting sexuality is a misapplication of a highly potent God-given human capability.

## Qur'anic Depictions of Intercourse

The Qur'an describes, in narrative, an act of sexual relations on just one occasion, as follows: "When he covered her (*taghashshāhā*), she bore a light burden, and carried it about" (Q 7:189).[27] The verse seems literally to describe a sexual position with a man on top of a woman, but the verb in this passage meaning "he covered her," *taghashshāhā*, also appears in other grammatical forms with reference to the night, which "covers" the day.[28] Another verse, as discussed earlier, also evokes the notion of covering, potentially intimating sexual intimacy: "They [your women] are a garment (*libās*) for you, and you are a garment (*libās*) for them" (Q 2:187). The reciprocity of covering in this verse contrasts with that of the man "covering" the woman in the previously cited verse.

Another verse likens sexual intercourse to plowing a field: "Your women are a tilth to you (*ḥarthun lakum*), so go to your tilth (*fa'tū ḥarthakum*) as you will" (Q 2:223). This metaphor could implicitly liken the male sperm to seed and the ovum or uterus to a field, wherein an agricultural laborer cultivates the fecund soil. From the vantage point of an ecologically pillaged modern world, this agricultural metaphor may initially conjure up an idea of exploitation, but images of exploitation do not align with the many Qur'anic verses that point to the wondrous nature of cultivated earth and the sanctity of the womb.[29] The metaphor need not be explicitly reproductive: in other verses, the *ḥarth* is equated not with the act of tilling, but with bounty, enjoyment, or the metaphorical act of harvesting. For example, God promises: "Whoever desires the harvest (*ḥarth*) of the hereafter, We shall increase for him his harvest. And whoever desires the harvest of this world, We shall give him some thereof, but he will have no share in the hereafter" (Q 42:20). In this case, the bounty could be the enjoyment of sexual intercourse itself or the likeness thereof, as discussed later.

The Qur'an also employs the notion of "inclining" as a euphemism for sexual seduction, as in the story of Joseph and the wife of the Egyptian viceroy, which reaches a narrative climax in a moment of extreme—but ultimately unfulfilled—attraction: "She inclined toward him, and he would have inclined toward her . . ." (*hammat bihi wa-hamma bihā law lā . . .*) (Q 12:24).[30] Sexual relations are often discussed with such intimations, but intercourse is mentioned specifically in a lengthy verse that permits "intercourse with your women" (*al-rafathu ilā nisāʾikum*) during the nights of the fast and states that women are "garments for you and you are garments for them" (Q 2:187), as noted earlier.[31] This verse permits sexual relations in the context of the nights of the fast: "lie with them (*bāshirūhunna*) and seek what God has prescribed for you"; however, during optional days of retreat in the mosque the verse explicitly prohibits intercourse (*lā tubāshirūhunna*) (Q 2:187).[32]

We can observe a pattern in the Qur'anic use of euphemisms versus direct references to sexual intercourse. In the stories and poetic descriptions of sexual relations, the Qur'an evokes intimations and metaphors, but for matters of purity and acts of worship, it employs more direct language for sexual relations that pertains specifically to intercourse, not to other modes of "inclining" or intimacy more generally. In this way, the Qur'an distinguishes multiple aspects of human sexuality, ranging from the emotional-cognitive dimensions of attraction and companionship to the physicality of contact.[33]

## Qur'anic Terms for Spouses

I outlined the Qur'anic idea of "pairing" at the cosmic level in the beginning of this chapter. In speaking about Adam's mate, for instance, the Qur'an consistently uses the term "spouse" (*zawj*). Other spouses, including those of the Prophet Muḥammad, are referred to in the Qur'an with the term *zawj* or its plural, *azwāj*; however, several other Qur'anic terms also pertain to female spouses (or to households more generally).

In addition to *zawj*, the word *imraʾa* (lit., "woman") can mean "wife," depending on context and interpretation.[34] The word *nisāʾ* refers to women categorically and appears frequently in the Qur'an in verses related to legal matters in the family; it can also refer to the wives of a given figure or to female members of the extended family, including in verses 33:30 and 33:32, where it refers to the women of the Prophet Muḥammad's household, as explored in later chapters.[35] The word for "companion" (f., *ṣāḥiba*) can also signify a wife (as in Q 70:12 and 80:36).[36]

Finally, in addition to the previously mentioned terms (*zawj*, *imraʾa*/*nisāʾ*, *ṣāḥiba*), the word *ahl* may also designate a wife specifically, or members of a household, or even people of a kinship group more generally.[37] Given the term's wide semantic range, we must take context into consideration to determine to whom the term refers in any given instance. A closely related word, *āl*, is also used in a titular sense in multiple verses (twenty-six to be exact) to refer to the household and kin of a specific man, as in the surah titled *Āl ʿImrān* (Q 3). In fourteen of these instances (just over half), the term is used in the context of the "House of Pharaoh" (*āl Firʿawn*). Notably, the term *āl* is always directly attached to the household of a specific man in the Qur'anic discourse, unlike the term *ahl*, which refers directly to a woman figure at times, or to the people of a particular city, for instance. Attempting to generalize the distinction between the two terms in the Qur'anic discourse, *ahl* suggests association by kinship, geography, or religious belonging, while *āl* refers to association with a particular patriarch.[38]

Consider again the word *zawj*, which can refer to a mate, spouse, or a pair or variety of something. Of the eighty-one times the root *z-w-j* appears in the Qur'an, the term is used only once to refer explicitly and exclusively to a husband; in this case, the husband (referred to as *zawj*) is a man whose wife complained to the Prophet, prompting a Qur'anic verse to address the situation and affirm the woman's rightful complaint against her negligent husband (Q 58:1).[39] The term *baʿl* refers to husbands specifically on six occasions.[40] On one occasion (Q 12:25), a female personality refers to her spouse not as *zawj* or *baʿl* but as *sayyid*, a polysemous term that can mean master, husband, and leader.[41]

## Regulating Sexuality and Licit Partnerships

In Qur'anic stories, the regulation of sexuality appears as a major test for human beings, female and male alike. The urgency of sexual ethics in the context of Qur'anic stories is also mirrored in direct Qur'anic injunctions: one segment of *Sūrat al-Nisā'* (Q 4) outlines verses on fornication and ends with the following caution about human beings as a collective:

> God desired to make [this] clear unto you (*li-yubayyina lakum*), and to guide you to the traditions (*yahdiyakum sunan*) of those who went before you, and to return you [to His favor]. And God is Knowing, Wise.
>
> God desires to return you [to His favor], but those who follow lusts (*al-shahawāt*) desire that you go tremendously astray.
>
> God desired to lighten [your burden] for you, for the human being (*al-insān*) was created weak. (Q 4:26–28)

God's "desire" (*irāda*) is contrasted to the desires of those who follow "lusts" (*shahawāt*) and succumb to their inherent human weaknesses; these verses discussing God's guidance, knowledge, and wisdom follow detailed restrictions on legitimate sexual partners.

Given this emphasis on proper restraint as an aspect of God's munificent desire for humankind, what factors, in particular, make sexual activity licit in God's benevolent scheme? Many Qur'anic verses discuss the circumstances and the necessary legal commitments between parties that are prerequisites for licit sex, including but not limited to the religious affiliation of the individual and the necessity of the bridewealth transaction.[42] The Qur'an also clarifies matters of licit versus illicit sexual engagement through multiple narratives.

One story (that of a woman marrying Moses) models the ideal dispositions involved in negotiating a marital contract. When Moses flees retributive justice in Egypt, he becomes dejected and seeks God's favor. He then arrives at a watering hole in Midian. Despite his own disheveled and desperate state, he chivalrously helps two women water their flock when the local shepherds were not appropriately attentive. He then withdraws to rest in the shade and beseech God for succor. The Qur'an describes the encounter that unfolds:

> Then one of the two [sisters at the watering hole] came to him [Moses], walking bashfully.[43] She said, "Truly my father summons you, that he might

> render to you a reward for having watered [our flocks] for us." When he [Moses] came and recounted his story to him [the father], he [the father] said, "Fear not. You have been saved from the wrongdoing people."
>
> One of the two [sisters] said, "O my father! Hire him. Surely the best you can hire is the strong, the trustworthy." (Q 28:25–26)[44]

As his daughter enthusiastically suggests, the father indeed offers to hire Moses on flexible terms, but first he offers to marry Moses to "one of these two daughters of mine" (Q 28:27). Curiously, the identity of the two sisters is not differentiated, and the sister who invites Moses to speak with her father may or may not be the same sister who also advocates Moses's employment with her father. The Qur'an gives no indication which of the two sisters initially spoke with Moses, which one urged her father to hire him, and which one eventually married Moses. The listener or reader is left to speculate. In any case, the father, as a potential in-law, maintains an exceptionally cordial demeanor in offering options and reassuring Moses of his compassionate intentions and humble virtue: "I desire not to be hard on you. You will find me, if God wills, to be among the righteous" (Q 28:27). All of the figures in the narrative exercise proper decorum, and they are, in turn, shown favor by God. As if to emphasize the woman's decorum, the Qur'an only intimates her desire; she does not, for instance, directly implore Moses to marry her. She is assertive, but with dignity. The mannerism of her walking toward Moses is also echoed in the modesty of her speech when she urges her father to retain Moses as an employee.

## Guarding against Illicit Sexual Desire

The sisters at the watering hole may be seen as exemplars of decorum, but the Qur'an also offers an example of catastrophically misplaced female sexuality. The story begins with the power of desire: "She in whose house he was staying sought to lure him from himself," that is, to seduce him against his better judgment (Q 12:23). Here, even a righteous person such as Joseph, who was explicitly given "wisdom and knowledge" by God (Q 12:22), risks being "lured from himself" and inclining toward illicit sex. Instead of inclining, however, Joseph affirms the Qur'anic ideal of prudent sexual behavior by taking refuge in God and by demonstrating how to fulfill the instruction to "guard the private parts."[45]

The notion of guarding the private parts is oft repeated in the Qur'an, as in the following verses, listed here in the order of their appearance in the compiled Qur'an: in Q 21:91 in reference to Mary, "who fortified her pudenda" (*allatī aḥṣanat farjahā*); in Q 23:5 in reference to human beings who preserve (gender inclusive pl., *ḥāfiẓūn*) their private parts; in Q 24:30 (as a plural verb, *yaḥfaẓūna*); in Q 24:31 as specifically directed to believing females (*yaḥfaẓna*); in Q 33:35 as "male preservers of their private parts and female preservers" (*al-ḥāfiẓīna furūjahum wa-l-ḥāfiẓāt*); in Q 66:12 regarding Mary, "who fortified her pudenda" (*allatī aḥṣanat farjahā*) (a repetition of Q 21:91); and in Q 70:29 (a repetition of Q 23:5). In these verses, both women and men "guard" their external sexual organs, but a female alone "fortifies" her pudenda. Both sexes are responsible for preserving their chastity, presumably against the inclinations of the self and the potential advances of others. It is the woman *herself* who is the "fortifier" and the "guardian." The woman has a proactive, defensive role in protecting herself against sexual aggression and eschewing illicit interactions.

The mentions of "fortifying" (for women) and "preserving" (for women and men) pudenda all come *after* the story of Joseph encountering the viceroy's wife—in terms of both the approximate revelatory schema of the surahs and the order of the final, compiled Qur'an; the issue of chastity is first broached in narrative form. Both structurally in terms of the final organization of the Qur'an and chronologically in terms of the revelatory order, verses with direct injunctions often emphasize prior narratives. The driving moral thrust of a captivating narrative is reinforced by a direct command.[46]

In this way, Qur'anic readers, reciters, and listeners grasp the issue in context before the Qur'an begins to reinforce the driving moral theme: avoid illicit sex. The initial audience of the Qur'an, those in the Prophet Muḥammad's milieu, could have experienced just such an unfolding of the Qur'anic discourse: they could first reflect on a narrative and its moral implications and, later, resolve to abide by the corresponding direct injunctions. Direct commandments reinforce moral lessons that are initially delivered in narrative form; thus, Qur'anic storytelling and Qur'anic commandments are intimately interconnected.[47]

## Vice, Virtue, and the Viceroy's Wife

The Qur'an gives examples of women who "fortify" themselves, but it also gives an example of a woman who exceeds appropriate boundaries. In the figure of the wife of the Egyptian viceroy, we see a woman who is a willing adulteress. Rather than fortifying herself, she invites Joseph: "She locked the doors and said, 'Come, you!'" (Q 12:23). Here, the viceroy's wife explicitly uses the power of her speech to seduce him (as discussed further in Chapter 3). This woman may be proactive in her immoral sexual pursuits, but the viceroy's wife stands in stark contrast to a number of other Qur'anic women who pursue sexual relations through lawful means or who avoid transgression in potentially compromising situations.

Mary, for instance, is a woman celebrated for her chastity; when a strange intruder enters her private quarters, she exclaims, "I seek refuge from you in the Compassionate, if you are reverent!" (Q 19:18).[48] The contrast between Mary and the wife of the viceroy is stark: Mary seeks refuge in God when a male figure suddenly appears in her private chamber, and the viceroy's wife seeks to lock a man in her chamber. Mary seeks refuge in God *from* someone; the wife of the viceroy *causes* someone to seek refuge in God.[49] The juxtapositions continue: the viceroy's wife attempts to have an affair with a virtuous young man and then accuses him of attempted fornication; Mary is chaste but then is accused of fornication: "Then she came with him [the infant Jesus] to her people, carrying him. They said, 'O Mary! You have brought an amazing thing! / O sister of Aaron! Your father was not an evil man, nor was your mother unchaste'" (Q 19:27–28).[50] In the case of the viceroy's wife, a "witness from among her family" points to the presence of physical evidence against her in the form of Joseph's shirt, torn from the back as he tried to escape from her. In the case of Mary, her son defends her honor by testifying (as an infant) that he was not the result of an illicit affair.

## Negotiating Marriage Arrangements

The previously mentioned narrative involving Moses's (eventual) wife is another example that contrasts with the inappropriate actions of the wife of the viceroy. Moses—like Joseph—was stranded and far from home, and it is not unreasonable that one of the women at the watering hole in Midian could be attracted to this young stranger; however, she does not impiously attempt to seduce him. The sister in Midian seemingly falls for this strong, trustworthy young man, a future prophet of God. But unlike the wife of the viceroy, she acts with discretion and pursues her interest through licit means from beginning to end.

In the context of this narrative, the Qur'anic audience is privy to the marital negotiations between a prospective husband and his prospective father-in-law. We can infer that this future wife of Moses serves as a model for how to licitly pursue a relationship. She approaches the matter with appropriate discretion by speaking with her father, and she licitly—and even quite swiftly as the story progresses—attains a spouse of prophetic caliber. In her ability to advocate for her interests (or alternatively, in her sister's ability to be an advocate), the Qur'anic audience sees a positive example of female desire and pursuit.

## A Marriage Made in Heaven

In another partnership depicted in the Qur'an, God intervenes directly to ensure that a specific woman is licit to marry a particular man (in this case, the Prophet Muḥammad himself). In this episode, the Prophet initially encourages his adopted son Zayd to remain married to his wife: "retain your wife for yourself and reverence God" (Q 33:37). The Prophet, the Qur'an explains, is concerned that he might be accused of illicit sexual behavior if marries the former wife of his adopted son. But the Qur'an discloses that it is, in fact, God's will that Zayd should divorce his wife and that his former wife be married to the Prophet. The Qur'an even gives explicit reasons for this incident, highlighting its didactic purpose: "so that there should be no restriction for the believers in respect to the wives of their adopted sons when the latter have relinquished their claims upon them" (Q 33:37).[51] Thus, the revelation of the verse enacts the marriage and then also confirms that the prohibition against incest does not apply to cases of fostering or adoption.[52]

The Prophet Muḥammad and Zayd's former wife are married by God *directly*: "We wed her to you. . . . And the Command of God shall be fulfilled" (Q 33:37).[53] These circumstances are also juxtaposed to the circumstances of the wife of the Egyptian viceroy. She faced the inverse problem: she was attracted to Joseph, an enslaved young man who entered her home as a foster son (Q 12:21). (Zayd, too, was initially an enslaved person of the Prophet Muḥammad's household before he was taken as a foster son.) In the case of the viceroy's wife, however, God does not intervene to make her love interest licit for her.[54] Despite her ardent efforts, her desire remains unsatisfied in the Qur'anic account.

## Sexual Slander

The viceroy's wife commits slander by lying about Joseph's intentions. Another Qur'anic episode involves the sexuality of an upright woman who is slandered. ʿĀʾisha bt. Abī Bakr (d. 58/678), the wife of the Prophet Muḥammad, was accused of adultery by members of her community, but was then declared—by the Qur'an itself—to be upright and innocent.[55] In this instance, the Qur'an condemns—at length—those who gossiped and accused a chaste woman of indecency:

> Why, when you heard it, did not the believing men and women think well of their own, and say, "This is a manifest lie"?
>
> Why did they not bring forth four witnesses? For when they brought not the witness, it is they who were then liars in the eyes of God.
>
> And were it not for God's bounty upon you, and His mercy, in this world and the hereafter, a great punishment would have befallen you for having engaged [in vain talk] concerning it,
>
> when you accepted it with your tongues, and spoke with your mouths that of which you had no knowledge, supposing it to be slight, though it is great in the eyes of God.
>
> And why, when you heard it, did you not say, "It is not for us to speak of this! Glory be to You! This is a tremendous calumny!" (Q 24:12–16)[56]

This episode includes a cadre of gossipers who were also implicated; in biographical literature, the full story also mentions that family members bore testimony to ʿĀʾisha's upright character.

Both these women, the wife of the viceroy and the wife of the Prophet Muḥammad, were wives of important statesmen and politically prominent individuals; however, in several key ways, ʿĀʾisha's situation stands in direct contrast to that of the wife of the viceroy. The viceroy's wife followed her caprice, slandered the person she herself had accosted, consorted with accomplices among the women in the city to exacerbate the situation, and caused an innocent person to be imprisoned. Later, the Qur'an relates the testimony of the wife of the viceroy about her wrongdoing: "The viceroy's wife said, 'Now the truth has come to light. It was I who sought to lure him from himself, and verily he is among the truthful'" (Q 12:51). In direct contrast, ʿĀʾisha acts with discretion when she finds herself alone with an unrelated young man, is accused of infidelity by her people, and the Qur'an *itself* testifies to her innocence: "Truly those who brought forth the lie were a group among you . . . " (Q 24:11; discussed further in Chapter 4). Both episodes address communal responses to alleged sexual impropriety; in the first instance, the woman in the relationship is indeed a seductress, and in the second instance, she is chaste. One story is derived from pre-Qur'anic sacred history, and the other story takes place in the nascent Muslim polity. From another perspective, the very theme that was initially raised in the story of Joseph's encounters with the viceroy's wife then has a direct moral bearing on an event transpiring in the emerging Muslim polity, a dynamic that I will address further in Chapter 4.

## Sexual Assault

The failed seduction of Joseph by the wife of the viceroy has an undeniable theatrical quality.[57] However, by approaching this story from another angle—as a narrative about what is commonly referred to as sexual assault—we can gain insights into the dynamics of sex, political power, coercion, testimony, and the pursuit of justice. The narrative also prompts an examination of these underlying power dynamics in a manner that involves, but then ultimately blurs and transcends, categories of female identity, male identity, masculinity, femininity, and womanhood. At the same time, the gender of the figures cannot be overlooked: Why does the Qur'an's most detailed account of what we might refer to in contemporary terms as "attempted sexual assault" involve a female perpetrator and a male victim?[58]

In Joseph, we see a person who represents several socially disadvantaged identities that make him particularly vulnerable to exploitation: he was subjected to violence, displacement, and migration (his brothers intended to kill him out of jealousy and then to leave him for dead in a well) (Q 12:15–18); he was a youth in a foster situation without familial protections; he was enslaved (Q 12:19–20); and he was an ethnic minority, a Hebrew under an Egyptian aristocracy.[59] The "women in the city" even refer to Joseph by highlighting his youth and his status as a "slave boy" when they gossip: "The viceroy's wife sought to lure her slave boy (*fatāhā*) from himself!" (Q 12:30).[60]

The power dynamics between the socially powerful and the wrongfully oppressed become a driving force in the narrative. This is evident, for instance, when Joseph is imprisoned by the sovereign, even in light of the clear physical evidence that supports his innocence and his good faith efforts to resist and flee from the sexual advances of the viceroy's wife:

> He [Joseph] said, "It was she [the viceroy's wife] who sought to lure me from myself." And a witness of her own people testified: "If his shirt is torn from the front, then she has spoken the truth and he is among the liars.
>
> But if his shirt is torn from behind, then she has lied and he is among the truthful." (Q 12:26–27)

Notably, someone from the family of the viceroy's wife comes forward to offer this empirical method of examining the evidence. The testimony of her relative against her reinforces the Qur'an's ethical commandment to the believers to advocate for justice even against blood ties:

> O you who believe! Be steadfast maintainers of justice (*kūnū qawwāmīna bi-l-qisṭ*), witnesses for God, though it be against yourselves, or your parents and kinsfolk, and whether it be someone rich or poor, for God is nearer to both. Follow not caprice (*al-hawā*), that you may act justly. If you distort or turn away, truly God is aware of whatever you do. (Q 4:135)[61]

In these verses, the command to "steadfastly maintain justice," even against kin or those with financial capital, is directly followed by a reference to caprice (*hawā*), a term that can also indicate, more specifically, lusts or sexual desires.[62] In Joseph's case, the female protagonist not only follows her lusts, but then also exacerbates her moral failing by initially distorting the truth and declining to admit to her wrongdoing, until years later, when she testifies against herself when put under social pressure. The phrase "distort or turn away" can even be understood as applying to the content of the testimony, thereby reinforcing the importance of bearing true witness, as in the sense of, "Do not distort justice by turning away from the truth." The merit of testifying truthfully corresponds to her relative, "a witness from her own people (*ahlihā*)," who stands up for justice even against kin and even against a figure with stature.

At several junctures, the viceroy's wife and others in influential positions, including her husband, decline to do justice. For instance, the women in the city who witnessed firsthand the pressure that the viceroy's wife exerted on Joseph enabled the exploitive dynamic. They did not stand up for the vulnerable individual who was threatened and placed in a compromising situation by a politically influential person. "And if he does not do as I command, he shall surely be imprisoned; and he shall be among those humbled," boasts the viceroy's wife to her consorts (Q 12:32). The husband even blames the situation on the guile of women generally, exclaiming, "Verily this is among the schemes of you [women] (*kaydikunna*)—your scheming is great indeed!" (Q 12:28).[63]

Here the sovereign evokes a stereotype of women, even if, to his credit, he does seem to recognize that his wife was culpable: "Joseph, turn away from this. And you [my wife], seek forgiveness for your sin. Truly you were among the wrongdoers" (Q 12:29). Yet, despite the physical evidence attesting to Joseph's victimization and despite the many witnesses to the transgressive intentions of the viceroy's wife, the more powerful member of society was only lightly chastised. The one who was assaulted and then threatened was unjustly imprisoned, where he remained "for a number of years" (Q 12:42). The Qur'anic narration makes it clear that Joseph's punishment was an intentional, not an accidental, oversight of justice: "It occurred to them [presumably the viceroy and his consorts], after they had seen the signs, to imprison him [Joseph] for a time" (Q 12:35). Those in authority acted punitively toward Joseph even *after* they had clear evidence of what had transpired. The narrative highlights the impetus to exert power over the vulnerable and to cover potential scandals rather than to pursue the truth with upright intentions and integrity. It also points to the role of enablers (in this story, the women and the husband) in cases of sexual coercion and domination.

## Sexual Misconduct, Advocacy, and Redemption

Initially, Joseph's situation is bleak on account of the harassment he experiences; he refuses to submit to the advances of the viceroy's wife and spends a number of years in prison due to the schemes against him. However, the wife's misconduct and lies are ultimately exposed when the women finally testify to Joseph's upright character, saying, "God be praised! We know no evil against him" (Q 12:51). Then, the viceroy's wife finally admits her culpability. She declares, "Now the truth has come to light. It was I who sought to seduce him, and verily he is among the truthful" (Q 12:51). Despite the delay in securing this truthful testimony, and despite the years that Joseph spent in prison, a modicum of justice eventually prevails.

At the end of this Qur'anic narrative, the wife of the viceroy redeems herself, to some extent; yet she expresses no remorse and gives no apology. She does testify against herself and affirms Joseph's good character. It takes her years—and it only comes about because of Joseph's insistent message to the king from his prison cell and the testimony of her consorts—but she does, eventually, take the morally correct course of action.[64]

Joseph's reputation is redeemed, but in a theological sense, the viceroy's wife has also—by admitting to her improbity—taken an important first step in her own redemption. Ultimately, we do not know anything more about her fate from the Qur'anic account. However, the larger narrative arc of the surah *is* one of redemption (and forgiveness), as demonstrated by the final scene of the story, in which the family of Jacob is peacefully and joyously reunited. In Q 12:97, after the passage of significant time and after receiving the sign of the shirt from Joseph, the brothers admit their fault in Joseph's disappearance. Similarly, in Q 12:51, after a number of years, the truth "comes to light" regarding Joseph's imprisonment and the wife of the viceroy admits her guilt. There is one key distinction between the two instances of the truth coming to light: the brothers explicitly beseech their father to "seek forgiveness for us from our sins" (Q 12:97), whereas the viceroy's wife, however contrite her words, does not explicitly ask for forgiveness.

In this narrative, the perpetrator initially denied and concealed the wrong, and then those with political authority failed to uphold justice. Yet, the truth prevailed in large part because Joseph insisted on bringing it to light. At opportune moments, he pressed his case with those in positions of influence. When the king sent a messenger to summon him from prison, Joseph said, "Return to your lord and ask him, 'What of the women who cut their hands? Surely my Lord knows well their scheming!'" (Q 12:50). Joseph appealed to the sovereign to pursue truth and seek justice. His self-advocacy reifies and elevates the communal standards that protect human dignity. The Qur'anic commandment for believers to "bid what is right and forbid what is wrong" (*yaʾmurūna bi-l-maʿrūf wa-yanhawna ʿan al-munkar*) is axiomatic.[65] In this example, the wife of the viceroy and her cohorts are brought to justice; however, it is only at Joseph's insistence that the truth is revealed. In this sense, from an affective perspective, the story could be particularly powerful for individuals reckoning with the impacts of sexual harassment.[66]

## Beauty: Virtue, Not Aesthetics

The way in which the wife of the viceroy and her consorts are smitten by Joseph's angelic presence leads us to contemplate the Qur'an's depiction of physical attractiveness. With the exception of the beings in paradise, as discussed later, the Qur'an does not describe the physical beauty of any figure.[67] Mary is characterized by beauty; it is not physical beauty, however, but rather that which relates to her piety: "So her Lord accepted her with a beautiful acceptance, and made her grow in a beautiful way" (Q 3:37).[68] In a series of verses that address the sexual and marital life of the Prophet Muḥammad, he is described as a "beautiful example" (*uswa ḥasana*) for the believers (Q 33:21).[69] Such verses extend the concept of beauty beyond aesthetics to a moral plane.

Later in the same surah (Q 33), the Qur'an explicitly affirms the Prophet's appreciation of the beauty of women; after detailed instructions to the Prophet forbidding incest and permitting concubinage, the Qur'an asserts, "Women are not lawful for you [Muḥammad] beyond that, nor [is it lawful] for you to exchange them for other wives, though their beauty impress you (*aʿjabaka ḥusnuhunna*), save those whom your right hand possesses. And God is Watcher over all things" (Q 33:52). Here, the beauty (*ḥusn*) of women impresses the Prophet, who is also described as a "beautiful example"—in terms similar to the Qur'anic description of Abraham "and those with him."[70] Appreciating the "beauty" (*ḥusn*) of women is virtuous: recognizing the beauty of women is part of the Prophet's beautiful example. Why should we assume that in the case of women, the beauty mentioned is superficial or aesthetic rather than a reference to an elevated, beautified character, as in the other instances in the Qur'an?

From the Qur'anic depictions of human beauty, we see that this is not primarily an aesthetic quality; rather, it relates, in a fundamental way, to virtue. With the exception of beings in paradise, who are described in the Qur'an by their distinctive eyes and youthfulness, no Qur'anic story focuses on physical traits as a function of human desirability; even Joseph, the only character whose attractiveness is a driving theme of a Qur'anic story, is not described in terms of his physical appearance. The viceroy's wife and the group of women surrounding Joseph are enraptured by an angelic quality about him; yet, they do not refer to his physical appearance per se. Here again, attractiveness, even sexual appeal more narrowly, is articulated in terms of character, not aesthetic appearance. Beauty is never merely—or even primarily—an aesthetic quality; beauty is, more precisely, the epitome of virtue.

## Otherworldly Sexualities

In the Qur'an, references to the "seen" or "witnessed realm" (*ʿālam al-shahāda*) are consistently accompanied—and, in fact, preceded—by mention of the "unseen" or "unknown realm" (*ʿālam al-ghayb*), which is occupied by other, non-human beings, such as *jinn* (beings created of "smokeless scorching fire," Q 15:27) and *malāʾika* (angels, beings made of light).[71] In Qur'anic narratives, angelic beings occasionally appear with human form in the seen realm. In addition, the Qur'an contains multiple descriptions of beings that exist in the realm of paradise. How is sexual difference marked somatically in paradise? What can these beings of the unseen realm tell us about human sex, sexuality, and gender? We now consider these questions with regard to Qur'anic discourse, but also with an appreciation for the ultimate impossibility of clarifying "what no soul knows" (Q 32:17). My aim is not to assign unseen beings a definitive sex, but rather to enable a deeper engagement with gendered language in the Qur'an.

## Sex, Gender, and Angelic Beings

In Arabic, referring to a being with a masculine pronoun is not sufficient, on its own, to presume the ontological maleness of that being, though angelic figures mentioned in the Qur'an all appear in seemingly masculine forms and names.[72] The messengers that visit Abraham and Lot and their families seem to be manifest as men (given that other men are reproached for desiring them in place of women). Mary interacts with a "spirit from God" that delivers the news of her impregnation, who "assumed for her the likeness of a perfect human being (*bashar*)" (Q 19:17); while *bashar* can refer to humans in a general sense, it can also refer to a man specifically.[73] Even Joseph is equated to an angel by the enraptured women who exclaim, "God be praised! This is no human being (*bashar*). This is naught but a noble angel!" (Q 12:31). Moreover, disbelieving people are condemned for fabricating female angels: "And they have made the angels, who are servants of the Compassionate, females. Did they witness their creation? Their witnessing shall be recorded, and they will be questioned" (Q 43:19). In the instances of angels appearing in the seen realm as messengers, it is unclear if they come embodied as fully sexed beings, or if they occasionally assume some distinctive features that signify a male identity.[74]

## Ethereal Creations and Virginity in an Eternal Abode

Angels may not be female—or may not have a sex—but what can be said of the ethereal beings in paradise? Do beings in paradise have sexed bodies in ways akin to earthly bodies? What purposes do they serve vis-à-vis paradise's other inhabitants? Are they heavenly re-creations of earthly females and males? Do beings in paradise have intercourse or experience something akin to sexual pleasure? Few of these questions can be definitively answered based on Qur'anic verses alone, yet it is still useful for our purposes to examine precisely what the Qur'an does—and does not—state about beings in paradise.

In Qur'anic verses about human telos, in verses about the primordial couple, and also in references to the coupling of beings in the realm of paradise, the term for spouse that connotes "one of a pair" (*zawj,* pl. *azwāj*) is consistently employed. (*Zawj* can refer to the male or the female human spouse as well as non-human mates, depending on context.) The Qur'an also employs other terms for wives and husbands, but none of these other terms are used in relation to paradisal beings. No term that exclusively means "wife," "woman," or "maiden" is used in reference to paradisal beings. The Qur'an refers to some beings in paradise with grammatically feminine adjectives, but in Arabic, a grammatically feminine adjective does not necessarily signify the state of being female, ontologically speaking. Hence, it is more accurate to describe "women" in Qur'anic discourse as belonging specifically to the earthly realm and to appreciate the high degree of ambiguity with regard to the nature of paradisal beings.[75]

This brings us to a key question: Do beings in paradise actually have intercourse, or do they experience something akin to sexual pleasure? The Qur'an uses sensual language and sexual intimations on multiple occasions to describe the pleasure experienced by those in paradise. They are depicted as reclining "upon embroidered couches" and "facing one another" (Q 56:15–16), while "immortal youths (*wildān mukhalladūn*) wait upon them / with goblets, ewers, and a cup from a flowing spring" (Q 56:17–18).[76] The verse is specifically about youth offering alimentary delights, but imagination could conjure up sexual delights as well.[77] Adding to the ambiguity, *wildān,* a plural of the word *walad,* can be inclusive of female youth, but can also refer to exclusively male youth.

One rhyming segment describes beings referred to as *ḥūr ʿīn* that have "the likeness of concealed pearls" who are a reward, "a recompense for that which they used to do" (Q 56:22–24).[78] While this verse is typically read through the lens of male desire, the beings are not specifically "women," and the pronoun "they" can be understood in a gender-inclusive sense. The *ḥūr ʿīn* could even be the resurrected humans themselves in a newly created state. The segment goes on to describe the beings in paradise: "Truly We [God] brought them into being (f., *anshaʾnāhunna*) as a [new] creation, / then made them [as] virgins (*fa-jaʿalnāhunna abkāran*), / amorous peers (*ʿuruban atrāban*) / for the companions of the right" (Q 56:35–38).[79] These sensuous verses give rise to a host of questions and possibilities.[80] Does the term *abkār* signal the qualities of youthfulness and sexual inexperience simultaneously? Moreover, does the description necessarily exclude male or male-like virgins?[81]

It could be that former human beings are made into a "new creation" specifically for paradise and that this state itself is virginal (in its newness).[82] This interpretation could be seen as consistent with imagery later in the surah, imagery that alludes to a kind of replacement after death: "We have decreed death among you, and none outstrips Us / in replacing [you with] your likenesses and bringing you into being again in what you know not. / You have indeed known the first creation. Why, then, do you not reflect?" (Q 56:60–62). This passage emphasizes human inability to comprehend this new "likeness," but then urges the human being to reflect on cosmic and human origins. In this process of the re-creation of earthly human beings, it might be the *quality* of being new and virginal that the Qur'an is evoking, not necessarily virginity in the material sense of a woman with an intact hymen. Moreover, there may be female-like beings in paradise, but to describe these beings as "women" is not a precise use of Qur'anic terms.

## Sexed Bodies and Sexual Pleasure in Paradise

In just one instance, the term *kawāʿib*, which refers to beings in paradise, potentially evokes an anatomical part of the sexed body: "Truly the reverent shall have a place of triumph, / gardens and vineyards, / *kawāʿib* of like age, / and an overflowing cup" (Q 78:31–34).[83] Some have rendered *kawāʿib* as "buxom maidens"; however, the verse may be better understood as evoking newness and youthfulness, as this description is more consistent with the notion of "like age" that immediately follows.[84] This interpretation also reinforces the multiple other Qur'anic references to the youthfulness and sprightliness of beings in paradise. If *kawāʿib* indeed signifies a voluptuous woman, how would her "peer" or her partner "of like age" be somatically marked? Also, why should the reference to the "reverent" (*muttaqīn*) in the preceding verse (Q 78:31) be interpreted through an androcentric lens as pertaining only to reverent men?[85] Surely, spritely, devoted companions are a potential motivating factor for women, too?

In other instances, the Qur'an is explicit about the equity of the reward: "whoever, whether male or female, performs a righteous deed and is a believer shall enter the garden wherein they will be provided for without reckoning" (Q 40:40).[86] The "companions of the right" (a gender-inclusive term) will be recompensed with pleasure in the gardens of the next world for properly restraining their sexuality in this worldly life, and for other praiseworthy qualities. A similar Qur'anic segment describes the pious (*abrār*) (again using a gender-inclusive term). The "immortal youths" (*wildān*) serve the pious—immortal youths who, "when you see them (m. pl., *-hum*) you would suppose them to be scattered pearls" (Q 76:19). The sensuality and majesty of the scene—in spite of, or perhaps even because of, all the ambiguous elements—give rise to literal or metaphoric ecstasy: "And when you look there, you will see bliss and a great kingdom" (Q 76:20).[87] Certainly, there is sensuousness, but does the act of sex occur in the paradisal garden? Is there something akin to earthly sexual pleasure?

Qur'anic descriptions of paradise make no explicit mention of sexual intercourse. Imagery of beings reclining on luxurious seating with "abundant fruit, / neither out of reach, nor forbidden" (Q 56:32–33)[88] could be interpreted as consistent with the use of sexual euphemisms in the Qur'an. One segment of verses mentions raised seating or reclining areas (*furush*), immediately followed by the discussion of heavenly spouses (Q 56:34–35). Another two verses mention that God will "pair" (or "marry") (*zawwajnāhum*) inhabitants, here employing the word that is regularly used in the Qur'an for human and non-human mates.[89]

Ultimately, from the Qur'anic assertions, it is unclear if heavenly beings have sexual relations akin to human beings on earth.[90] There could be—perhaps like the tasty fruit in paradise—some semblance:

> And give glad tidings to those who believe and perform righteous deeds that theirs are gardens with rivers running below. Whenever they are given a fruit therefrom as provision, they say, "This is the provision we received aforetime," and they were given a likeness of it. Therein they have spouses (*azwāj*) made pure,[91] and therein they shall abide. (Q 2:25)

Likewise, in one verse, the Qur'an depicts paradisal beings as "possessing restrained glances" (*qāṣirāt al-ṭarf*), "whom neither human nor jinn has ever touched (*lam yaṭmithhunna*)" (Q 55:56).[92] This assertion strongly implies that among the earthly aspirants of this paradise, the ones admitted to the abode will be able to "touch" these previously untouched beings, though the Qur'an never explicitly makes such a promise.

The notion of having intercourse with heavenly virgins also creates an interpretive dilemma; that is, once "deflowered," a virgin is no longer a virgin, and so the notion of having one or more virginal maidens for all of eternity and the notion of having intercourse with her or them are mutually exclusive propositions (at least with reference to a basic understanding of intercourse and virginity in the earthly realm). Having a great number of virgins would allow for sex with virgins for a time, but in an *eternal* realm, would not virginity be exhausted? If the female-like beings are spontaneously restored to a state of virginity after sexual intercourse, do male-like beings in paradise experience a similar spontaneous renewal that is not possible on earth? In paradise, how is virginity marked somatically or otherwise? Is "virginity" in the Qur'anic discourse only applicable and desirable for females?

The Qur'an describes the *ḥūrīs* and the youth who are made eternal (*wildān mukhalladūn*) using the metaphor of pearls, which evokes their purity and aesthetic appeal, but possibly also their sexual appeal.[93] These beings have aesthetic—potentially erotic—appeal, but perhaps they do not have a practical function with regard to intercourse. On numerous occasions, heavenly beings are depicted with abundant fruits and drinks and golden goblets, and the Qur'an specifies that the fruits are consumed: "abundant fruit from which you will eat shall be yours therein" (Q 43:73).[94] The inhabitants of Paradise are told: "Eat and drink in enjoyment for that which you used to do" (Q 52:19). In contrast, the Qur'an provides intimations, but it does not explicitly specify that beings in paradise have sexual intercourse.

On one occasion, the Qur'an describes the bliss of the pious in paradise who are "upon couches, gazing" (Q 83:23) and who are "given to drink of pure wine sealed, / whose seal is musk—so for that let the strivers strive" (Q 83:25–26). Here, the parallels between "sealed wine" and sexual naïveté are suggestive. However, there is no indication that the verse should be understood exclusively through the lens of male desire. Another verse (Q 5:5) describes lawful food and licit sexual partners in the earthly realm. In this verse, the two (food and sex) are connected as pleasurable and sensual activities, but no Qur'anic verses specifically address sex in paradise. In one instance, the Qur'an states, "No soul knows what comfort is kept hidden for them as a recompense for that which they used to do" (Q 32:17).[95] In this case, it is possible that part of the "comfort" of paradise could be sexual intimacy, but this is not made explicit. Notably, it is the pious "soul" (*nafs*) who receives this hidden comfort. If earthly male "souls" receive the "comfort" of sexual intimacy in paradise, it would be reasonable to include earthly females too in this category of "souls" who receive this comfort.

The sensuality in the descriptions of paradise is ostensibly intended to motivate pious action, but in what ways are heavenly beings constituted, somatically, to allow for sexual intercourse? Do they look and function like human beings on earth? Is there some kind of action which these beings engage in that is comparable to sex on earth? Without a need for reproduction, and hence no need for reproductive organs, perhaps the paradisal gardens, with their amenities, comforts, and company, are pleasure enough without the need for somatic pleasure derived from sexual acts. In this case, the beings in paradise may be aesthetically pleasing but potentially do not have a teleological purpose of bringing inhabitants sexual pleasure.

The "wide-eyed" *ḥūr ʿīn* are described by the shape of their eyes, and the *qāṣirāt al-ṭarf* are described by the gesture of their eyes. In both cases, their eyes indicate their attentive presence and desirability. The behavior of the *qāṣirāt al-ṭarf*, in particular, extends the virtue of restrained glances from the earthly realm to the realm of paradise. This would suggest that some semblance of sexuality exists in paradise in order to have beings who are seemingly reserved about it. With the exception of the eyes of these heavenly beings (whatever their sex), the Qur'an does not offer much by way of details about the embodiment or physical traits of figures in paradise. The *qāṣirāt al-ṭarf* are, however, likened to "well-guarded" or "hidden" eggs (Q 37:49). Like the metaphor of the pearl, this reference suggests qualities of delicacy, purity, and richness, but it does not conjure up a specific bodily form.

We can posit that *ḥūrīs* should be understood as a subset of the more general category of immortal youths, since *ḥūrīs* are both youthful and immortal inhabitants of the gardens of paradise. The "beings of restrained glances" (*qāṣirāt al-ṭarf*) and the "wide-eyed" beings (*ḥūr ʿīn*) may be one and the same, but it is also possible that the *qāṣirāt al-ṭarf* are a subset of the *ḥūr ʿīn*, and that both are a subset of the "immortal youth" (*wildān mukhalladūn*). The most internally consistent possibility, given the various Qur'anic verses, is that humans are creatures bound exclusively to this present world, whereas in the gardens of the next world, all former human beings are varieties of the "immortal youths" (*wildān mukhalladūn*), that is, former human beings in a transformed state. Notably, the Qur'an does not explicitly mention "women" in paradise and does not explicitly promise sexual intercourse in paradise. These observations may disenchant earthly aspirants, but could paradise, by definition, possibly disappoint its inhabitants?

## Sexual Difference, Sexual Intercourse, and Regulating Desire

This chapter has provided an intra-textual reading of Qur'anic narratives involving women's sexuality. I have focused on the Qur'anic concept of pairs, on Qur'anic narratives involving couples, and on the aesthetic and erotic appeal of sexualized beings in paradise. We have seen that multiple Qur'anic stories involve sexual relations or sexual desire in some way, and narratives complement verses that directly permit and proscribe. Several Qur'anic stories involve female figures and impart details pertaining to sexual ethics: Adam and his spouse, the wife of the viceroy, the Prophet Muḥammad's wives, the wife of Moses, Lot's daughters, and others are all evoked in narratives that pertain to sex. Taken together, Qur'anic narratives reinforce the idea that intercourse is gratifying when it falls within certain ordained guidelines and moral limits. In summary, the concept of "guarding the private parts" is first illustrated by the primeval couple, who, in a dramatic moment, develop awareness of their sexual embodiment and hasten to cover their nakedness. Mary and Joseph are epitomes of sexual restraint.[96] Moses's future wife serves as a model for how to advance a licit relationship. The issue of the remarriage of divorcees is addressed in an episode involving the former wife of Zayd, who is eventually married to the Prophet Muḥammad by God directly.

Zayd's wife is the only female figure who is divorced in the context of a narrative, and her divorce works in her favor when God directly marries her to the Prophet Muḥammad. From the vantage point of social ethics, the story reinforces what other verses of the Qur'an plainly state: separation between spouses is one divinely sanctioned solution.[97] Moreover, the episode of the (former) wife of Zayd reinforces the lack of prohibition on divorcees remarrying[98] (with the notable exception of the Prophet Muḥammad's wives being forbidden to remarry after his death).[99]

The Qur'an contains many verses discussing the circumstances and conditions involved in licit sex, and includes multiple narratives that involve marriage or marital partners. Two new marriages are contracted in the course of Qur'anic narratives. The first one (in the order of both revelation and the compiled Qur'an) is Moses's marriage to one of the sisters of Midian. This story emphasizes the honorable manner in which parties should negotiate a marriage. The second marriage, that of the Prophet Muḥammad to the former wife of Zayd (as just discussed), emphasizes the divine will in the selection process and neutralizes a previous social taboo related to marriage eligibility. Both stories are brief but, in keeping with the didactic style of Qur'anic discourse, contain considerable practical lessons for the community of believers.

With regard to spousal relations, Qur'anic narratives include a full spectrum of possibilities: righteous couples, iniquitous couples, righteous husbands with iniquitous wives, and one case of a righteous wife (the wife of Pharaoh) with a reprobate husband. The Qur'an describes spouses in a variety of terms, the most frequent being *zawj*, a term that carries the sense of being one of a pair; the frequent use of this term can be understood as an indicator of the ideal reciprocity in marital relationships. All Qur'anic couples mentioned are pairs of women and men, in keeping with the Qur'an's emphasis on females and males as spouses for one another. In this respect, there is a direct mapping of sex onto gender roles.

Beyond marital unions, how should illicit sexual attraction or activity be addressed on the interpersonal and communal levels? On this question, several Qur'anic stories are relevant. One incident involved the Prophet Muḥammad's wife ʿĀʾisha, who was falsely accused of having engaged in adultery.[100] The ever-chaste Mary was herself accused of illicit sex when she encountered her people as an unmarried woman carrying her infant son. Add to these instances the attempted conquest of Joseph by the viceroy's wife and the encounters of Lot's daughters with a drunken mob and we see the broad range of Qur'anic stories that somehow involve the prospect of illicit sex. In fact, more Qur'anic stories are devoted to these themes than stories bearing on other aspects of sexual relations or even family relations. Judging by the sheer number of stories that relate to the topic, the issue of illicit sex is a major human dilemma in the Qur'anic worldview, both for the chaste who are unjustly accused of illicit sex and for immoral people who create havoc for themselves and others through their profligacy and moral bankruptcy.

The viceroy's wife, with her unbridled desire for the angelic-like Joseph, stands out as an exemplar of impropriety. With her susceptibility to her whims, her moral failings, her impulse to save face, and her later struggle to make amends, her flawed moral constitution renders her relatable. In fact, the vast majority of Qur'anic readers, reciters, or listeners may be more able to relate to her than to a figure like Mary, who represents an aspirational level of piety. When the female figures here are considered as a cohort, it is clear that the Qur'an does not emphasize the trope of the seductress; in fact, of the dozens of female figures mentioned in the Qur'an, only one plays the role of the temptress, and even she can be directly contrasted to women in similar, potentially compromising situations who take the correct moral action. With regard to sexual etiquette, there are other morally troubled women figures; for example, the consorts of the viceroy's wife are complicit, as they did not act when Joseph faced the sexual advances of the viceroy's wife. This cohort of women who (at least initially) act impiously can be compared to the mob of men who desire Lot's angelic guests and who are examples of impropriety.[101]

The Qur'an does not explicitly depict any female figure enduring sexual violence;[102] however, the possibility is alluded to, arguably, in the context of Pharaoh's abuse of his power: "Indeed, Pharaoh exalted himself in the land, and made its people into factions, oppressing a party among them, slaying their sons and sparing their women. Verily he was among those who work corruption" (Q 28:4). This context of a genocide (as described here and also in Q 7:141) is clearly rife for sexual violence, particularly given that the women are explicitly left alive when their men are murdered.

On a less austere note, narrative tropes involving sexual desire are not limited to the earthly plane; sensual delights—if not sex itself—await pious believers in paradise. In this eternal realm, where there seems to be no need for—and certainly no mention of—reproduction, sexual difference and gender are more fluid, and the gratification of sexual desire is intertwined with the gratification of other sorts of aesthetic and sensual pleasures. The Qur'an strikes a balance between, on the one hand, offering a preview of the afterlife to humans, who are privy to the "seen realm," and, on the other, safeguarding the mysterious aspect of the unseen realm (*al-ghayb*). Many ambiguities arise with regard to sexual differentiation and sexual encounters in paradise, but we can draw one clear observation: in describing a realm that, by its nature, eludes human comprehension, the Qur'an conjures up particular affects, without divulging its secrets.

This chapter has served as a preliminary frame for themes related to sex and sexuality. I have focused on sexuality in and beyond the confines of marriage, including the aesthetic and erotic appeal of sexualized beings in paradise. I have examined how sex, as a feature of embodiment and as an act of intimacy, factors into Qur'anic narratives. I next delve into detail on the importance of Qur'anic female figures in the context of the family (in Chapter 2), in the context of women's speech (in Chapter 3), and in the context of moral and ethical precedents involving women (in Chapter 4).

## Notes

1. This is the first attempt I have found to consider sexuality in the Qur'an through a comprehensive analysis of narratives involving female figures. A number of previous studies consider only a few figures or consider sex and sexuality in the Qur'an primarily from the vantage point of legal studies. See, for instance, Ziba Mir-Hosseini, Mulki al-Sharmani, and Jana Rumminger, eds., *Men in Charge? Rethinking Authority in Muslim Legal Tradition* (London: Oneworld Publications, 2015). See also Ali, *Sexual Ethics*.
2. The root *z-w-j* occurs eighty-one times in the Qur'an and has a wide semantic range; it can signify an even number, a pair, two things that are connected in some way, a spouse, one of a pair, or simply a variety of something (as in Q 56:7). See *AEDQ*, 405–6.
3. The root *ʾ-n-th* occurs thirty times in the Qur'an, twenty-four times as a singular noun (*unthā*) and six times as a plural noun (*ināth*); see, for example, Q 42:50. See also *AEDQ*, 56. The noun that means "male" (*dhakar*, pl. *dhukūr/dhukrān*) is mentioned in the Qur'an eighteen times. Overall, the root *dh-k-r*—with the general meaning of "mention" or "remember, recall"—is mentioned 292 times in fourteen different grammatical forms. See *AEDQ*, 328–32. For a feminist analysis of Q 4:1, see, for example, Osman, *Female Personalities*, 16–22, and Bauer, *Gender Hierarchy*, 101–57. For a reflection on dualism in descriptions of creation, see Wadud, *Qur'an and Woman*, 20–23.
4. On the genesis of human beings from an initial pair, see, for example, Q 49:13 and 75:39. Regarding verse 75:39, *The Study Quran* translates *al-zawjayn* as "two genders"; however, the translation "two sexes" is more precise, as preceding verses reference sexual fluids and clots, thereby situating Q 75:39 in a biological, rather than a social, context. On the pairing of human beings, see also Q 4:1, 7:189, 30:21, 39:6, 51:49. The Qur'an consistently depicts sex as binary and does not directly address intersex persons (*khunthā* in Arabic), a topic that is, however, taken up by Muslim jurists. See Marion Katz, "Gender and Law," in *Encyclopaedia of Islam, Three*, ed. Kate Fleet et al. (2017), online at: http://dx.doi.org.ezproxy.library.tufts.edu/10.1163/1573-3912_ei3_COM_27397 (accessed May 27, 2019).
5. For an in-depth discussion of human nature as it relates to the rest of the created world in Qur'anic discourse, see Murata, *The Tao of Islam*, 23–37. For a discussion

of the motif of duality, see Todd Lawson, "Duality, Opposition and Typology in the Qur'an: The Apocalyptic Substrate," *Journal of Qur'anic Studies* 10, no. 2 (2008): 27–35; see p. 30 for a long list of common Qur'anic dualities.

6. See Q 112:4. This word and its root, *k-f-ʾ*, appear only once in the Qur'an. See *AEDQ*, 809.
7. For further discussion of this "single soul" and the creation of the primal pair as discussed in the commentary literature, see Osman, *Female Personalities*, 19–36. For a discussion of the tendency of translators to change the feminine pronoun (*hā*) for soul into a masculine pronoun or neuter pronoun, see Barazangi, *Women's Identity and the Qur'an*, 44. Notably, these verses immediately follow an absolute refutation of the concept of God taking a child. See Q 39:3–4 as well as discussions of parenting in Chapter 2.
8. For a poetic rendering of this concept, see, for example, Q 55:26–27.
9. For a more detailed discussion of wombs, see Chapter 2. See also Kathryn M. Kueny, *Conceiving Identities: Maternity in Medieval Muslim Discourse and Practice* (Albany: State University of New York Press, 2013), 19–49.
10. For an analysis of this and related verses, see Jerusha Tanner Lamptey [Rhodes], "From Sexual Difference to Religious Difference: Toward a Muslima Theology of Religious Pluralism," in *Muslima Theology*, 231–45. A similar verse refers to the multiplicity of human skin tones and languages as part of the divine design: "And of God's signs is the creation of the heavens and the earth and the diversity of your tongues and your colors. Indeed, in that are signs for those of knowledge" Q 30:22.
11. This point has long been a cornerstone of feminist scholarship on the Qur'an. See, for instance, Wadud, *Qur'an and Woman*, 36–38.
12. The grammatical case endings create consonance for the words "human being" (*basharan*), "lineage" (*nasaban*), "kinship" (*ṣihran*), and "powerful" (*qadīran*). The root *ṣ-h-r* that translates as "kinship" earlier appears twice in the Qur'an and also means fusing or bonding, as in Q 22:20. The term *ṣihr* (pl. *aṣhār*/*ṣuharāʾ*) can be used more generally in Arabic to refer to in-laws. The verse cited is the one Qur'anic use of the word in the context of family relations, with the metaphorical sense of becoming joined or fused to a new family through marriage. See *AEDQ*, 539. The root *n-s-b*, as in the word *nasab* (pl. *ansāb*) in this verse, refers to family relations through descent. See *AEL*, 1737–38. Other terms for kinship relations include *ʿashīra* (e.g., Q 26:214), and *qurbā* (e.g., Q 2:83, 2:177, 4:36). See also Anver Giladi, "Family," *EQ*, 2:173–76. Several other Qur'anic terms also refer to various aspects of familial relations, as discussed further in Chapter 2. Arguably the many terms and multiple occurrences of words related to family relations underscore their conceptual importance in the Qur'anic worldview.
13. See also Q 80:19.
14. See also Q 35:12 for another verse that uses the imagery of seas (and that directly follows a verse on reproduction): "Not equivalent are the two seas: one is sweet, satisfying, pleasant to drink, and the other is salty, bitter. Yet from each you eat fresh meat, and bring out ornaments that you wear. . . ." Subsequent verses describe other binaries in creation.

15. The imagery of the heavens and earth being metaphorically sewn together and torn apart is complemented by the rhyme of the roots *r-t-q* (to mend, join together, repair, patch up, stick together) and *f-t-q* (to split, rip open, slash lengthwise). This verse is the only occurrence of either of these words or their roots in the Qur'an. See *AEDQ*, 346 and 691, respectively. For philosophical and mystical discussions of the heavens and the earth, see Murata, *The Tao of Islam*, 117–41.
16. See Q 4:1, 6:98, 7:189, 31:28, and 39:6.
17. *Arḥām* (sing. *raḥim*) literally means "wombs" or can be symbolic of family relations. For analysis of this verse in classical commentary, see Osman, *Female Personalities*, 32–34. This verse is widely recited at the beginning of the communal Friday prayer, a liturgical use that is attributed to the Prophet himself and one that underscores the importance of the verse in inculcating piety (*taqwā*).
18. See Lamrabet, *Women and Men in the Qur'ān*, 39. Feminist commentators have been quick to point out that the Qur'an does not identify the original single soul as being a specific person, even if subsequent interpretations identify this single soul as Adam. See, for instance, Wadud, *Qur'an and Woman*, 20.
19. Language of complementarity can be deployed to create hierarchical schema rather than a robust recognition of reciprocity. Language of complementarity may at times be used to justify subjugation, but the premise of complementarity itself does not necessitate hierarchy. See Celene Lizzio, "Courage at the Crossroads," in *A Jihad for Justice: Honoring the Work and Life of Amina Wadud*, ed. Juliane Hammer, Laury Silvers, and Kecia Ali, 85–89 (2012), https://www.bu.edu/religion/files/2010/03/A-Jihad-for-Justice-for-Amina-Wadud-2012-1.pdf (accessed August 10, 2019).
20. For poignant reflections on the theological significance of this verse, see Lamrabet, *Women and Men in the Qur'ān*, 73. See also Barlas, *Believing Women*, 153.
21. With regard to the word *anfusihim* (themselves), the *anfus* (selves) is plural and grammatically feminine, and the possessive suffix is plural and grammatically masculine; the composite word is inclusive of human beings generally. On this point, there are dozens of other Qur'anic examples.
22. Here, as in many other places, a grammatically masculine verb does not necessarily correspond exclusively to an ontologically male actor or actors. The second-person pronoun suffix *-kum* in the verse must be gender inclusive for the verse to refer to male–female intimacy.
23. See also Lamrabet, *Women and Men in the Qur'ān*, 74. Asma Barlas argues that the Qur'an counterbalances the regulation of sexual praxis by not depicting sex itself as "dangerous or dirty," but as "fulfilling and wholesome" even beyond its procreative aspects. See Barlas, *Believing Women*, 153.
24. This narrative is the first in Qur'anic sacred history; Q 2:35 is just over forty verses into the Qur'an when reading/reciting the Qur'an sequentially. The last verses that mention a couple are in Q 111, just over a dozen verses before the Qur'an closes. Even sequentially in the composite Qur'an, couples have a presence at the beginning, at the end, and in many places in between.
25. See also Q 20:121. For provocative discussions about bodily covering in the Qur'an, see Barazangi, *Women's Identity and the Qur'an*, 62–67. For an analysis of early depictions

of Adam's spouse, see Catherine Bronson, "Eve in the Formative Period of Islamic Exegesis: Intertextual Boundaries and Hermeneutical Demarcations," in *Tafsīr and Islamic Intellectual History: Exploring the Boundaries of a Genre*, ed. Andreas Görke and Johanna Pink (New York: Oxford University Press and the Institute of Ismaili Studies, 2014), 27–61. For an analysis of this prototypical female in both medieval and contemporary commentary traditions, see Bauer, *Gender Hierarchy*, 101–57. See also discussions of recent feminist scholarly analysis in Jardim, *Recovering the Female Voice*, 40–44. See further discussions in Chapter 2.

26. See Q 20:118, where God says, "Truly it [the garden] is for you that you will neither hunger there, nor go naked (*lā taʿrā*)." See also discussions in Osman, *Female Personalities*, 29–30. For a provocative literary analysis of this story, including of the role of transgression, shame, and moral failure, see Sarah R. bin Tyeer, *The Qurʾan and the Aesthetics of Premodern Arabic Prose* (London: Palgrave Macmillian, 2016), 95–99. See also Bodman, *The Poetics of Iblīs*, 213–14. For discussions of the pudenda of Adam and Eve in relation to purity, see Brannon M. Wheeler, *Mecca and Eden: Ritual, Relics, and Territory in Islam* (Chicago: University of Chicago Press, 2006), 56–58.
27. Some have speculated that this unnamed couple is Adam and Eve because of the mention of one soul and its bifurcation, but the verse seems more likely to be a parable. For commentary, see *SQ*, 476 nn. 189–90. The story is not taken to mandate a normative sexual position, in which the man necessarily "covers" the woman; on the contrary, with the exception of prohibiting anal sex, Islamic jurisprudence does not regulate sexual positions. Anatomically speaking, the female sexual organ "covers" the male sexual organ in intercourse.
28. For example, Q 7:54. There are a multitude of literal and metaphorical usages and eleven different grammatical forms of the root *gh-sh-w/gh-sh-y* in the Qur'an, but of the twenty-nine occurrences of this root, it is only used explicitly in the aforementioned verse in reference to having sexual relations. In Islamicate poetry, the night is often equated to a lover. See *AEDQ*, 666–68. See also *AEL*, 790.
29. For example, Q 22:5 connects *turāb* (soil, dirt, dust) to the creation of the human being in stages in the womb. Over a dozen verses echo the idea that human beings were created from *turāb*; furthermore, human beings, like the remains of the cultivated fields, return to the earth in death. See also Q 18:37, 33:11, 65:7, and multiple other verses on human origins and material mortality. See related discussions in Wills, *What the Qur'an Meant*, 183–84, and in Barlas, *Believing Women*, 161–64. See also discussions in Lamrabet, *Women and Men in the Qur'ān*, 74–76.
30. The verse goes on to stress that he "would have" inclined toward her "had he not seen the proof of his Lord" (*law lā an raʾā burhāna rabbihi*). The parallel structure of the language here (*hammat bihi wa-hamma bihā*) and the use of the conditional structure stress that this inclination almost happened. See Q 22:52 for a verse that discusses the desires of messengers and prophets in general and the way in which "God makes firm His signs" to them.
31. *The Study Quran* renders *al-rafathu ilā* as "to go unto," but the word "intercourse" is arguably a clearer translation. See also Q 2:197 for the only other Qur'anic occurrence of the word *rafatha* in the context of a prohibition of sexual relations (*lā rafatha*) for

pilgrims. These are the only two instances of this term or its root, *r-f-th*, in the Qur'an. In addition to sexual intercourse, the term can mean "obscenity, indecency, indecent action or speech, to behave in an obscene manner." See *AEDQ*, 373–74. In addition, *The Study Quran* renders the occurrence of *nisāʾikum* in this verse as "your wives," but I have used "your women"; in later chapters, I examine this distinction between "wives" and "women" as categorical references.

32. The root *b-sh-r* appears in the Qur'an 122 times in thirteen grammatical forms. See *AEDQ*, 92–94. A primary meaning of the root is skin, possibly evoking the image of sexual intimacy as skin-to-skin contact. The root also has the connotation of giving good tidings, as in Q 41:30. *The Study Quran* renders *bāshirūhunna* as "to lie with" but translates the negative form of the command (*lā tubāshirūhunna*) euphemistically as "do not approach." For a discussion of this verse, see Shuruq Naguib, "Horizons and Limitations of Muslim Feminist Hermeneutics: Reflections on the Menstruation Verse," in *New Topics in Feminist Philosophy of Religion: Contestations and Transcendence Incarnate*, ed. Pamela Sue Anderson (Dordrecht: Springer, 2010), 33–50.
33. Kecia Ali, for instance, emphasizes "meaningful consent and mutuality" as "crucial for a just ethics of sexual intimacy" and argues that sex should embody such virtues as "kindness, fairness, compassion, and generosity." See Ali, *Sexual Ethics*, 193–94.
34. The root *m-r-ʾ* occurs thirty-eight times in the Qur'an in five forms: once as an adjective (see Q 4:4), eleven times in gender-inclusive usages to mean "person" (*imruʾ*/*imraʾ*/*imriʾ* in different grammatical cases), twenty-four times to mean "woman" or "wife" depending on the context, and two times in the feminine dual. See *AEDQ*, 874.
35. The word is from the root *n-s-w*. It appears fifty-nine times in the Qur'an, including twice, in Q 12:30 and 12:50, in the form *niswa* (a so-called plural of paucity) in reference to the women in the city who are consorts of the viceroy's wife. See *AEDQ*, 935–36. The word is also used as the title of the fourth surah of the Qur'an, *al-Nisāʾ* (The women).
36. See also Q 6:101 and 72:3 for the word *ṣāḥiba* to negate the claim that God has a female companion.
37. Examples of this usage include Q 3:33, 11:73, 15:65, 15:67, 19:6, 33:33, and others; *ahl* is from the root *ʾ-h-l*, which occurs 127 times in the Qur'an; it has various meanings, depending on context. These meanings range from "people" generally, to family or household, to a euphemism for wife, or as a designation of individuals or groups who possess some thing or some quality. See *AEDQ*, 61. See also Appendix B for a list of usages pertaining to female figures and their families.
38. Some theorize that the letter *hāʾ* in the root of the word *ahl* was contracted to become the letter *hamza*, and that the two *hamza*s of the new word *ʾ-ʾ-l* then contracted to a *hamza-alif* to form the word *āl*. See *AEDQ*, 64–65. *The Study Quran* renders *āl* as "people" in some instances and as "House" or "family" in other instances. I have used the term "House" consistently in this work. For illustrative examples of the terms *ahl* and *āl* with reference to the same family, see Q 15:65–67 and 55:33–34, regarding the family and House of Lot. See Appendix B for relevant verses containing these terms.

39. This surah (Q 58) is widely known as "*al-Mujādila*" (f., lit. "the disputer") after this phrase in the first line that describes the woman, widely identified in the commentary literature as Khawla bt. Thaʿlaba, who "disputes with you [Muḥammad]." See *SQ*, 1342 nn. 1–4 for the context of this episode, and see discussions in Chapter 4. For a reflection on the contemporary significance of this (female) disputer (*mujādila*), see Mohja Kahf, "She Who Argues: A Homily on Justice and Renewal," *Muslim World* 103, no. 3 (2013): 295–304.
40. The word *baʿl* appears twice in the context of divorce negotiations (Q 2:228 and 4:128), three times in Q 24:31 in the context of modesty (and which men women need to dress more modestly around), and once in a Qur'anic narrative involving the wife of Abraham addressing Abraham as such in Q 11:72. The root appears a seventh time (Q 37:125) as the name for a false god worshiped by misguided peoples—ostensibly an overt reference to the biblical use of the word in this same context. Other meanings of the root include being perplexed or confounded. See *AEL*, 228.
41. The term *sayyid* occurs in the context of the climactic interactions between the adolescent Joseph and the aristocratic Egyptian couple, as discussed later in this chapter and in subsequent chapters. It is derived from the root *s-w-d*, a root occurring in the Qur'an ten times. It occurs with the meaning of master, leader, or chief in Q 12:25 and 33:67; it carries the meaning of noble in Q 3:39 to describe the Prophet John. In other instances, it occurs with the connotation of darkness, blackness, or the process of becoming black. See *AEDQ*, 464–65.
42. For an excellent historiographical approach to themes of intent (*irāda*) and consent (*riḍā*) in Islamic legal discourse on licit and illicit sex, including a discussion of unfree persons, see Hina Azim, *Sexual Violation in Islamic Law: Substance, Evidence, and Procedure* (New York: Cambridge University Press, 2015). Notably, marriage is not the only contractual agreement that makes sex licit between a man and a woman. Enslaved persons, known in the Qur'an literally as "what your right hands possess" (*mā malakat aymānukum*; see, for instance, Q 2:221, 4:25, and 24:32), are also licit sexual partners, with some important exceptions. For a detailed discussion, see Kecia Ali, *Marriage and Slavery in Early Islam* (Cambridge, MA: Harvard University Press, 2010). On the religious affiliation of potential partners, see Ali's discussion in *Sexual Ethics*, 14–22; see also my discussions in Chapter 4 below. For a contemporary interpretation that shifts the Muslim marriage contract from a premodern notion of "ownership" to a framework of "partnership," see Asifa Qureishi-Landes, "A Meditation on *Mahr*, Modernity, and Muslim Marriage Contract Law," in *Feminism, Law, and Religion*, ed. Marie A. Failinger, Elizabeth R. Schiltz, and Susan J. Stabile (Burlington, VT: Ashgate, 2013), 189–91. A number of Qur'anic verses deal in general terms with the issue of financial agreements in marriage. See, for example, Q 4:24–25; in both verses (4:24 and 4:25), the word "their [f.] bridewealth" (*ujūrahunna*) is the twenty-seventh word, suggesting therein (by structure, perhaps) the principle of balance.
43. The Qur'anic narrative indicates her virtue by noting that the sister was "walking bashfully." For a discussion of the virtue of modesty in Islamic ethics, see Marion Holmes Katz, "Shame (*Ḥayāʾ*) as an Affective Disposition in Islamic Legal Thought,"

*Journal of Law, Religion and State* 3 (2014): 139–69. Katz posits a definition of *ḥayāʾ* as "anticipatory shame," noting that "in its broadest usage, the word does not suggest the possession of a retiring or self-effacing personality"; rather, it denotes the possibility that a "specific action may be unbecoming" (143). Furthermore, Katz observes that having *ḥayāʾ* is "an affective disposition rather than simply an evanescent feeling" (144). As a desirable quality for a young woman entering a marriage, see Katz's discussions, 153–54. See also previous discussions of the paradisal female-like "beings of restrained glances" (*qāṣirāt al-ṭarf*) in Q 37:48, 38:52, and 55:56.

44. For a discussion of the figure of Moses's father-in-law in the exegetical tradition, including references to the corresponding biblical verses, see Younus Y. Mirza, "Ibn Taymiyya as Exegete: Moses' Father-in-Law and the Messengers in *Sūrat Yā Sīn*," *Journal of Qur'anic Studies* 19, no. 1 (2017): 39–71. For discussions of the figure of Moses, see Brannon M. Wheeler, *Moses in the Qur'an and Islamic Exegesis* (London: RoutledgeCurzon, 2002).
45. For an extensive discussion of the word *ḥāfiẓāt* and its historical interpretations, see Chaudhry, *Domestic Violence and the Islamic Tradition.*
46. In Q 4:34, pious women are "guardians" (f. pl., *ḥāfiẓāt*) of the "unseen" (*al-ghayb*), but in approaching the Qur'an as a complete recitation, it is *after* the encounter between the viceroy's wife and Joseph that the Qur'an mentions guarding the pudenda specifically. Arguably, narrative sets the stage for the direct ethical injunction.
47. I discuss this dynamic again in Chapter 3, and Karen Bauer makes a similar argument in "Emotion in the Qur'an," 24.
48. Mary's chastity is again emphasized in the Qur'an in 66:12.
49. In Chapter 3, I highlight similarities in the language Mary and Joseph use to confront their respective intruders.
50. For reflections on the terminology "sister of Aaron," see Michael Marx, "Glimpses of a Mariology in the Qur'an: From Hagiography to Theology via Religious-Political Debate," in *The Qurʾān in Context: Historical and Literary Investigations into the Qurʾānic Milieu*, ed. Angelika Neuwirth, Nicolai Sinai, and Michael Marx (Leiden: Brill, 2010), specifically 539–41 and 553–54. See also Gregg, *Shared Stories, Rival Tellings*, 541–42 and 549–50, and Reynolds, *The Qur'ān and Its Biblical Subtext*, 132–34. For reflections on the births of Jesus and Moses as subversive, see Geissinger, "Mary in the Qur'an," 388–91.
51. The Qur'an does not mention the woman by name, but the story is widely narrated in the early biographical literature, where her identity is Zaynab bt. Jaḥsh. As Karen Bauer notes regarding verse Q 33:37, some verses "tell the believers, even including the Prophet, that they need guidance to calibrate their emotions, and this guidance may lead them against their own emotional urges. They must submit their own feelings to God's authority." See Bauer, "Emotion in the Qur'an," 14. I discuss this episode in more detail in Chapter 4.
52. In Q 33:3–5 and 33:37, the Qur'an clarifies that adoption, as an attempt to alter the ancestral lineage of an individual, is prohibited. Fostering, however, is encouraged as a pious act. As I discuss in Chapter 2, Qur'anic narratives include cases of several foster child–parent relationships.

53. This is one of many verses in which God as the Qur'anic narrator speaks in both the first and third persons. The word for marriage also signifies copulation: *nikāḥ*, from the root *n-k-ḥ*, means to commingle, to copulate, and to take in marriage; it refers to "coitus; and coitus without marriage; and marriage without coitus." See *AEL*, 2848.
54. Various commentators speculate that Joseph married the wife of the Egyptian viceroy after her husband passed away. Other exegetes depict the wife as a "lover in progress," meaning that her feelings evolved from a lust-based attraction to Joseph's outer beauty to an appreciation of his inner beauty, his character, qualities, and station. See Osman, *Female Personalities*, 53–55. The Qur'an does not provide information about Zayd's wife's desires, but subsequent works of exegesis do describe her relief and satisfaction with the Prophet Muḥammad as a new husband.
55. For a critical overview of the biographies of ʿĀʾisha throughout Muslim intellectual history, with attention to aspects of sexuality, see Ali, *The Lives of Muhammad*, 155–99. See also Jardim, *Recovering the Female Voice*, 51–57.
56. See also the later verses Q 24:23–24, "Truly those who accuse chaste and heedless believing women are cursed in this world and the hereafter, and theirs shall be a great punishment / on the day their tongues, their hands, and their feet bear witness against them as to that which they used to do." The incident that led to the accusations, the accusations themselves, and the accusers are not recounted in the Qur'an, though the Qur'an does relate the moral and ethical lessons of the episode for the different parties involved, as I discuss in more detail in later chapters.
57. See Mustansir Mir, "Irony in the Qur'ān: A Study of the Story of Joseph," in *Literary Structures of Religious Meaning in the Qur'an*, ed. Issa J. Boullata (New York: Routledge, 2000).
58. For a feminist perspective on this question, see Gayane Karen Merguerian and Afsaneh Najmabadi, "Zulaykha and Yusuf: Whose 'Best Story?'" *International Journal of Middle East Studies* 29, no. 4 (1997): 485–508.
59. For an analysis of the biblical "ambivalent and self-contradictory masculinity of Isaac and Jacob," see Lori Hope Lefkovitz, *In Scripture: The First Stories of Jewish Sexual Identities* (Plymouth, UK: Rowman & Littlefield, 2010), 85. See also Lori Lefkovitz, "'Not a Man': Joseph and the Character of Masculinity in Judaism and Islam," in *Gender in Judaism and Islam: Common Lives, Uncommon Heritage*, ed. Firoozeh Kashani-Sabet and Beth S. Wenger (New York: New York University Press, 2015), 175–78, and Shalom Goldman, *The Wiles of Women/The Wiles of Men: Joseph and Potiphar's Wife in Ancient Near Eastern, Jewish, and Islamic Folklore* (Albany: State University of New York Press, 1995).
60. Here, as Osman points out, the term *shaghafa* (which is used in Q 12:30 in a verbal form) is "literally the layer of fat that veils the heart"; the viceroy's wife's heart becomes afflicted with love (*qad shaghafahā ḥubban*) for Joseph. See Osman, *Female Personalities*, 55. Although the cause of the affliction is very different, this description of the metaphorical heart of an afflicted woman can be compared with descriptions of the distraught feelings of the mother of Moses, as we see in Chapter 3. It is not until this verse that Joseph's assaulter is specifically identified as the "viceroy's wife" by her

gossiping friends; at the outset of the narrative, in verse 21, the Qur'anic audience knows only that she is the wife of "the man from Egypt who bought him [Joseph]."

61. In this verse, all believers are commanded to be "maintainers" (*qawwāmīna*) of justice; this is relevant to feminist analysis of Q 4:34, which also contains this term. See Celene Ibrahim, "Verse 4:34: Abjure Symbolic Violence, Rebuff Feminist Partiality, or Seek Another Hermeneutic?" in *Muslim Women and Gender Justice*, 174–75. The clause, "God is nearer to both," could be understood in the sense that God is more entitled to reverence than either a rich person or a poor person. In other words, standing for justice, no matter whom it requires standing against, is a form of witness before God.
62. The root of *hawā* (*h-w-y*) signifies falling down, literally and metaphorically. Its derived grammatical forms can mean to seduce or enrapture. Aside from caprice, other possible translations include affection, passion, longing, and so forth. See the reference to *hawā* as related to the Prophet David in the Introduction to this work; see also discussions on familial ethics in Chapter 2.
63. See also discussions of female guile, women's passion, and women's sexuality in Osman, *Female Personalities*, 51–56. For discussions of guile (*kayd*), see Ashley Manjarrex Walker and Michael A. Sells, "The Wiles of Women and Performative Intertextuality: Aisha, the Hadith of the Slander, and the Surah of Yusuf," *Journal of Arabic Literature* 30, no. 1 (1999), 69–71.
64. Sarah bin Tyeer observes: "this complexity creates a balance in the story whereby the representation of life is not a one-dimensional caricature of moral characters only, nor is life represented as depraved with only morally failed characters. Even the plotting brothers, who are morally questionable characters in the story, develop as they are forgiven and given a second chance at the end." See bin Tyeer, *The Qur'an and the Aesthetics of Premodern Arabic Prose*, 17. See also provocative discussions in Osman, *Female Personalities*, 56–60.
65. For example, Q 3:104, 3:110, 31:17, and others. The command to "bid what is right and forbid what is wrong" is also preceded by an explicit reference to gender in one instance: "The faithful men and the faithful women are protectors (*awliyā'*) of one another; they bid what is right and forbid what is wrong" (Q 9:71).
66. For an analysis of the narrative in relation to the experience of contemporary sexual assault survivors and perpetrators, see Celene Ibrahim, "Sexual Violence and Qur'anic Resources for Healing Processes," in *Sexual Violence and Sacred Texts*, ed. Amy Kalmanofsky (Cambridge, MA: Feminist Studies in Religion, 2017), 80–88.
67. The Qur'an mentions only a few specific body parts of women personalities. In the case of the Queen of Sheba, in Q 27:44, "It was said to her, 'Enter the pavilion.' But when she saw it, she supposed it to be an expanse of water and bared her legs." In relation to the wife of Abū Lahab in hell, a "rope of palm fiber" will be around her neck (Q 111:5). The women with the viceroy's wife cut their hands (Q 12:31, 12:50), and the wife of Abraham slaps her face (Q 51:29). The nakedness of the primordial couple is also mentioned.

68. See discussions of this verse in subsequent chapters. The word signifying beauty comes from the same root (*ḥ-s-n*) as the words denoting goodness, probity, and spiritual excellence (e.g., *iḥsān, muḥsin*). See also Q 33:52 for a reference to female beauty (*ḥusn*). For further explorations of the concept of beauty, see bin Tyeer, *The Qur'an and the Aesthetics of Premodern Arabic Prose*, 43–47 and 50–55.
69. For reflections on the significance of the Prophet as an exemplar, see Lamptey, *Divine Words*, 127–28 and 141–43. See also Kecia Ali, "'A Beautiful Example': The Prophet Muhammad as a Model for Muslim Husbands," *Islamic Studies* 43, no. 2 (2004): 273–91; in particular, see 289–90 for the compelling distinction Ali draws between the exemplary and exceptional qualities and actions of the Prophet.
70. The term *uswa ḥasana* appears with regard to Abraham "and those with him" in Q 60:4. A subsequent verse reiterates that the beautiful example is both Abraham and his companions: "You have a beautiful example in them . . ." (Q 60:6). See further discussions in Chapter 4.
71. See Q 15:27 for a description of the *jinn*. See also Amira El-Zein, *Islam, Arabs, and the Intelligent World of the Jinn* (Syracuse, NY: Syracuse University Press, 2009). The composition of angels from light is derived from a hadith attributed to ʿĀʾisha. References to angels, from the root *m-l-k*, occur 73 times in the Qur'an; this root occurs a total of 206 times with other meanings. See *AEDQ*, 893–95. See also El-Zein, *Islam, Arabs, and the Intelligent World of the Jinn*, 32–52 and Gisela Webb, "Angels," *EQ*, 1:84–92.
72. For instance, see Q 2:97–98 for references to Gabriel (Jibrīl) and Michael (Mīkāʾīl), angelic personalities that also appear in the biblical tradition. See also Q 43:77 for the name Mālik, a guardian of hell who is held to be an angel. (On this verse, differences of vocalization could render this word a description and not a proper name.) For a brief discussion of gender as it pertains to angels, see also De Sondy, *The Crisis of Islamic Masculinities*, 97–98.
73. See also Q 3:42 for the angels who call out to Mary.
74. Organ systems, including reproductive organs, are perhaps not suited to the messengers' constitution (see, for example, Q 51:26–28 and 11:70, in which angelic messengers refuse food). Moreover, as pointed out by Gabriel Reynolds, the Qur'an describes Mary and Jesus as eating food in Q 5:75, which is offered as evidence of their full humanity. See Reynolds, *The Qurʾān and Its Biblical Subtext*, 95.
75. For detailed accounts of heavenly beings in Islamic sources, see Nerina Rustomji, *The Garden and the Fire: Heaven and Hell in Islamic Culture* (New York: Columbia University Press, 2009), and Christian Lange, *Paradise and Hell in Islamic Traditions* (New York: Cambridge University Press, 2016). See also *Roads to Paradise: Eschatology and Concepts of the Hereafter in Islam*, 2 vols., ed. Sebastian Günther, Todd Lawson, and Christian Mauder (Leiden: Brill, 2017).
76. See Muhammad A. S. Abdel Haleem, "Quranic Paradise: How to Get to Paradise and What to Expect There," in *Roads to Paradise*, 57–61. For a discussion of how Qur'anic descriptions of paradisal banquets (and their attendees) relate to tropes in pre-Islamic literary genres, see Lange, *Paradise and Hell*, 66.

77. As Christian Lange observes, "the Qurʾān delicately intimates congress," but "in comparison with the culinary pleasures and the extravagant material riches enjoyed by the blessed, sexuality in the Qurʾānic paradise is a rather subdued affair." See Lange, *Paradise and Hell*, 45.
78. See Q 44:54, 52:20, and 56:22 for three instances of the phrase *ḥūr ʿīn*. See also *AEDQ*, 241–42. For further discussion on the depictions of the *ḥūr ʿīn* in literary and oratory sources, see the work of Maher Jarrar in "Strategies of Paradise: Paradise Virgins and Utopia," in *Roads to Paradise*, 271–94. For a chronological analysis of verses involving houris and heavenly spouses, see Lange, *Paradise and Hell*, 51–52. Lange argues that earlier verses on houris (which he regards as a pagan element) are "replaced by the resurrected wives of the believers" in later verses (56). Again, I would contend that no expression in the Qur'an itself clearly and specifically identifies these "spouses" as wives. For reflections on the ambiguity surrounding these beings as well as their sensuality, see Nerina Rustomji, *The Garden and the Fire*, 95–96. See also discussions of servants and fare in Rustomji, 91–97; for a discussion of symbolism and metaphor regarding the pearl, see esp. 92–93. In her analysis of a different historical context, Raber notes that "unlike other gems, the pearl is notoriously ephemeral, fragile"; see Karen Raber, "Chains of Pearls: Gender, Property, Identity," in *Ornamentalizing the Renaissance*, ed. Bella Mirabella (Ann Arbor: University of Michigan Press, 2011), 162.
79. Notably, the root *ʿ-r-b* and the root *t-r-b* have consonance and are both used in twenty-two instances in the Qur'an. (On a more esoteric level, this parallel could subtly reflect the meaning of *atrāb*, that is, to be "equal" or "well matched.") Concerning the root *ʿ-r-b*, this verse represents the only use of this particular adjectival form; other meanings of this root, as used in the Qur'an, include Arab and Arabic. See *AEDQ*, 131–32. A primary meaning of the root *ʿ-r-b* is to have or to revert to speech that is pure and free from error. Another meaning is to be lively and sprightly. A derived meaning that pertains specifically to women, according to Lane's lexicon, is "to act amorously." In addition, the term refers to "a woman who is eager for play, or sport" and to "a woman who is a great laugher," among many other usages given by Lane. See *AEL*, 1991–95. In terms of the root *t-r-b*, the word *atrāb*, which is the plural of *tirb*, meaning "well-matched" or "equals in age," also occurs in Q 38:52 and 78:33. The word *turāb*, derived from the same root, also means "dust"; it appears seventeen times in the Qur'an, including as the metaphorical or primordial substance from which humans are made. The root appears in the form *tarāʾib* to refer to the upper chest or rib area in Q 86:7. See *AEDQ*, 131–32.
80. For a further discussion of the history of exegetical debates on this topic, see Jarrar, "Strategies of Paradise." My analysis here considers Qur'anic terminology; for a discussion of hadith involving virgins in paradise, including discussions of authenticity, see Brown, *Misquoting Muhammad*, 238–46. For descriptions of Muslim women in paradise (and hell) according to well-known premodern sources, see also Lange, *Paradise and Hell*, 158.
81. *The Study Quran* translates *fa-jaʿalnāhunna abkāran* as "then made for [*sic*] them virgins"; Bakhtiar translates "made them virgins." See Bakhtiar, *The Sublime Quran*, 624. (Bakhtiar's translation is also that of Badawi and Abdel Haleem in *AEDQ*, 108.)

I have interpolated the word [as] in the preceding to signify my reading that this is a rhetorical use of the term "virgin," as I describe later. The word *abkār* (sing. *bikr*) is derived from the root *b-k-r*, which can also mean "unprecedented, novel, new." The root relates to youngness in age, particularly in animals (as used once in Q 2:68 in reference to a cow). See *AEDQ*, 108–9; see also *AEL*, 239–41; *LA*, 332–35; and *SQ*, 1323 nn. 35–40. See Q 66:5 for the only other use of the word *abkār* in the Qur'an; it appears in the context of spouses from those previously married and virgins.

82. The pronoun "them" (*hunna*) in *ansha'nāhunna* is a grammatically feminine plural, although here the feminine plural could pertain to the individual souls (f., *nafs*; pl. *nufūs* or *anfus*). If the feminine pronoun used here is seen as referring to the souls, this would be consistent with the sentiments of the remainder of the verse, since "companions of the right" is not a term that is generally restricted to men: "Truly We brought them (the souls, f.) into being as a [new] creation, / then made them virginal (*abkāran*), / amorous peers (*ʿuruban atrāban*), / for the companions of the right."
83. As Abdel Haleem observes, "any physical description of the people of paradise is very sparse" ("Quranic Paradise," 61). We can make a similar observation about Qur'anic depictions of human beings in the earthly realm, where the emphasis is on character traits and actions over appearances. When physical features are described, they often have metaphorical aspects (e.g., Q 3:106 and 80:38–41, among other verses describing faces). At the same time, this focus on rhetoric does not negate the potential for sex and sexual difference in the heavenly realm.
84. The term *kawāʿib* (sing. *kāʿib*) occurs just once in the Qur'an, making it a *hapax legomenon*. The term *kawāʿib* is translated in *The Study Quran* as "buxom maidens" and explained in the commentary as "maidens with full breasts" who are "fully mature" (*SQ*, 1466 n. 33). Bakhtiar translates this as "swelling breasted maidens" (*The Sublime Quran*, 683). Abdel Haleem argues that in its Qur'anic use, the term indicates the *onset* of puberty when a female *begins* to develop breasts. See Abdel Haleem, "Quranic Paradise," 60–61. For the connotation of youthfulness, see also *AEL*, 2616.
85. On the dominance of an androcentric lens in this regard, see Lange, *Paradise and Hell*, 158.
86. For analysis of the "recompense" for virtuous women and men, see Wadud, *Qur'an and Women*, 48–49.
87. In analyzing the Qur'an's apocalyptic language, Todd Lawson highlights the role of indeterminacy, vagueness, and ambiguity in producing its binary opposite, certainty. See Lawson, "Duality," 28. For a discussion of how interpreters embellished descriptions of these heavenly beings, see Lange, *Paradise and Hell*, 111, 130, 135, 140–41, and 152.
88. The lack of forbidden fruit in this paradise is in direct contrast to the primeval garden where Adam and his spouse ate of the forbidden tree. See Q 7:22 and 20:121 for their eating from the tree. The rudimentary clothing quickly stitched (from plant matter) by the primordial couple contrasts with the elaborate silk garments and jewelry worn by

beings in paradise. For descriptions of clothing in paradise, see Q 18:31, 22:32, 76:12, and 76:21.

89. See Q 44:54 and 52:20. *The Study Quran* translates *zawwajnāhum* as "wed" and renders the verse "we shall wed them to wide-eyed maidens." The masculine plural object pronoun *hum* in *zawwajnāhum* could be understood as gender inclusive, and in a literal translation of the verse, there is no word "maiden"; the spouses are simply described as "wide-eyed" (*ḥūr ʿīn*). Both spouses from among the paradisal immortal youth could have wide eyes; yet, the term is commonly taken by commentators to refer exclusively to females. See *AEL*, 666. Bakhtiar renders the phrase in question as, "we shall give in marriage lovely-eyed houris." See *The Sublime Quran*, 578.
90. As Abdel Haleem observes, "nowhere are they [beings of paradise] seen in any sexual situations or even sleeping" ("Quranic Paradise," 61).
91. Some exegetes emphasize that the *ḥūrīs* do not menstruate, procreate, or have bodily excretions. See Jarrar, "Strategies of Paradise," 277–78.
92. I prefer Bakhtiar's more precise choice of "those who restrain their glances" for the *qāṣirāt al-ṭarf* instead of *The Study Quran*'s translation, "of modest gaze." For Bakhtiar's translation, see *The Sublime Qur'an*, 621. The verb *ṭamatha*, from the root *ṭ-m-th*, is used only in the form *yaṭmith* in this verse and in an exact repetition of the verse in Q 55:74 (in keeping with the repetitive style of the surah as a whole). Primary meanings of the root *ṭ-m-th* are agricultural and pastoral, including metaphorical uses pertaining to the female body: "to place a halter on a horse or camel for the first time; to graze a piece of land for the first time; to deflower; to menstruate"; see *AEDQ*, 571. See also *AEL*, 1878, which specifies that the term can signify the onset of menses or a first experience of coitus that causes bleeding.
93. As discussed in Abdel Haleem, "Quranic Paradise," 64–65. See Q 55:58 for *qāṣirāt al-ṭarf* compared to rubies and coral. See also Jarrar, "Houris," in *EQ*, 2:456–58.
94. For a mention of golden goblets, see Q 43:71. For other mentions of elaborate alimental fare in paradise, see Q. 37:45–47, 47:15, 56:29–33, 76:15–18, and multiple other verses.
95. See also Abdel Haleem, "Quranic Paradise," 61.
96. On the "restrained virility" of Joseph and the sexuality of the Prophet Muḥammad, see De Sondy, *The Crisis of Muslim Masculinities*, 108–9 and 115. As De Sondy observes: "As ends on a continuum of what sexual ethics look like when played out, these male paragons Joseph and Muḥammad are able to illustrate that masculinity can look different in its outworkings—which is permissible so long as the core of one's identity is submission to God" (115).
97. See, for example, Q 4:128–30: "If a wife fears animosity or desertion from her husband, there is no blame upon them should they come to an accord, for an accord is better. Souls are prone to avarice, but if you are virtuous and reverent, surely God is aware of whatever you do. / You will not be able to deal fairly between women, even if it is your ardent desire, but do not turn away from one altogether, so that you leave her as if suspended. If you come to an accord and are reverent, truly God is

forgiving, merciful. / If the two separate, God will enrich both out of His abundance, and God is All-Encompassing, Wise."

98. See, for instance, Q 2:226–32 and 65:1–7 (a surah named "Divorce"). Qur'anic verses are also emphatic about the care and respect that widows are due and explicitly render remarriage permissible according to guidelines to ensure that remarriage happens "in an honorable way." See Q 2:234–35.
99. See Q 33:53. As a side note, the Qur'an itself does not relate stories of widows remarrying, but biographical traditions relate that the Prophet Muḥammad married a number of widows.
100. For further analysis of this episode, see Walker and Sells, "The Wiles of Women," esp. 55–56 and 59.
101. This story is discussed in the subsequent chapter in the context of father–daughter relationships. Male–male sexual desire is addressed in the story of Lot, his daughters, and the townspeople, who are "confused in their drunkenness" (Q 15:27); however, female–female sexual desire is not specifically addressed in any Qur'anic story.
102. For Abrahamic perspectives on this issue, see Amy Kalmanofsky, ed., *Sexual Violence and Sacred Texts* (Cambridge, MA: Feminist Studies in Religion Books, 2017).

# 2
# Female Kin, Procreation, and Parenting

Nearly all the female figures mentioned in the Qur'an appear in conjunction with a family member—a spouse, parent, sibling, or child, and often a combination of such relations. In this context, the present chapter considers Qur'anic descriptions of childbearing, childrearing, and kinship. I build on the previous chapter's discussion of sexual difference and gendered bodies and further probe "male–female relationships within the broader context of human relationships of dependency."[1] I provide a female-centric lens on kinship relations in the Qur'an. I look at Qur'anic descriptions of mothers, daughters, sisters, wives, and female extended kin that constitute relationships of dependency, affection, familial discord, and heroism. I demonstrate that female figures are not just auxiliaries or helpmates in the domestic and reproductive spheres; some bear children, but often women use their wit to provide vital lifelines to male figures. From daring rescues to offers of employment, the Qur'an depicts several female figures leveraging their kinship networks to the benefit of vulnerable male figures in distress.

In its narratives and in its direct ethical injunctions, the Qur'an reinforces the idea that human beings, both women and men, are responsible to strive for justice in their families and societies—and in their souls. To that end, Qur'anic narratives regularly feature wives, mothers, and sisters whose characters demonstrate God's ultimate wisdom, who provide guidance on family affairs, and whose narratives serve to inculcate piety in the Qur'anic reader, reciter, or listener. Ethical lessons pertaining both to familial cooperation and to intra-familial struggles involve mothers, daughters, sisters, and wives interacting with one another and with their male family members. Foster parents and nursemaids also enter the Qur'anic discourse.

The Qur'an includes figures that epitomize nearly all the different constellations of parent–child dynamics, including foster relationships. In fact, the vast majority of Qur'anic narratives involve some kind of family dynamic.[2] For all the main figures considered "messengers" (*rusul*, sing. *rasūl*), at least one female figure is associated with that messenger (and sometimes

*Women and Gender in the Qur'an*. Celene Ibrahim, Oxford University Press (2020). © Oxford University Press.
DOI: 10.1093/oso/9780190063818.001.0001.

more).[3] It is not only prophets, but also prophets' *families*, who figure prominently in Qur'anic stories.

In light of this centrality of kinship in the Qur'an, we must elucidate the roles of women figures as mothers, daughters, and sisters. Multiple other works study individual figures or compare a few figures; however, previous works have not approached female figures in the Qur'an comprehensively in the context of kinship ethics.[4] As a point of orientation, this chapter begins by surveying God's role as a caretaker in relation to human beings. I then survey key ethical directives that pertain to family relations. I then discuss narratives pertaining to mothers, daughters, and sisters in turn. I also make comparisons between female family members and the fathers, sons, brothers, and husbands with whom the women and girls interact.

## God and Procreation

Procreation, including the role of women therein, is repeatedly evoked in the Qur'an as a "sign" (*āya*) of God's power and majesty. A few words about divine–human relations are in order, by way of comparison. As we have seen in Chapter 1, God has no consorts, and moreover, "God begets not, nor was He begotten" (Q 112:3). Accordingly, the Qur'an never refers to God as "father" or "mother," nor does it refer to human beings as "children of God"; instead, it employs the phrase "Children of Adam" (e.g., Q 2:40).[5] The Qur'an depicts a different degree of intimacy between God and human beings than that of kinship metaphors. God is no "father" or "mother" in the Qur'anic discourse, but God is the "best of providers," among other such attributes of munificence.[6] Unlike God, beings in God's creation have partners and procreate: "The Originator of the heavens and the earth, He has appointed for you mates (*azwāj*) from among yourselves, and has appointed mates also among the cattle. He multiplies you thereby; naught is like unto Him, yet He is the Hearer, the Seer" (Q 42:11). Verses refuting the idea that God has consorts, or female children, or children in general are numerous.[7]

Multiple verses celebrate the miracle of procreation, human and otherwise, as a reflection of God's attributes of majesty as manifest in the created world: "God knows that which every female bears, how wombs diminish and how they increase. Everything with Him is according to a measure— / Knower of the Unseen and the seen, the Great, the Exalted" (Q 13:8–9). The

Qur'an echoes this idea of God's intimate awareness of each and every female (human and otherwise) in a verse depicting sex and procreation as part and parcel of the powerful sovereignty of God: "Unto God belongs sovereignty over the heavens and the earth; He creates whatever He will, bestowing females upon whomever He will, and bestowing males upon whomever He will, / or He couples males and females and causes whomever He will to be barren. Truly He is Knowing, Powerful" (Q 42:49–50). Procreation, in the human and non-human realms, is a sign of divine power, majesty, and knowledge; the selection of female or male, or both, or neither is God's prerogative.[8]

God is not a parent-God, but God is involved in each being in each womb: "God created you from dust, then from a drop, then He made you pairs; and no female bears or brings forth save with His knowledge . . ." (Q 35:11). In addition to the role of Omniscient Creator, God assumes nurturing roles vis-à-vis human beings, as expressed in names such as the Bestower (al-Wahhāb) and the Sustainer (al-Razzāq).[9] Similarly, the divine appellation Rabb (commonly translated as "Lord") includes, in addition to the sense of "possessor" or "owner," the sense of "caretaker," one who properly orders affairs and establishes someone firmly—in God's case, by bestowing spiritual knowledge and material provisions.[10] This nurturing relationship is exemplified in the case of the child Mary, when "her Lord (*rabbuhā*) accepted her with a beautiful acceptance, and made her grow in a beautiful way, and placed her under the care of Zachariah," and then supplied her with regular divine provisions in her sanctuary (Q 3:37). Blessings and divine care are also a means by which God tests the gratitude of the faithful: "And God brought you forth from the bellies of your mothers (*ummahātikum*), knowing naught. And He endowed you with hearing, sight, and hearts, that perchance you may give thanks" (Q 16:78).

Here, external sensory faculties (such as the hearing and sight evoked earlier) combine with corresponding internal faculties such as discernment and insight (as evoked by the metaphor of the heart) to provide the human being with information about the seen and unseen dimensions of the created world. By employing these senses, human beings are capable of moral judgment, discernment, and ethical action.[11] However, human beings' knowledge and awareness—even in adulthood—are limited. One verse bluntly reinforces this differential: "I [God] did not make them witnesses to the creation of the heavens and the earth, nor to their own creation" (Q 18:51). Multiple such verses emphasize the need for human beings to eschew pretentiousness, but at the same time, the Qur'an encourages its readers, reciters, and listeners to use their intellects to reason about the unique place and purpose of human beings in the created world.

## Family in Life, Death, and Eternity

Alongside establishing this relationship between God and human beings, the Qur'an provides moral injunctions by which human beings should abide to achieve their ultimate potential. The Qur'an reminds its listeners/readers that each individual with sound faculties of reason is held accountable for behavior, including maintaining upright family relations. Family relationships, and the human life cycle itself, are situated in the larger Qur'anic apocalyptic schema:

> O humankind! If you are in doubt concerning the resurrection, [remember] We created you from dust, then from a drop, then from a blood clot, then from a lump of flesh, formed and unformed, that We may make clear for you. And We cause what We will to remain in the wombs for a term appointed. Then We bring you forth as an infant, that you may reach maturity. And some are taken in death, and some are consigned to the most abject life, so that after having known they may know nothing. And you see the earth desiccated, but when We send down water upon it, it stirs and swells and produces every delightful kind. (Q 22:5)

Human beings must remember their humble origins, prepare for their death, and must "guard against a day that would make children go grey-haired" (Q 73:17). And God's judgment is not swayed (like a person's might be) toward nepotism: "Your family relations and your children will not benefit you on the day of resurrection; He will distinguish between you. And God sees whatever you do" (Q 60:3). God holds to account those who pervert justice or deliberately turn away from the divine decree.[12]

One rhetorically powerful rhymed surah reinforces this accounting with a chilling description of the testimony that the innocent female child will bear when she is vindicated against her oppressor:

> When the female infant buried alive is asked
> for what sin she was slain;

when the pages are spread,
and when heaven is laid bare;
when hellfire is kindled,
and when the garden is brought nigh,
each soul shall know what it has made ready. (Q 81:8–14)

In this context of warning human beings of an impending day of judgment, the Qur'an includes descriptions of nursemaids made negligent and women made to miscarry as indications of the onset of the upheaval of "the hour" (*al-sāʿa*):

> O humankind! Reverence your Lord. Truly the quaking of the Hour is a tremendous thing.
>
> On the day you see it, every nursing woman will forget that [infant] she nurses, and every pregnant woman will deliver her burden, and you will see humankind drunk, though drunk they will not be. Rather, the punishment of God is severe. (Q 22:1–2)

In these verses, women's bodies undergo traumatic experiences as a sign of the end times. Similarly, another symptom of the duress and havoc of "that day" is people fleeing from family members:

So when the piercing cry does come,
that day when a person (*al-marʾ*) will flee from his sibling,
and his mother and his father,
and his companion (f., *ṣāḥibatihi*) and his children;
for every person that day his affair will suffice him. (Q 80:33–37)[13]

Such Qur'anic imagery, including parent–child relationships, sibling relationships, and kinship in general, encourages human beings to accumulate good credit in order to receive favorable treatment and recompense on the day of judgment (*yawm al-dīn*).[14]

Family relationships remain important well beyond earthly life, death, and judgment, particularly for the pious. The Qur'an describes familial relationships as continuing in the afterlife, when the righteous are reunited: "Gardens of Eden that they shall enter along with those who were righteous from among their forebears, their spouses, and their progeny; and angels shall enter upon them from every gate" (Q 13:23).[15] Familial relationships are even enhanced in paradise. Companions drink together in good company and abundance without suffering the ill effects of intoxication (Q 56:17–19), and relationships troubled in worldly existence can be ameliorated: "We shall remove whatever rancor lies within their breasts—as brethren (*ikhwān*), upon couches, facing one another" (Q 15:47).[16] In this ideal case, the individual soul earns divine rewards, including reunion with morally upright kin. Yet the Qur'an also describes grim possibilities—including the loss of family—for those on the other end of the arc of moral justice, "those who lose their souls and their families on the day of resurrection" (Q 39:15).[17]

## Guidance for Parents and Caregivers

In light of the overarching Qur'anic framework for moral accountability, a plethora of Qur'anic verses offer guidance for parents, both women and men, and many verses discuss children, including female children specifically.[18] For instance, infanticide is condemned in no uncertain terms, and the cultural motives surrounding female infanticide are denounced:

> And when one of them receives tidings of a female (*unthā*), his face darkens, and he is choked with anguish.
>
> He [the person] hides from the people on account of the evil of the tidings he has been given. Shall he keep it [the infant] in humiliation, or bury it in the dust? Behold! Evil indeed is the judgment they make! (Q 16:58–59)[19]

With a similar emphasis on protecting vulnerable girls, the Qur'an expresses a special concern for protecting orphaned girls from being taken advantage of sexually, and it outlines prohibitions against incest and directives to men about women they are prohibited from taking as sexual partners (Q 4:22–23).[20] In a related passage that addresses the righteous division of inheritance, the Qur'an urges parents to have empathy for the children of others: "Let those who would dread if they left behind their own helpless progeny have fear; let them reverence God and speak justly" (Q 4:9).[21] This verse is followed immediately by a caution against consuming the wealth of orphans (Q 4:10).

Many other verses urge concern for and protection of the material interests of the vulnerable. For example, Q 4:75 admonishes the indolent and gives voice to the beleaguered:

> And what ails you that you fight not in the way of God, and for the weak and oppressed—men, women, and children—who cry out, "Our Lord! Bring us forth from this city whose people are oppressors, and appoint for us from You a protector, and appoint for us from You a helper." (Q 4:75; see also discussions in Chapter 3)

A few verses later, Q 4:98 stresses God's inclination toward clemency for those who are "weak and oppressed among men, women, and children, who neither have access to any means nor are guided to any way." Notably, this surah, entitled *al-Nisāʾ* (The women, Q 4), contains frequent references to the plight of vulnerable populations.

Qur'anic emphasis on the moral imperative to protect those who are socially vulnerable is found in tandem with verses that exhort human beings to virtue and humility. For example, the Qur'an stresses that parents should not be deluded by pride in material matters, including their progeny: "Wealth and children are the adornments of the life of this world, but that which endures—righteous deeds—are better in reward with your Lord, and better [as a source of] hope" (Q 18:46). This cautionary lesson is highlighted in a story of the fate of an arrogant man who boasted about his wealth and progeny (Q 18:39–41). (This episode occurs in *Sūrat al-Kahf*, a surah that is commonly recited each Friday as a weekly reminder of the temporal nature of blessings and the swift recompense for wrongdoers.) The Qur'an also cautions the Prophet Muḥammad—and, by extension, the Qur'anic audience as a whole—against looking at the children of others with envy: "And let not their wealth or their children impress you. God desires but to punish them thereby in the life of this world, and that their souls should depart while they are disbelievers" (Q 9:55).[22]

The primary message, that life is a test and the world is the testing ground, extends to interactions with and attitudes toward one's progeny: "And know that your property and your children are only a trial, and that God—with Him is a great reward" (Q 8:28).[23] Children are akin to property here in that both are delights that could prompt vanity or distract from life's central purpose: "O you who believe! Let neither your property nor your children divert you from the remembrance of God. Whoever does so, it is they who are the losers"

(Q 63:9). In short, parenting numerous children may indicate virility and confer worldly esteem (and several righteous individuals, including Abraham and Zachariah, are explicitly rewarded with progeny), but in general, offspring are not portrayed as a measure of a person's standing with God.[24]

Moreover, family can be a source of anxiety or can even be part of a trial from God. The prophet Job, for instance, patiently perseveres in affliction, calls out to God for mercy, and is explicitly rewarded by his family being returned to him: "And We bestowed upon him his family (*ahlahu*) and their like along with them as a mercy from Us and a reminder for possessors of intellect" (Q. 38:43).[25] His family was enlarged out of God's providential care and instruction. In other situations, the Qur'an warns that dealings with family can be a source of distraction, or worse; even in the nuclear family, individuals can be a source of direct malice: "Among your spouses and your children there is indeed an enemy unto you; so be wary of them" (Q 64:14). Karen Bauer summarizes how "the believer is encouraged to go against his natural feelings," where "love of family, worldly goods, wives, children, and even his own life, must be put second to his love for God"; this requires human beings to "re-calibrate their natural affections, transferring them from the life of this world to God and the hereafter."[26]

## Gendered Dimensions of Child–Parent Relations

Many Qur'anic verses discuss infancy and dependent children, but the Qur'anic notion of a "child" is not limited to a specific period of youth. A "child" (*walad*) can indicate a young person, but more broadly, it evokes a kinship relation whose importance transcends the early years of life, and even worldly life altogether.[27] Considering the obligations upon parents, the Qur'an outlines some divisions of labor. For instance, wet-nursing is permissible for mothers who do not or cannot nurse, and fathers are assigned the material costs of dependent children's clothing and provisions (Q 2:233).[28] This same verse emphasizes several principles related to child care:

> Let mothers nurse their children two full years, for such as desire to complete the suckling. It falls on the father to provide for them and clothe them honorably. No soul (*nafs*) is tasked beyond her capacity. Let no mother be harmed on account of her child, nor father on account of his child. And the like shall fall upon the heir. If the couple desire to wean, by their mutual

> consent and consultation, there is no blame upon them. And if you wish to have your children wet-nursed, there is no blame upon you so long as you give payment according to what is acceptable. And reverence God, and know that God sees whatever you do. (Q 2:233)

In addition to stressing "mutual consent and consultation" between parents, these passages clearly put a material value on the work involved in nursing, in this case wet-nursing specifically.[29]

Multiple other lengthy verses acknowledge the demands of gestation. In this way, the Qur'an values women who birth and potentially also nurse infants (theirs or others', through wet-nursing). This is in addition to the labor of parenting in general that falls upon both women and men:

> And We have enjoined the human being (*al-insān*) to be virtuous unto his parents. His mother carried him in travail and bore him in travail, and his gestation and weaning are thirty months, such that when he reaches maturity and reaches forty years he says, "My Lord, inspire me to give thanks for Your blessing with which You have blessed me and have blessed my parents, and that I may work righteousness such that it please You; and make righteous for me my progeny. Truly I turn in repentance unto You, and truly I am among those who submit." (Q 46:15)[30]

This verse emphasizes the physicality and exertion required in pregnancy, birthing, and nursing; it also reminds the human being of her duties toward her parents, particularly when they reach old age.

Verses that stress the physical exertion and investment involved in childrearing also call for care and patience with aging parents, mothers and fathers alike. In one verse, the command to be virtuous to aging parents immediately follows the central Qur'anic command to worship God:

> Your Lord decrees that you worship none but Him, and be virtuous to parents. Whether one or both of them reach old age, say not to them "Uff!" nor chide them, but speak unto them a noble word.
>
> And lower to them the wing of humility out of mercy and say, "My Lord! Have mercy upon them, as they raised me when I was small." (Q 17:23–24)

Likewise, in the broader Qur'anic context, the ethics of being righteous, whether as a daughter or son, include being virtuous to parents and to extended kin, remembering parents and relatives properly in bequests (Q 2:180), and steadfastly maintaining justice, even if it is against parents and kinsfolk (Q 4:135).[31] Such ethical mandates are not dependent on biological sex or gendered social roles.

## Motherhood in Qur'anic Metaphors

The Qur'an is not just emphatic about the elevated status of parents generally and mothers specifically, but it also affirms and defends the concept of motherhood in other ways. For instance, several Qur'anic verses explicitly condemn husbands for repudiating their wives by the custom of *ẓihār*, a pronouncement by which a man effectively declares his wife to be akin to the backside of his mother.[32] This custom of repudiation disgraces the wife, but from another angle, it also constitutes a derogatory reference to the concept of motherhood.

Notably, verse Q 33:4, which condemns the practice of *ẓihār*, closely precedes the verse establishing that the Prophet Muḥammad's wives are the "mothers" (*ummahāt*) of the believers (Q 33:6).[33] These verses both involve motherhood metaphors, as applied to wives. The metaphor "mothers of the believers," a specific valuation of the Prophet's wives, demonstrates an ethically appropriate representation of the concept of motherhood; in the context of its placement in proximity to Q 33:4, the honorific appears in contrast to the derogatory evocation of motherhood implied in the pronouncement of *ẓihār*.

Whether in the actual role of mothering, or even in the linguistic associations with motherhood, the Qur'an celebrates women's maternal status. Along with emphasizing pious mother figures, the Qur'an presents other affirmative connotations related to motherhood; the language of the Qur'an celebrates the capacity of the womb (*raḥim*) and employs the concept of wombs (*arḥām*) in connection with the importance of kinship ties.[34] The Arabic word for "womb" is closely linked to the word for "mercy" or "compassion" (*raḥma*), as well as to the divine names al-Raḥmān and al-Raḥīm, which signify aspects of God's merciful and compassionate nature.[35] Other semantic associations with the word for "mother" also have positive valances. For instance, the Qur'an evokes the term *umm* to confer the grandeur and sacred origins of revelation: "Truly We have made it an Arabic Qur'an, that perchance you may understand, / and truly it is with Us in the mother of the

Book (*umm al-kitāb*), sublime indeed, wise" (Q 43:3–4).[36] In a similar sense, the "blessed" city of Mecca is the "mother of cities" (*umm al-qurā*) (Q 6:92 and 42:7).[37]

## Forebears in Qur'anic Narratives

Dozens of verses depict prophets struggling against the objections of their people who are heedless and ignore prophetic warnings in favor of the beliefs and practices of their forebears.[38] A plethora of verses depict theologically misguided polytheistic peoples who attribute their beliefs to their forebears with statements like: "our forebears (*ābāʾunā*) ascribed partners unto God beforehand, and we were their progeny after them" (Q 7:173).[39]

Other verses caution against taking disbelieving fathers and brothers (understood as ancestors/parents and siblings in a gender-inclusive reading) as protectors (*awliyāʾ*). The verse cautions against placing family bonds of any kind above commitment to religion, love of God, and love of the Prophet Muḥammad; in this example, the familial circle is explicitly expanded and contemporaneous family relations are emphasized through references to ancestry, procreation, sibling relations, and marriage. In this verse, family relations could have a negative net effect on a person's spiritual standing; family—like wealth—could drive an otherwise upright believer toward iniquity:

> O you who believe! Take not your forebears (*ābāʾakum*) and your siblings (*ikhwānakum*) as protectors if they prefer disbelief to belief. As for those among you who take them as protectors, it is they who are the wrongdoers.
>
> Say, "If your forebears (*ābāʾukum*), your children (*abnāʾukum*), your siblings (*ikhwānukum*), your spouses (*azwājukum*), your tribe [kin] (*ʿashīratukum*), the wealth you have acquired, commerce whose stagnation you fear, and dwellings you find pleasing are more beloved to you than God, and His Messenger, and striving in His way, then wait till God comes with His Command." And God guides not iniquitous people. (Q 9:23–24)[40]

The final message is echoed in numerous edicts, parables, and stories: theological commitments must take precedence over familial bonds if the two come into conflict.

As important as family relations are, a believer's relationship with God is of paramount importance in the hierarchy of relationships. Accordingly, one verse describes the adoration of forebears in a slightly more positive light, but then urges the believer instead to channel dedication and enthusiasm toward the worship of God over ancestral pride: "Remember God as you remember your forebears, or with more ardent remembrance" (Q 2:200). The implicit rationale is that forebears (or progenitors) may benefit their heirs in this worldly life, but God provides better benefits in worldly life and in the hereafter. The copious number of verses describing God as Provider, Protector, Guardian, and more can be seen as redirecting patriarchal impulses into a theological framework of accountability.[41]

Having provided a general topical introduction to procreation, parenting, childrearing, and familial relations, it is now possible to explore Qur'anic narratives involving mothers, daughters, and sisters in more detail.

## Jesus's Grandmother and Other Qur'anic Matriarchs

Four women in the course of Qur'anic narratives are impregnated with children who become prophets or otherwise exceptional individuals: the mother of Isaac (wife of Abraham), the mother of John (wife of Zachariah), the mother of Mary (wife of ʿImrān), and the mother of Jesus (Mary).[42] The Qur'an even mentions two figures who are grandmothers, both of prophets: the mother of Mary is the grandmother of Jesus, and the mother of Isaac is the grandmother of Jacob (and the great-grandmother of Joseph). God informed Isaac's mother of her future status as a grandmother through angelic visitors: "We gave her glad tidings of Isaac, and after Isaac, of Jacob" (Q 11:71).[43]

Abraham's wife, Zachariah's wife, and Mary were all surprised by pregnancies that resulted in righteous babies.[44] None of these three women is depicted as being particularly desirous of children before her miraculous impregnation. Nonetheless, at least in the case of Abraham's wife, the news from God (as related in the first person) is described as joyous: "We gave her glad tidings" (Q 11:71). In the case of Zachariah's wife, the focus is on Zachariah's desire for progeny; he prays, "My Lord! Leave me not childless, though You are the best of inheritors" (Q 21:89), and then God directly intervenes (as related again in the first person): "We set his wife aright for him" (Q 21:90). The root of the word "set aright" (*ṣ-l-ḥ*) is also the root for "righteousness"; the verse continues by pointing out the nature of the righteousness of the family: "Truly they vied in good deeds. They called upon Us with desire and with fear, and they were humble before Us" (Q 21:90). The righteousness of this family is an echo of the righteousness of Abraham, Isaac, and Jacob in a preceding verse: "And each of them We made righteous (*ṣāliḥīn*)" (Q 21:72).

## Additional Positive Depictions of Mother Figures

Aside from Joseph's lustful foster mother, the Qur'an does not explicitly refer to any incompetent mothers, nor does it depict daughters or sons disobeying their mothers or otherwise being disrespectful toward a mother. For instance, Adam and his spouse had a son who commits fratricide, but in this episode, the brothers are referred to as the "sons of Adam," and Adam's spouse is not mentioned at all in conjunction with the conflict.[45] God destroys Noah's wife and his son for their disobedience, but the Qur'an does not explicitly connect the son's faults to incompetent parenting on the part of Noah or his wife. The wife of Lot, another female figure who, like the wife of Noah, is destined to damnation, is mentioned at least ten times, but is never depicted as interacting with Lot's daughters.[46] Of the three Qur'anic women who are explicitly damned for their inequity (the wives of Noah, Lot, and Abū Lahab), none is ever depicted interacting with progeny. Similarly, with the exception of Joseph's foster mother (as discussed in Chapter 1), the Qur'an does not contain a single narrative depicting a woman as verbally abrasive or unscrupulous in her capacity as a mother.

Many exemplary figures interact with their progeny or perform acts of devotion toward their parents or mothers specifically. For instance, Joseph, a grown son, expresses his physical affection for his parents when he joyously embraces them after years of separation: "he drew his parents close to himself and said, 'Enter Egypt in security, if God wills!'" (Q 12:99). He then proceeds to "raise his parents up to the throne" together (Q 12:100).[47] John is also "dutiful toward his parents" and "was not domineering, rebellious" (Q 19:14). In another example, Jesus declares as an infant that he was made to be "dutiful toward my mother" (Q 19:32).[48] These sentiments are reinforced by other prophets who pray for their parents, including Noah (in Q 71:28), Abraham (in Q 14:41), and Solomon (in Q 27:19).[49] Although in some instances women do pray (as discussed in Chapter 3), no female figure prays specifically for her parents. The sister of Moses, however, shows loyalty in deed by supporting her mother in dire circumstances; her mother utters a one-word command and the daughter springs into action to help rescue her brother (as discussed in the section on siblings later in this chapter).

## Parenting and Piety in Qur'anic Narratives

In the examples of Qur'anic infants who become prophets, as mentioned earlier, a righteous woman begets a righteous child; examples include the mother of Moses, the mother of Mary, and Mary herself. However, a pious parent does not guarantee a pious child. In several Qur'anic stories, children turn out to be morally delinquent despite having an exemplary parent. For instance, when Noah beckons his son to join him on the ark to avoid the rising floodwaters, his son is aloof; then, Noah pleads with God on behalf of his son in vain and earns a reproach from God:

> And Noah called out to his Lord and said, "O my Lord! Truly my son is from my family. Your promise is indeed true, and You are the most just of judges."
>
> He [God] said, "O Noah! Truly he is not from your family; surely such conduct was not righteous. So question Me not concerning that of which you have no knowledge; truly I exhort you, lest you be among the ignorant." (Q 11:42–46)

In this exchange between God and Noah, God redefines the concept of family, in that Noah's son "is not from your [Noah's] family." Noah's son is drowned.[50]

Similarly, Abraham, the prophet and "friend of God" (*khalīl Allāh*) (Q 4:125), attempts to secure the fate of his progeny after God informs him of his own elevated status as a leader (*imām*): "He [God] said, 'I am making you [Abraham] an imam for humankind.' He [Abraham] said, 'And of my progeny?' He [God] said, 'My covenant does not include the wrongdoers'" (Q 2:124).[51] On another occasion, Abraham prays for his children and descendants, this time more fully acknowledging that each soul bears its own burdens but may hope to benefit from the mercy of God: "And whoever follows me, he is of me. And whoever disobeys me, surely You are Forgiving, Merciful" (Q 14:36).

In contrast to Abraham's concern for the well-being of his offspring, Abraham's hard-hearted and verbally abusive father disavows him, saying, "Do you reject my gods, O Abraham? If you cease not, I shall surely stone you. Take leave of me for a long while!" (Q 19:46).[52] This harshness on the part of Abraham's father follows a long segment of verses in *Sūrat Maryam* that relate and celebrate the nurturing bonds between other central Qur'anic personalities and their parental figures.

The difficulties the young Abraham experiences amidst an unrighteous people, with a father who is described in no uncertain terms as an "enemy of God" (*ʿaduwwun li-llāh*) (Q 9:114), stands in contrast, for instance, to the young Mary, who is dedicated by her prayerful mother to the cause of monotheistic worship and is raised in the temple by Zachariah, a prophetic figure.[53] We learn that Mary's mother dedicated her unborn child to the service of her Lord (Q 3:35). Qur'anic narratives of the young Abraham do not refer to his mother specifically. He does, however, pray for his parents (Q 14:41) and, when he is exiled, promises to ask God for forgiveness for his father specifically (Q 60:4).[54] Solomon (Sulaymān), a figure who is a prophet and the son of a prophet, thanks God for the blessings upon his parents.[55]

## Additional Narratives of Parental Negligence

In one Qur'anic narrative, a set of parents have a child who is destined to become corrupt. This child is slain by a mysterious servant of God while still in his youth, before the boy can grow up to create havoc and heartache for his pious parents (Q 18:74 and 18:80–81). This narrative depicts a set of righteous parents with an insubordinate child and stands in contrast to a couple who pray for a healthy child and then are ungrateful and negligent themselves. This story is related in the Qur'an as follows:

> When he covered her, she bore a light burden and carried it about. But when she had grown heavy, they called upon God, their Lord, "If You give us a healthy child, we shall surely be among the thankful."
>
> Then, when He gave them a healthy child, they ascribed partners unto Him with regard to that which He had given them. Exalted is God above the partners they ascribe.
>
> Do they ascribe as partners those who created naught and are themselves created? (Q 7:189–91)[56]

The narrative involves a couple who begin as pious supplicants but then attribute partners to God; it is the only instance in the Qur'an in which a mother figure lapses in piety, and in this story, it is the couple together who lapse. In this example, like the example of Adam and his spouse, it is the couple *together* who make a mistake.[57] No mother figures, acting alone, are depicted negatively. By way of comparison, fathers are represented in Qur'anic narratives both positively and negatively. We find depictions of the shortcomings of Abraham's theologically misguided and incompetent father and, as mentioned earlier, even references to this father figure as an "enemy of God" (Q 9:114).

## Father–Daughter Relations in Qur'anic Narratives

The Qur'an contains depictions of both mother–daughter and father–daughter relations. Perhaps most striking is the fact that of all the various family configurations, the Qur'an does not depict a corrupt daughter figure, nor any instance of a parent who has a strained relationship with a daughter. Two praiseworthy mothers, the mother of Mary and the mother of Moses, are mentioned in conjunction with their praiseworthy and obedient daughters. The Qur'an mentions the daughters of Lot, and Mary's father is also mentioned once in dialogue (Q 19:28). The Prophet Muḥammad's daughters appear briefly in the context of God's commands to the Prophet to instruct them (and his wives and female followers in general) to wear modest clothing, "to draw their cloaks over themselves" so as not to be harassed by "those in whose hearts is a disease" (Q 33:59–60).[58]

As introduced in the previous chapter, an endearing father–daughter interaction occurs when two sisters meet the wandering, dejected, but still good-natured Moses at a watering hole. One of the sisters encourages her father to retain Moses as an employee: "O my father! Hire him. Surely the best you can hire is the strong, the trustworthy" (Q 28:26). The father, potentially reading the unstated intent of his daughter's words, makes Moses a two-part offer for marriage and employment: "I desire to marry you to one of these two daughters of mine, on [the] condition that you hire yourself to me for eight years" (Q 28:27). By requiring that Moses work for him for such a substantial period, he kept his daughter under his watchful care while securing her a "strong" and "trustworthy" spouse of prophetic caliber.

When Lot, a prophetic figure, discusses *his* daughters, the circumstances are quite different. The Qur'an describes the circumstances in several surahs, including in one instance as follows:

> When Our [God's] messengers came to Lot, he was distressed on their account, and felt himself powerless concerning them. And he said, "This is a terrible day!"
>
> And his people came hurrying toward him, while earlier they had been committing evil deeds (*kānū yaʿmalūna al-sayyiʾāt*). He said, "O my people! These are my daughters; they are purer for you (*hunna aṭharu lakum*). So reverence God, and disgrace me not with regard to my guests. Is there not among you a man of sound judgment (*rajulun rashīd*)?" (Q 11:77–78)

Consider the nature of Lot's rhetoric, as well as the dimensions of thematic intra-connectivity in the Qur'an. Lot's offer is clearly rhetorical mockery, not a solemn offer of marriage and not a sacrificial offering.[59]

The derision in Lot's offer is captured in his words in *Sūrat al-Ḥijr* (Q 15): "These are my daughters (*banātī*), if you must act (*in kuntum fāʿilīn*)" (Q 15:71). Lot's disdain is not lost on his people, who respond with a taunt of their own: "*Certainly you know* that we have no right to your daughters, and *surely you know* that which we desire" (Q 11:79, emphasis added). Several cues, including the abundance of emphatic language (rendered in italics), strongly suggest that Lot's offer of his daughters was not intended or received as an earnest proposal for sex or marriage. Note that Lot's people themselves assert that they have no "right" (*ḥaqq*) to his daughters. If a father figure were sincerely offering his daughters in marriage (as we saw with the father of the two young women in Midian who made an offer to Moses), there would be no need for a categorial denial of the possibility of rights on the part of the men (*mā lanā fī banātika min ḥaqq*, lit., "we have not, in the matter of your daughters, any right").

Interestingly, people who are depicted as committing other sorts of iniquities and lacking in sound judgment still maintain a discourse of rights and boundaries in relation to these daughters. Consider the "evil deeds" (*sayyiʾāt*) and disreputable moral condition of the group of his people that Lot encountered; they are "iniquitous" (*fāsiqīn*). The notion that a prophet of God would compel his daughters into marriage with people described as lacking "sound judgment," as "committing evil deeds," and then in the subsequent verse as "confused in their drunkenness" (Q 15:72) is entirely inconsistent with Qur'anic mandates pertaining to sexual relationships and marital ethics.[60] And it is utterly inconsistent with the station of prophethood as depicted in the Qur'an.[61] Again, Lot's language can be contrasted to the manner in which the father in Midian offered one of his daughters to Moses—at *her* subtle prompting.

Did Lot introduce his daughters to the men for the purposes of making them into sexual decoys so that his angelic guests could be spared? Again, given what we have seen of sexual ethics and parental ethics in the Qur'an, the idea that Lot would offer his daughters to iniquitous men for sex and then, in his next words, admonish these same people in no uncertain terms (see Q 11:78) is not a coherent interpretation. The idea that Lot was offering his daughters up to be raped in order to protect God's messengers is not a convincing explanation of his intentions on a literary level, putting aside creedal definitions of prophetic character or the ability of God's messengers to handle the issue of the townsmen themselves. (In the course of the narrative, the messengers did, after all, destroy the entire city.) Lot's words are also not an indication that he places the well-being of his daughters beneath the well-being of his guests or in some way seeks to sacrifice his daughters out of preference for his guests. Lot's phrase "disgrace me not with regard to my guests" (*lā tukhzūni fī ḍayfī*) can be understood as an expression of a deep shame at the behavior of his people (*qawmuhu*). Both the Qur'anic narrator and Lot himself stress Lot's connection to his people. Understood in this light, Lot's words are a condemnation of the behavior of his people and an expression of deep shame at this behavior; they are not an offer to subjugate his daughters to iniquitous people.

As previous commentators have suggested, in these instances, "daughters" could be understood metaphorically as referring to the young women of Lot's tribe, but the subsequent depiction of Lot fleeing with his family (here and in several other surahs) suggests that the reference to "daughters" in this case is to the members of his family with whom he escaped.[62] The narrative of a prophet escaping persecution with his family also has notable parallels to the situation of the Prophet Muḥammad, who was also experiencing difficulties; according to the biographical literature, the Prophet Muḥammad emigrated with his own daughters on account of persecution of their family at the hands of his people. (See discussions in Chapter 4.)

At one point in the encounter with his people, Lot states that his daughters are "purer" (*aṭhar*) (Q 11:78) for his guests.[63] Lot's words are typically understood by exegetes as reinforcing male–female sexual complementarity, and much has been written about the implications of Lot's condemnation with regard to same-sex relationships in the Qur'an's moral schema.[64] It is beyond the scope of this book to enter into this debate; however, we can observe here some similarities between the indecency of Lot's unruly townspeople and the women who accompany the Egyptian viceroy's wife.

With regard to the narrative trope in which individuals are enthralled or seduced, recall that the group of women are overcome at the sight of Joseph, as noted in Chapter 1. The group conspires against this innocent young man when he refuses the sexual advances of the viceroy's wife. Lest this small group of women give women at large a poor reputation, we also have a Qur'anic story about a group of poorly behaved men.[65] In Lot's estimation, there is not among them "a man of sound judgment" (*rajulun rashīd*) (Q 11:78). Certainly the behavior of this small group of men does not imply that men, writ large, possess poor judgment. Both stories depict forms of corrupt behavior and involve human susceptibility to dynamics of coercion, and both involve intense human sexual desire for figures with angelic qualities, but neither episode ultimately results in forced sex.[66] In one instance, divine messengers in human form awaken the desire of a group of men, and in the other instance, a human being with angelic characteristics enchants a group of women. Once again, an intra-textual reading of Qur'anic narratives reveals rich juxtapositions.[67]

## Foster Mothers and Foster Daughters

Continuing with the theme of binary juxtapositions, with regard to foster mother figures, the Qur'an includes one epitome of vice and one paragon of virtue. The foster mother of Joseph, who attempts to seduce her charge and only years later exonerates him when she is coerced into speaking the truth, is presented as a lustful, lying, and failed mother character. This image is counterbalanced with the example of a God-fearing foster mother who is called "an example for those who believe" (Q 66:11). This wife skillfully convinces her husband, the tyrannical Pharaoh, to spare Moses's life; she uses her influence to save the baby from certain doom. Ultimately, she appeals to the lure of kinship: "A comfort (*qurratu ʿayn*) for me and for you! Slay him not; it may be that he will bring us some benefit, or that we may take him as a son" (Q 28:9).

Her desire for a child is similar to that of Zachariah, who seeks a child who is "well-pleasing" (Q 19:6).[68] The distress of his unfulfilled desire is epitomized by his "secret cry" (Q 19:2–3).[69] At the time, he was the guardian of Mary, whose keen awareness of God's blessings (Q 3:37) seems to inspire Zachariah to pray for a biological heir with the following poetic entreaty:

> My Lord! Verily my bones have grown feeble, and my head glistens with white hair. And in calling upon You, my Lord, I have never despaired.
>
> Truly I fear my relatives after me, and my wife is barren. So grant me from Your Presence an heir who will inherit from me and inherit from the house of Jacob. And make him, my Lord, well-pleasing. (Q 19:4–6)[70]

A dialogue between Zachariah and God ensues, and God grants Zachariah and his wife a righteous son and a future prophet named John (Yaḥyā).[71] Zachariah begins with a foster child and then is granted a biological child. Unlike the foster mother of Moses, we do not know if Zachariah desired to be the foster father of Mary with a passion similar to that with which the foster mother of Moses desired him. From the Qur'anic language alone, we just know that there was a casting of lots and a dispute: "This is from the tidings of the Unseen, which We reveal to you. You were not with them when they cast their lots [to choose] who among them would care for (*yakfulu*) Mary, and you were not with them when they were disputing" (Q 3:44).[72] Surrounding this verse are two verses in which angels speak with Mary and affirm her select status "above the women of the worlds" (Q 3:42). These verses could be interpreted to mean that Mary was so blessed that prospective caretakers disputed over the opportunity to care for her.[73]

In *Sūrat Āl ʿImrān*, God places Mary "under the care of Zachariah" (Q 3:37); in a verse in *Sūrat al-Aḥzāb* (Q 33:37), God addresses the situation in which the Prophet Muḥammad was a surrogate father. Both verses concern men who fostered children and women who received unique blessings from God. In *Sūrat al-Aḥzāb* (Q 33:37), a woman (Zaynab bt. Jaḥsh, according to the commentary tradition) is granted the unique honor of being married to the Prophet Muḥammad by God's direct decree. And in *Sūrat Āl ʿImrān* (Q 3:37), Mary is described as receiving direct provision from God. In being the beneficiaries of God's unique blessings, both women—Zaynab and Mary—break social and even material conventions. (Note the structural parallel in the verse numbers 3:37 and 33:37.)[74]

## Sister Figures in Qur'anic Narratives

On a number of occasions, the Qur'an depicts sibling relationships, both cooperative and dysfunctional ones. An older sister of Moses uses her courage and wit to ensure that her infant brother is returned to their mother after being cast into the river. The child is picked up by the "House of Pharaoh" (*āl Firʿawn*):

> And she [Moses's mother] said to his sister, "Follow him." So she watched him from afar; yet they were unaware.
>
> And We forbade him to be suckled by foster mothers before that; so she [Moses's sister] said, "Shall I direct you [pl.] to the people of a house who will take care of him for you and treat him with good will?"
>
> Thus We returned him to his mother, that she might be comforted and not grieve, and that she might know that God's promise is true. But most of them know not. (Q 28:11–13)[75]

Moses's sister is obedient when her mother utters one brief command: "Follow him" (*quṣṣīhi*) (Q 28:11). The girl is not only amenable to performing a potentially perilous task for the benefit of her family, but she also thinks quickly and intuitively in trying circumstances. She obeys her mother's word, but then also acts independently and decisively when the need arises, and her proposition ultimately brings about a desirable resolution to the imminent peril of losing her brother. She stands out in her capacity as both a daughter and a sister.

Interestingly, the Qur'an includes several stories that feature immoral brothers, but it does not mention sisters in a similar manner. The one relationship between sisters depicted in the Qur'an is that of the two sisters in Midian, a relationship characterized by collaboration as the sisters water the family flock together. The sisters even reply in unison when a disheveled Moses asks them brusquely, "What is your errand?" (Q 28:23).[76] In contrast, the sibling relationship of "Adam's two sons" (*ibnay Ādam*) is characterized by extreme jealousy that results in one murdering the other (Q 5:27–31).[77] Jealousy between brothers, verging on fratricide, again surfaces when Joseph's brothers dispose of him in a well and lie about his disappearance, saying that he had been slain by a wolf, all in order to gain the exclusive attention of their father (Q 12:8). In the beginning of the narrative, the malevolent subterfuge of Joseph's brothers creates the crisis, and Joseph's well-intentioned brotherly subterfuge is what ultimately restores family harmony. Joseph's saga ends better than that of Adam's two sons; it culminates with forgiveness and an affectionate reunion of Joseph, his brothers, and his parents, in fulfillment of Joseph's dream (see Q 12:90–100).

Moses also has a mostly cooperative relationship with his brother Aaron (Hārūn), another prophetic figure; however, in one dramatic instance, Moses becomes momentarily enraged and accosts his brother:

> And he cast down the tablets and seized his brother by the head, dragging him toward himself. He [Aaron] said, "Son of my mother! Truly the people deemed me weak, and they were about to kill me. So let not the enemies rejoice in my misfortune, and place me not with the wrongdoing people." (Q 7:151)

Moses is placated by the plea of the "son of his mother" and supplicates, "My Lord, forgive me and my brother and bring us into Your mercy, for You are the most merciful of the merciful" (Q 7:152). Here, the repetition of the concept of mercy three times is significant, as mercy (*raḥma*) is connected etymologically to the womb (*raḥim*), as discussed earlier.

In this instance, Moses's supplication to God as "the most merciful of the merciful" (*arḥam al-rāḥimīn*) is directly linked to Aaron's evocation of their connection through the womb. A second Qur'anic retelling of this encounter relates that Aaron placated the irate Moses by appealing to their close brotherly relation: "O son of my mother (*ya ibna umma*)! Seize not my beard nor my head" (Q 20:94). The phrase "O son of my mother" is a rather clunky English translation; the Qur'anic expression imparts meaning through the quickened cadence of the parties in an altercation. In contrast to this brotherly jousting, the brotherly subterfuge of Jacob's sons, and the eventual fratricide involving Adam's two sons (Q 5:27), the Qur'an does not depict a single instance of a conflict between sisters.

The metaphor of sisterhood has both positive and negative connotations. For instance, God's signs (*āyāt*) are metaphorical sisters: "Not a sign did We show them but that it was greater than its sister" (Q 43:48); the word *āyāt* (sing. *āya*) also refers to verses of the Qur'an, which are considered "signs" in their own right. In contrast to this positive metaphor, the metaphor of sisterhood also extends to wrongdoing communities who enter hell and grumble there:

> Every time a community (*umma*) enters, it curses its sister (*ukhtahā*), till, when they have all successively arrived there, the last of them will say of the first of them, "Our Lord, it was they who led us astray; so give them a double

> punishment in the fire." He will say, "For each of you it shall be doubled, but you know not." (Q 7:38)

These two evocations of metaphorical sisterhood, one positive and one negative, are the only metaphorical uses of the concept of sisterhood in the Qur'an that I noted. Of the fourteen references to sister(s) in the Qur'an, the majority are in the context of legal rulings on marriage and inheritance.

## The Womb and Beyond

Reproduction, pregnancy, and birthing are repeated Qur'anic themes; however, upon closer examination, we see that in the Qur'an, women figures are not just auxiliaries in the reproductive and domestic spheres. They may occasionally bear progeny, but they also, for instance, provide vital lifelines to male family members in distress. Intimate mother–daughter interactions are highlighted, and sister figures also factor into Qur'anic stories in a consistently positive light. Daughters display courage and obedience, collaborate with parents on important matters, and are sources of wisdom. The Qur'an never depicts theologically or ethically corrupt daughters or sisters, whereas it does present narratives involving corrupt sons and brothers.

Qur'anic stories epitomize nearly all the diverse constellations of parent–child relationships, including some foster relationships. References to family and extended kin also appear in the context of depicting prophets, messengers, and their nemeses. Female kin—even when they remain anonymous—are present as social actors in a larger story. The Qur'an depicts a number of women becoming impregnated, including two aging female figures who conceive prophets (the mothers of John and Isaac). The Qur'an also depicts one birth scene (Mary birthing Jesus) in some detail. The status of motherhood is reinforced in numerous verses and even in metaphors.

The Qur'anic depictions of women in the context of family cover a variety of scenarios, but only a brief parable directly depicts a mother figure (along with her spouse) engaged in blameworthy behavior, namely, forgetting God's blessings on them, in the form of their righteous child, and associating partners with God. Joseph's foster mother has a long-term problematic relationship with him, but Moses's foster mother encouraged his adoption and is depicted as a paragon of virtue. Even the women who are treacherous in their capacity as wives are not depicted in negative relationships with their progeny. For instance, the wife of Lot is not depicted interacting with children in Qur'anic accounts, even though Lot's daughters are mentioned briefly. The wife of Noah, whose children are mentioned in other verses, is also not depicted interacting with them.[78] The wife of Noah and the wife of Lot—two irrevocably corrupt women—are never depicted in their capacity as mothers in the Qur'an. With the exception of the behavior of the viceroy's wife toward her foster son, Joseph, the Qur'an does not provide an archetype of an abusive mother figure.

Having covered Qur'anic depictions of women vis-à-vis issues of sex and sexuality in Chapter 1 and women as kin in the present chapter, we next turn to women as interlocutors in Chapter 3.

## Notes

1. See Hidayatullah, *Feminist Edges*, 191. See also Shaikh, *Sufi Narratives of Intimacy*, 131.
2. See Appendix B for a complete list of female figures and references to the families of various figures. These family relations are sometimes subtle. For instance, as noted in Chapter 1, in Q 12:26, the wife of the Egyptian viceroy has "a witness from among her family" (*shāhidun min ahlihā*). Other than the Queen of Sheba, female figures without relatives are all peripheral characters, including the "women in the city" who tempt Joseph, Moses's unsuccessful wet nurses, and the woman who "unravels her yarn," as mentioned in a brief parable in Q 16:92.
3. See Q 46:35 for the term "the resolute among the messengers" (*ulū al-ʿazmi min al-rusul*). See also Q 33:7 for the specific prophets (namely, Noah, Abraham, Moses, Jesus, and Muḥammad) with whom God made a "solemn covenant" (*mīthāqan ghalīẓan*), who are commonly given special status by exegetes.
4. For reflections on the importance of family to Islamic sacred history in comparison to biblical texts, see David S. Powers, *Muhammad Is Not the Father of Any of Your Men* (Philadelphia: University of Pennsylvania Press, 2009), 1–10. For an excellent overview of Qur'anic ethical and legal directives on the family as a unit of society, see Maria Massi Dakake, "Quranic Ethics, Human Rights, and Society," in *The Study Quran*, 1785–1804. For encyclopedia entries on specific kinship roles, see works by Avner Giladi, "Children," *EQ*, 1:301–2; "Family," *EQ*, 2:173–76; and "Parents," *EQ*, 4:20–22; as well as Talal Asad, "Kinship," *EQ*, 3:95–100. For an analysis of male figures and masculinity more generally in the context of select families of prophets, see De Sondy, *The Crisis of Islamic Masculinities*, 95–120.
5. For multiple examples of the use of the phrase "Children of Adam" from one surah alone, see Q 7:26–27, 7:31, 7:35, 7:172. On the progeny of Adam being misled by Satan, see Q 17:64.
6. See, for instance, Q 5:114, 21:26, 22:58, 23:72, and 62:11 for the epithet "best of providers" in context. See also Q 2:126 for the patriarch Abraham beseeching God as

"provider" for his family. For a Qur'anic metaphor for God's immanence, see Q 50:16: "We did indeed create the human being, and We know what his soul whispers to him; and we are nearer to him than his jugular vein."

7. See, for example, Q 2:116, 5:17, 5:116, 6:100, 9:30, 10:68, 16:57, 17:40, 18:4, and others.
8. See also Q 42:50. De Sondy summarizes: "Procreation is then to be understood as a way to highlight God's divinity, as 'the One'"; see *The Crisis of Islamic Masculinities*, 104.
9. This is illustrated, for example, in Q 6:98: "And He it is who brought you into being from a single soul, and then [gave you] a dwelling place and a repository. We have expounded the signs for a people who understand." See, for instance, Q 3:8 for the Bestower (al-Wahhāb) and 51:58 for the Sustainer (al-Razzāq). Other names that relate to this nurturing role include the Guardian (al-Wālī), the Trustee (al-Wakīl), the One Who Responds (al-Mujīb), and the One Who Averts Harm (al-Māniᶜ). For an analysis of the ways in which human genders can be seen as reflections of God's attributes and appellations, see Shaikh, *Sufi Narratives of Intimacy*, 172–84.
10. See *AEL*, 1008–9.
11. For a discussion of Qur'anic imagery involving the heart, breast, and similar such terms, see Bauer, "Emotion in the Qur'an," 14–16.
12. For God as Lawgiver (al-Shāriᶜ), see, for example, Q 42:13; for God as Arbitrator (al-Ḥakam), see Q 22:69.
13. In Q 80:35, the mother is mentioned before the father (*ummihi wa-abīh*), which fits the rhyme scheme of the surrounding verses.
14. See Q 1:4, among many other such references.
15. I have translated *ābāʾ* as "forebears," while *The Study Quran* uses "fathers"; I elaborate on the term *ābāʾ* in detail later in this chapter.
16. The verse describes the beings in paradise as being at peace and as beneficiaries of the mercy of God; thus, there is no reason to exclude females and restrict such verses to males. *Ikhwān* carries the meaning of "brethren," in an arguably gender-inclusive sense, for instance in Q 49:10: "The believers are but brethren; so make peace between your brethren, and reverence God, that perchance you may receive mercy." See also Q 3:103: "And hold fast to the rope of God, all together, and be not divided. Remember the blessing of God upon you, when you were enemies and He joined your hearts, such that you became brethren." See *AEL*, 34.
17. Emphasis added. This is echoed in Q 42:45: "And those who believe will say, 'Truly the losers are those who have lost themselves and their families on the day of resurrection.'"
18. For an analysis of Qur'anic injunctions, see Barlas, *Believing Women*, 172–77. For secondary literature on social history, as well as on relevant hadith and subsequent Islamic legal discourses related specifically to parenting, see the works by David Powers and Avner Giladi [also Gilᶜadi]. See also Janan Delgado and Celene Ibrahim, "Children and Parents in the Qur'an and in Premodern Islamic Jurisprudence," in *Religious Perspectives on Reproductive Ethics*, ed. Dena Davis (New York: Oxford University Press, 2020).
19. Condemnations of infanticide occur in multiple other verses, including Q 6:137, 6:140, 6:151, and 60:12. Q 17:31 mentions economic motivations for infanticide. In

16:58–59, the Qur'an specifically mentions a female infant, but the next verse refers to the infant with the generic/masculine pronoun (*hu*). The use of the generic pronoun (when a female pronoun would otherwise be expected) could suggest here that the speaker described in these verses does not cognitively recognize the daughter's unique personhood. The pronoun could also simply be read as a gender-inclusive pronoun. See also Barlas, *Believing Women*, 180–81.

20. See Q 4:3–4 and 4:127. Note that in the Qur'an and subsequent Islamic law, suckling for a designated period confers kinship status, and as such, milk-siblings are prohibited from sexual engagement.
21. Siblings are prescribed a share of inheritance upon the passing of either parent (or their agnates) without preference for birth order but with some consideration given to sex. Women, as wives, daughters, and agnates, have Qur'anic rights to inheritance. For an overview of normative Islamic principles of inheritance and their Qur'anic basis, see Lamrabet, *Women and Men in the Qur'ān*, 131–41; see also *SQ*, 192–95 nn. 7–14.
22. See also Q 9:69 and 9:85.
23. See also Q 2:155, 6:53, 6:165, 7:168, and others.
24. See Q 37:112 and 3:38–39, respectively.
25. See also Q 21:84: "So We answered him and removed the affliction that was upon him, and We gave him his family (*ahlahu*), and the like thereof along with them, as a mercy from Us and a reminder to the worshipers." For a succinct comparative perspective and summary of the wife of Job in later Muslim exegetical traditions, see Kaltner and Mirza, *The Bible and the Qur'an*, 91–93. For an excellent analysis of passages involving Job in the Qur'an, see A. H. Johns, "Narrative, Intertext and Allusion in the Qurʾānic Presentation of Job," *Journal of Qurʾanic Studies* 1 (1999): 1–25. Some commentators relate Q 38:44 to Job's wife, who is said to have provoked Job into making an oath against her, but this backstory does not occur in the Qur'an or extant hadith. For commentary, see *SQ*, 1111 n. 44.
26. Bauer, "Emotion in the Qur'an," 13.
27. See Giladi, *EQ*, 1:301 for a list of Qur'anic terms specifying youth and progeny.
28. This division of labor could be seen as a sociologically based ruling, one that takes into consideration the biological realities of reproduction wherein women bear the greater burden in reproduction—literally, in an embodied sense. Presumably the material costs fall upon the biological father because the biological mother contributes to the development and nurturing of the child with her physical being through the period of gestation and potentially through the period of lactation. In certain cases, the male heirs receive a larger portion of inheritance, presumably because they likely have costs to cover related to supporting progeny, not to mention the marriage gift, the expenses of maintaining a spouse (which are also mandatory), and potentially also other kin who might fall to their charge. For a discussion of spousal roles, see Celene Ibrahim, "Family Law Reform, Spousal Relations, and the 'Intentions of Islamic Law,'" in *Women's Rights and Religious Law: Domestic and International Perspectives*, ed. Fareda Banda and Lisa Fishbayn Joffe (New York: Routledge, 2016), 111–13.

29. In another verse, the Qur'an outlines what may be thought of as a principle of equal opportunity with regard to the compensation of men and women, with regard to works with spiritual merit: "I will not let the work of any worker among you, male or female, be in vain; each of you is like the other" (Q 3:195). See also Q 4:124: "And whoever performs righteous deeds, whether male or female, and is a believer, such shall enter the garden, and they shall not be wronged so much as the speck on a date stone." See also Q 4:32, 16:97, 40:40, and 49:13 in relation to men and women having equal opportunity for God's pleasure and rewards. For a discussion of such verses, as narrated in hadith on the authority of women companions of the Prophet, see Geissinger, *Gender and Muslim Constructions*, 241–42.
30. See also Q 31:14–15.
31. This verse, 4:135, is topically related to 4:35, one of several places in the Qur'an (like 3:37 and 33:37, discussed earlier in this chapter, or 3:33 and 33:33, discussed in later chapters) in which verses with similar numbering correspond topically.
32. For an analysis, see Gerald Hawting, "An Ascetic Vow and an Unseemly Oath?: *Īlāʾ* and *Ẓihār* in Muslim Law," *Bulletin of the School of Oriental and African Studies* 57, no. 1 (1994): 113–25. See also further analysis in the next chapter.
33. For a discussion of the relationship between this honorific and female moral agency, see Barazangi, *Women's Identity and the Qur'an*, 81–82.
34. For example, Q 4:1, 31:34, 47:22, and others. See Marcia Hermansen, "Womb," *EQ*, 5:522–23. See Barlas, *Believing Women*, 178–79. See also discussions in Osman, *Female Personalities*, 32–35. For a compelling analysis of intertextual polysemy involving the womb and related imagery, see Abdulla Galadari, *Qur'anic Hermeneutics: Between Science, History, and the Bible* (New York: Bloomsbury, 2018), 55.
35. For a discussion, see *SQ*, 503–4.
36. See also Q 3:7, 13:39, and others. For a discussion of this "female discourse" as it relates to scripture (and in particular for analysis of the female-affirming verse Q 3:6 and its relationship to the "gender-oriented subtext" of Q 3:7), see Angelika Neuwirth, "Mary and Jesus, Counterbalancing the Biblical Patriarchs: A Re-reading of *Sūrat Maryam* in *Sūrat Āl ʿImrān* (Q 3:1–62)," *Parole de l'Orient* 30 (2005): 239–41.
37. See Q 48:24 for the one Qur'anic instance of Mecca, and see Q 3:96 for the term *bakka* (thought to be another name for Mecca), described by the Qur'an as the location of the "first house"; see *SQ*, 156 n. 96. For the use of this figurative language to refer to a group of towns having a "mother city," see Q 28:59. The root ʾ*-m-m* that forms the basis of the word "mother" (*umm*) occurs in the Qur'an in ten forms, for a total of 119 times; see *AEDQ*, 47. Notably, the root for the word for "father" and related concepts (ʾ*-b-w*) occurs a nearly matched total of 117 times in three forms. See *AEDQ*, 7.
38. For example, Q 2:170, 7:70, 11:87, 14:10, and others; Q 6:91 stresses forebears' lack of knowledge. See discussions in Lamptey, *Divine Words*, 126. For just one contrasting example, see God's support of the progeny of a righteous father in Q 18:82.
39. I render the term (*ābāʾ*) in a gender-inclusive translation; however, the term shares a root signification with the word "father," meaning that it could also be understood as referring to a direct male parent or a male lineage.

40. I have translated these terms here and elsewhere with gender-inclusive meanings. For instance, another possible rendering for *abnāʾukum* is "sons"; however, the inclusive translation arguably better captures the spirit of the verse.
41. For detailed analysis, see Barlas, *Believing Women*, 109–21.
42. See discussions in Osman, *Female Personalities*, 48–51. I do not include Hagar here, as her pregnancy and the birth of the prophet Ishmael are not explicitly related in Qur'anic stories, even though there are references to Abraham's family that would include Hagar.
43. Here, and in Q 11:71 as well, the choice of the first-person pronoun can even be seen as stressing the intimacy of the conferral. See discussions in Osman, *Female Personalities*, 47–48. See Chapter 3 for an analysis of God's speech to female figures.
44. See Q 11:71–73, 15:53–56, and 51:28–30 for the pregnancy of Abraham's wife. For analysis of these verses, see Moballegh, "Veiled Women Unveiling God." See Q 3:40, 19:5–7, and 21:90 for the pregnancy of Zachariah's wife. See Q 3:42–45 and 19:16–24 for Mary's pregnancy. For a contemporary treatment of the subject of barrenness with reference to the Qur'anic stories of these women, see Ayesha S. Chaudhry, "Unlikely Motherhood in the Qur'ān: Oncofertility as Devotion," *Oncofertility: Ethical, Legal, Social, and Medical Perspectives* 156 (2010): 3–6.
45. See Q 5:27–31. For detailed comparative perspectives on this story in Jewish, Christian, and Muslim sources, see Gregg, *Shared Stories, Rival Tellings*, 7–113.
46. Farid Esack observes that even in commentary traditions, sources do not mention "Lot and his wife's daughters" or "their daughters" and speculates that this might be "a subtle attempt to ignore any relationship between the 'good' daughters and father on the one hand and the 'bad' mother on the other." See Esack, "Lot and His Offer," 13.
47. For an analysis of the emotional resonance of this scene, see Bauer, "Emotion in the Qur'an," 19. The reference to Joseph's parents (dual, *abawā*) at the end of this surah functions as a structural bookend to the narrative; the narrative begins with Jacob telling Joseph about his forefathers (dual, *abawā*) Abraham and Isaac (Q 12:6).
48. For reflections on the masculinity of Jesus as compared to other prophetic figures, see De Sondy, *The Crisis of Muslim Masculinities*, 116–17.
49. For instance, other supplicants include Noah (in Q 71:28), Abraham (in Q 14:41), and Solomon (in Q 27:19).
50. See Q 17:3 for a general mention of Noah's progeny who do survive.
51. For Abraham's role in the establishment of Mecca, see 2:125–31.
52. Abraham's father is named in one verse as Āzar; see Q 6:74. Abraham's relationship with his father is narrated several times, therein dramatizing the conflict between monotheism and polytheism within a family; see Q 9:114, 11:69–104, 14:41, 19:42–49, 21:51–71, 37:85–99, 43:26–28, and 60:4.
53. For comparative perspectives on this motif in Christian literature, see Marx, "Glimpses of a Mariology," 554.
54. See also Q 9:114 and 19:47 for Abraham's prayers on behalf of his father.
55. See Q 27:19. See also Q 34:13 for a verse celebrating the gratitude and ingenuity of the "House of David." For further discussions, see Wright, "The Qur'anic David," 187–96.
56. For commentary, see *SQ*, 476 nn. 189–90.

57. For further discussion, see Denise Spellberg, "Writing the Unwritten Life of the Islamic Eve: Menstruation and the Demonization of Motherhood," *International Journal of Middle East Studies* 28, no. 3 (1996): 305–24.
58. This verse has stimulated a great deal of attention in the academic literature for its implications regarding veiling, a topic that is vast and ultimately beyond the scope of this book. Suffice it to note that the Qur'anic rationale for covering is provided: "thus is it likelier that they [aforementioned women] will be known and not be disturbed (*wa-lā yu'dhayna*)." Whatever arguments can be waged about the effectiveness of the strategy, the intention of the Qur'an's narrator is explicit. See also Q 2:222 for a verse employing the same root (*ʾ-dh-y*) with regard to men not having sexual relations with women during menstruation; here also, the verse refers to the well-being of women. For a critical reading of this verse and the subsequent commentary tradition, including interpretations of the word *adhā*, see Naguib, "Horizons and Limitations of Muslim Feminist Hermeneutics," 33–50.
59. Farid Esack explores the incident as an "apparent condoning—if not encouragement—of gang rape." See "Lot and His Offer," 12. I do not read Lot's words as condoning or encouraging rape; however, I appreciate how Esack unpacks potential ethical implications of the narrative. For other recent academic explorations of this episode, see Waleed Ahmed, "Lot's Daughters in the Qurʾān: An Investigation through the Lens of Intertextuality," in *New Perspectives on the Qurʾān: The Qurʾān in Its Historical Context 2*, ed. Gabriel Said Reynolds (Abingdon, UK: Routledge, 2011), 411–24.
60. See this argument in Esack, "Lot and His Offer," 26.
61. For a discussion of the concept of *ʿiṣma*, the protected status of prophets, as it pertains to this story, see Esack, "Lot and His Offer," 16–19. Also see the analysis of the ways in which *ʿiṣma* is gendered in Lamptey, *Divine Words*, 142–43.
62. See Esack, "Lot and His Offer," 22.
63. In this instance, females (here daughters) are described as "purer" (*aṭhar*) for Lot's guests as sexual partners than males. This is clearly not a general Qur'anic assertion that categorically ascribes a higher degree of purity to females over males; the degree of preference is situationally specific. Imagine how this assertion could be taken out of context by a misandrist and then offered as a general Qur'anic assertion that females have a degree over males categorically. I point out this instance simply to contrast other disputed verses (e.g., Q 2:228 and 4:34), in which males/boys/men are described as having some degree over females/girls/women. Arguably none of these verses is a categorical statement about male versus female worth. On this latter point, see Barazangi, *Women's Identity and the Qur'an*, 52–53.
64. For instance, see Amreen Jamal, "The Story of Lot and the Qurʾān's Perception of the Morality of Same-Sex Sexuality," *Journal of Homosexuality* 41, no. 1 (2001): 1–88. See also Osman, *Female Personalities*, 46. For citations to further academic literature on this issue, see also Esack, "Lot and His Offer," 21. The Qur'an does not depict female–female sexual desire or relationships. Some commentators have suggested that references in Q 4:15 may refer to females who have engaged in same-sex acts, but the verse itself can also be interpreted as pertaining to illicit heterosexual relations. See *SQ*, 196 n. 16.

65. The word "*niswa*" appears twice in Q 12:30 and once in 12:50 in reference to the "women in the city"; the grammatical form is the so-called plural of paucity, suggesting that this was not all the women in the city, but rather a select group of them. See *AEDQ*, 935–36.
66. For a discussion of the story of Lot and his family as it relates to sexual assault, see Celene Ibrahim, "Sexual Violence," 85–88.
67. Citing the work of Angelika Neuwirth, M. A. S. Abdel Haleem, and others, Todd Lawson rightly observes that "the interplay of conceptual and substantive oppositions and dualities is a prominent feature of both the form and content of the Qur'an." See Lawson, "Duality," 27. The play on dualities is not merely simple opposites (such as day and night, or heaven and hell); dualities are even manifest in the plots of Qur'anic narratives, as I show in this work.
68. This could be "well-pleasing" to Zachariah, to God, or to both.
69. See also Q 21:89–90 and Chapter 3 for an analysis of this secret cry in relation to a secret cry of Mary. For a general mention of barrenness, see Q 42:49–50.
70. I have used "despaired" rather than "been wretched" as it appears in *The Study Quran*, as it mimics something of the Arabic rhyme, according to the translation methodology laid out by Shawkat M. Toorawa in "*Sūrat Maryam* (Q. 19): Lexicon, Lexical Echoes, English Translation," *Journal of Qur'anic Studies* 13, no. 1 (2011): 25–78. In Arabic, the verses in question end with the long vowel *alif*, thereby adding to their consonance. As Geissinger further notes, "the aural similarity between the *-iyyā* verse-endings and the Arabic feminine suffix *-iyya* helps evoke associations with femaleness, and gives the recited text a gentle and compassionate tone overall." See Geissinger, "Mary in the Qur'an," 383.
71. On Yaḥyā, see Q 3:39, 6:85, 19:7–15, and 21:90.
72. Based on his analysis of pre-Qur'anic texts (namely the *Protoevangelium of James*), Reynolds raises the possibility that this reference to the casting of lots pertains to the marital "custody" of Mary and that the biblical Joseph is the recipient of the custody, even though there is no such mention of a spouse for Mary in the Qur'an itself. See Reynolds's arguments in *The Qur'ān and Its Biblical Subtext*, 142–43. The argument may be compelling based on a comparative reading of pre-Qur'anic texts, but it is ultimately unlikely from the perspective of an intra-textual reading of the Qur'an. In Q 3:37 we also find a nearly identical verb "to care for" (*kaffala*), and the context is clearly Zachariah fostering Mary as a girl-child. A form of the verb *kafala* is also used in reference to the fostering of Moses as an infant in Q 20:40 and 28:12. (The concept is also relevant in Islamic jurisprudence pertaining to the care of children; see Delgado and Ibrahim, "Children and Parents.")
73. On the other hand, it is also possible that those casting lots might have perceived the care of a girl child as a burden. In this case, the narrator's interjections recounting Mary's blessed status could serve as an ironic juxtaposition: the angelic messengers affirm her unique status, one that was perhaps not immediately evident to her people.
74. For a discussion of structure in the Qur'an as a methodology of exegesis, see Daniel A. Madigan, "Reflections on Some Current Directions in Qur'anic Studies," *Muslim World* 85 (1995): 345–62.

75. For a parallel account, see Q 20:39–40. For a discussion of this episode and of infant prophets who are depicted in the Qur'an, see Geissinger, "Mary in the Qur'an," 388–90. In the biblical account, the female figure who rescues Moses from the water is identified as the daughter of Pharaoh. While the daughter could be included in the Qur'anic reference to the "house of Pharaoh," Pharaoh's daughter is not specifically mentioned in the Qur'anic account.
76. The address is in the dual grammatical form. The translation could also be rendered, "What is your affair?" A more colloquial translation might render the question, "What's the matter with the two of you?"
77. For the account of "Adam's two sons," see Q 5:27–31. As noted, the sons are specifically attributed to Adam, and Adam's spouse is not mentioned in verses recounting this fratricide. For a detailed analysis of this story, see Bodman, *The Poetics of Iblīs*, 84–93.
78. For comparative perspectives on Noah and his family, see Christine Dykgraaf, "The Mesopotamian Flood Epic and Its Representation in the Bible, the Quran and Other Middle Eastern Literatures," in *Sacred Tropes: Tanakh, New Testament, and Qur'an*, ed. Roberta Sterman Sabbath, Biblical Interpretation Series (Leiden: Brill, 2009), 393–408. For comparative perspectives on Noah's wife, see Nora K. Schmid, "Lot's Wife: Late Antique Paradigms of Sense and the Qurʾān," in *Qurʾānic Studies Today*, ed. Angelika Neuwirth and Michael A. Sells (New York: Routledge, 2016), 52–81.

# 3
# Women Speakers and Interlocutors

From mothers-to-be and their angelic interlocutors to the gossiping accomplices of a viceroy's wife, this chapter focuses on the speech of Qur'anic women. I highlight patterns and explore didactic and affective dimensions of this speech. When, where, how, and to whom do women and girls speak? How do girls and women assert political, religious, and other types of epistemic authority through their speech? What information does their speech imply about their characters, values, and outlooks? What virtues does this speech aim at instilling? How does the speech of pious women compare to the speech of pious men?

I also discuss women's interactions with God and divine messengers. By way of comparison, Adam receives "words from his Lord" (Q 2:37), and Moses converses with God at length; the dialogue that transpires between God and Moses is, in one instance, nearly forty verses long (Q 20:11–48). The Prophet Muḥammad receives God's Word as the Qur'an. What then is the nature of God's communication with *women*? How do women speak with God's messengers? I begin with the authoritative speech of a singular ant, and the namesake of *Sūrat al-Naml* (Q 27), the surah with the most verses containing female speech.[1]

## Queenly Speech and Exemplary Leadership

Like his prophetic father David (Dāwūd), Solomon is given gifts of wisdom, eloquence, and a unique ability to commune with the natural world. In Solomon's case, these gifts are manifest in his ability to understand the speech of animals. This special ability to commune with animals is attested to in his encounter with a preoccupied ant:

> And gathered for Solomon were his hosts of jinn and men and birds, and they were marshaled [in ordered ranks], till when they came to the valley

*Women and Gender in the Qur'an.* Celene Ibrahim, Oxford University Press (2020). © Oxford University Press.
DOI: 10.1093/oso/9780190063818.001.0001.

> of the ants, an ant said, "O ants! Enter your dwelling, lest Solomon and his hosts crush you, while they are unaware."
>
> And he [Solomon] smiled, wondering at her words, and said, "My Lord! Inspire me to give thanks for Your blessing with which You have blessed me and my parents and to work righteousness pleasing to You, and cause me to enter, through Your Mercy, among Your righteous servants!" (Q 27:17–19)[2]

Not only does Solomon listen to the speech of the ant, but her speech also triggers a shift in consciousness for him, prompting him to pray: "My Lord! Inspire me (*awziʿnī*) to give thanks" (Q 27:19). Solomon's forces are already "marshaled" (*yūzaʿūn*)(Q 27:17); however, after hearing the ant's speech, Solomon is moved to communicate with his Lord and beseech God's inspiration. The two verbs, to inspire and to marshal, share a common root,[3] suggesting a subtle shift in Solomon's attention from managing his military expedition to attending to his relationship with his Lord. The ant inspires Solomon to remember the blessings of his parents and to beseech God for righteous actions, and in doing so, Solomon repeats nearly verbatim a formula of praise that appears in another Qur'anic verse that begins by extolling the role of the mother in gestation and weaning (as discussed in the previous chapter):

> And We have enjoined upon the human being to be virtuous to his parents. His [the human being's] mother carried him in travail and bore him in travail, and his gestation and weaning are thirty months, such that when he reaches maturity and reaches forty years he says, "My Lord! Inspire me to give thanks for Your blessings with which You have blessed me and have blessed my parents, and that I may work righteousness such that it pleases You, and make righteous for me my progeny. Truly I turn in repentance to You, and truly I am among those who submit." (Q 46:15)

With her minute stature and her sincerity, this ant reminds Solomon of his own dependency on the human beings whose union brought him into the world and of his dependency on the Lord who rules over him and his affairs. Even as Solomon prepares for military conquest, he is reminded of his blessings, his parents, his spiritual and teleological purpose, and his ultimate servanthood. His shift of consciousness in these verses foreshadows the shift of consciousness experienced by the Queen of Sheba, whose military perspective shifts to a theological outlook.

In another element of foreshadowing, the ant successfully protects her colony against the might of Solomon, and so, too, does the Queen of Sheba warn her advisors against the tolls of war and their potential abasement should the affair not go well. In this way, she avoids war:

> She [the Queen] said, "O notables! Give me your opinion in this matter of mine. I am not one to decide on any matter unless you are present."
>
> They said, "We are possessed of strength and possessed of great might. But the command is yours; so consider what you would command."
>
> She said, "Verily, kings, when they enter a city, corrupt it, and make the most honorable of its people the most abased. They will do likewise.
>
> I will send a gift to them and observe what the envoys bring back." (Q 27:32–35)

The ant and the Queen both use decisive voices to warn their respective constituents of the imminent danger brought on by Solomon's march.

The feminine voice of the ant protecting her people can be seen as a direct parallel to the Queen of Sheba seeking to protect her people. Solomon's interaction with the ant provides a subtle lens through which to interpret the subsequent narrative of Solomon and the Queen: Solomon is not a callous king assailing a queen who eventually capitulates to the conquest. Rather, all three leaders—the ant, Solomon, and the Queen—ascertain and embrace their respective responsibilities as heads of their particular polity. The Qur'an does not specifically refer to this ant as the queen of her colony; however, given what is known about the social organization of ant colonies, and given the narrative involving Solomon and the Queen that immediately follows the story of the ant, the correspondences are potent.[4]

In this encounter with the ant, Solomon is tested several times as to the intensity of his gratitude and humility toward God; his might and perception may be unparalleled among human beings, but he is subservient to God and attentive to an ant.[5] The Queen, too, is tested to see if she can recognize the truth regarding her throne, a metaphor that foreshadows her ability to recognize her worldly throne as metaphorically subservient to the throne of God.[6] Despite their respective lofty political stations and their immense worldly power, the Queen of Sheba and King Solomon are called on to see past the deceptive nature of material realities in order to perceive transcendent ones.[7]

Through her speech in particular, the Queen is depicted as a competent sovereign whose speech and actions engender the respect of her advisors.

She is balanced in her approach and diplomatic: she is eager to listen to advice, yet also persuasive when taking a stance; she is collaborative in soliciting feedback, but also decisive in her resolutions.[8] Upon receipt of the letter from Solomon, which threatens military aggression, the Queen is seemingly able to discern a "noble" implication in the message, even though, initially, she cannot discern the precise nature of the submission to which Solomon calls her.

In the letter that the Queen reads to her inner council, she delivers Solomon's message: "Do not exalt yourselves against me, but come to me in submission (*muslimīn*)" (Q 27:31). The polysemantic valances of the word *muslim* render the statement both an act of proselytization and an assertion of political dominance.[9] Despite initially "prostrating to the sun instead of God," as the hoopoe bird observes on his scouting mission, the Queen immediately recognizes that the letter Solomon sends is "a noble letter" (*kitābun karīm*) (Q 27:29), and this begins her journey toward submission (*islām*), a journey that ends with her repentance. She exclaims, "My Lord! Surely I have wronged myself, and I submit with Solomon to God, Lord of the worlds" (Q 27:44).[10]

As the most loquacious female in the Qur'an, the Queen's speech has a quality of nobility and clear prophetic resonances.[11] Her last speech in the Qur'an is a profession of submission: "I submit with Solomon to God, Lord of the worlds" (Q 27:44). This is preceded by a declaration of repentance, "Surely I have wronged myself," a formula that is even repeated verbatim by Moses in the following surah, *Sūrat al-Qaṣaṣ* (Q 28:16).[12] This sincere repentance is not the only time in which the Queen's speech in the Qur'an is prophetic in character. In reading the "noble letter" (Q 27:29) from Solomon to her circle of advisors, the Queen utters the *basmala*: "In the name of God, the Compassionate, the Merciful" (*bismi-llāh al-raḥmān al-raḥīm*) (Q 27:30); thus, the Queen's speech is honored and elevated with one of the Qur'an's most sacrosanct formulas of praise.[13]

## The Secret Cries

The narrative of the Queen is not the only case in which a female figure articulates, with words that come from a divinely inspired source, speech that affirms the compassionate attributes of God. Mary is also intimately aware of the compassionate divine presence, and when she gives birth to a child without a spouse, an angelic messenger instructs her to say, "Verily I have vowed a fast to the Compassionate (al-Raḥmān), so I shall not speak this day to any human being" (Q 19:26). Mary, like Solomon, is surrounded by pious people from birth, and like both Solomon and the Queen, she also has unique spiritual gifts and faces specific trials.

Aside from the Prophet Muḥammad, to whom the whole of the Qur'an is directed, Mary is the individual who has the most extensive conversations with divine messengers. In the course of her miraculous pregnancy and her delivery of Jesus, she communicates with messengers who share news of her lofty status, command her to piety, announce her miraculous pregnancy and prophetic child (Q 3:42–43 and 19:21), and even offer postpartum comfort (Q 19:24–26)—support that is akin to that provided by doulas or midwives.[14]

The Qur'an does not specify who delivers provisions to Mary as a girl (Q 3:37); we might infer that these provisions are also supplied by angelic messengers. The divine blessings that surround Mary from the time of her girlhood are such that even her guardian Zachariah, a prophet, is astounded. Zachariah inquires, "Mary, from where does this come to you?" and she answers with confidence, "It is from God. Truly God provides for whomever He will without reckoning" (Q 3:37). In this exchange, a young Mary reminds her guardian of the nature of God's lordship; as a girl, Mary seems to know, intuitively, about the nature of divine provisions. It is Mary's devotion in her sanctuary (*miḥrāb*) that "then and there" inspires Zachariah to "call upon his Lord" for "a good progeny" (Q 3:38).

In another place in the Qur'an, Mary's speech is juxtaposed with that of Zachariah. *Sūrat Maryam* begins with "a reminder of the mercy of your Lord to His servant, Zachariah, / when he cried out to his Lord with a secret cry" (Q 19:2–3). Here, the idea of a secret cry parallels a passage later in the surah when Mary, having conceived and withdrawn "to a far-off place," also cries out; like Zachariah's cry, Mary's cry is immediately answered. Zachariah cries with the agony of not having a child, while Mary cries from the agony of delivering a child. In her cry, the young Mary asks for death and seeks to be utterly forgotten, and in his cry, the aged Zachariah asks for a child to inherit from him and continue the lineage of the family of Jacob. Both Mary and Zachariah are in private prayer when the respective messengers speak to them carrying the news of the pregnancies. As if reinforcing this thematic connection on a structural level (and among many other thematic and structural parallels in the beginning of this surah), Zachariah's secret cry is located in Q 19:2–3 and Mary's is in Q 19:23.

Not only are their respective cries connected, but Mary's later vow of silence and gesturing in Q 19:29 is also a thematic echo of Zachariah's inability to speak and the need for him to gesture after he receives news of a child (Q 19:10–11). Whereas God rendered Zachariah unable to speak for a period of three nights after receiving news of the child (Q 19:10), Mary's vow of silence is undertaken out of voluntary obedience to God following the birth of Jesus (Q 19:26). These two periods of silence both contrast with God's generative speech, the single-word, single-syllable command that sets all of creation in motion: "Be!"[15] God describes this creative speech to Zachariah, and then also to Mary, as "easy for Me," seemingly in contrast to the wrenching inner struggles Zachariah and Mary both experience and give voice to in fraught moments of solitude.[16]

Mary's speech is directed only to God, the angels, and her guardian. When faced with the masses, God instructs her to remain silent; but lest her silence be taken as a model for female speech in general, we are also given the example of the Queen of Sheba, a military and political ruler who addresses her court and the court of Solomon with resolve. Mary receives messages and direction from angelic figures, yet she consistently addresses her speech not to the messengers but to God directly, as in the following verses:

> When the angels said, "O Mary, truly God gives you glad tidings of a Word from Him, whose name is the Messiah, Jesus son of Mary, honored in this world and the hereafter, one of those brought nigh.
>
> He will speak to people in the cradle and in maturity, and will be among the righteous."
>
> She said, "My Lord, how shall I have a child while no human being has touched me?" He said, "Thus does God create whatever He will." When He decrees a thing, He but says to it, "Be!" and it is. (Q 3:45–47)

The messenger speaks to Mary, but she answers with the address, "My Lord" (Q 3:47); she is possibly addressing God directly, not the angelic intermediary. Like Zachariah in Q 19:6, Mary seems to beseech God directly.

From an intra-textual reading, we can understand that Mary first hears the voice of the messenger, but then, when she cries out to her Lord, she actually sees the "spirit" in human form: "Then We sent unto her Our spirit, and it assumed for her the likeness of a perfect human being" (Q 19:17).[17] This messenger, appearing as a "perfect human being" (*basharan sawiyyan*), then conveys the mission: "I am but a messenger of your Lord, to bestow upon you a pure boy (*ghulām*)" (Q 19:19). In response to her justifiably confused state, the messenger responds with a definitive statement from God: "Thus shall it be. Your Lord says, 'It is easy for Me, and [it is thus] that We might make him [Mary's child] a sign for humankind, and a mercy from Us. And it is a matter decreed'" (Q 19:21).[18]

The emphatic nature of the language, "thus shall it be" and "it is a matter decreed" (Q 19:21), also echoes the message to the wife of Abraham (Q 51:30). She receives "glad tidings" of a child and also a grandchild (Q 11:71). The divine blessings are bestowed directly from God, and the first-person pronoun conveys the intimacy of the conferral. The blessing is followed by reassuring speech from (angelic) messengers of God, speech that reiterates the blessing on the "family of the house" (*ahl al-bayt*): "They [the angelic messengers] said, 'Do you marvel at the command of God? The mercy of God and His blessings be upon you, O family of the house! Truly He is praised, glorious'" (Q 11:73).[19] Here, given the semantic range of the word *ahl*, the address "*ahl al-bayt*" could refer specifically to Abraham's wife, or it could be a general address to those in Abraham's household.

## God's Revelations to a Woman

Many female figures are tested in obedience and resolve; many receive God's messages and submit. In the beginning of this work, I pointed out that Mary is described as delivering, literally (in the sense of birthing), the "Word" of God. Mary "was among the devoutly obedient" to God and "confirmed (*ṣaddaqat*) the words of her Lord and His books" (Q 66:12).[20] The mother of Moses receives a revelatory message that commands her to cast her infant into the river and trust in God's promise to bring the child back. In this respect—her ability to endure an onerous task, as inspired by God, with respect to her son—the mother of Moses bears a resemblance to Abraham, who also directly confronts the possibility of losing his beloved son (Q 37:102).

Like Mary's delivery of Jesus, the onus on the mother of Moses and her ability to fulfill the divine command constitute the beginning of an immense movement for divinely ordained social change; immediately preceding this address to the mother of Moses, we learn that God "desired to be gracious to those who were oppressed in the land, and to make them imams, and to make them the heirs, / and to establish them in the land" (Q 28:5–6).[21] As a first step toward this revolution, God sends revelation to a mother with an infant.

The Qur'an describes how Moses's mother received revelation (*waḥy*) using the intimate first-person pronoun: "So We revealed to the mother of Moses (*umm Mūsā*), 'Nurse him. But if you fear for him, then cast him into the river, and fear not, nor grieve. Surely We shall bring him back to you and make him one of the messengers'" (Q 28:7). The revelation to Moses's mother is similar to the revelation that Joseph receives in his time of tribulation; he has been cast into water (in his case, it is a well), yet God sends him a personal revelation prophesying his eventual triumph over those who oppressed him (Q 12:15). The mother of Moses, like Joseph, receives a prophecy from God.[22]

In another surah, God recounts this particular episode to Moses, emphasizing again the revelatory nature of the speech: "When We revealed to your mother that which was revealed . . ." (Q 20:37–39). Here, God's speech to the mother of Moses is embedded in speech to Moses. Stylistically, the prose in these verses displays an echo effect. For instance, several phrases reoccur: "We revealed . . . that which was revealed," "an enemy to Me and an enemy to him," "cast him . . . and cast it . . . I cast upon you," and other such examples. In addition to the aural echoes, the story is framed by a recurring emphasis on the idea of God's capacity for "seeing" (as al-Baṣīr).[23] Moses says, "Truly You do ever see us [Moses and his brother]" (Q 20:35). God, in turn, after relating the harrowing story of Moses being thrown into the river, says to him: "I cast upon you a love from Me, that you might be formed under My eye" (Q 20:39). Again, the theme of God as watchful is emphasized; Moses's mother was watchful over him, and God is watchful over the mother and her children.

In the next verse, it is Moses's sister who is the watchful and protective one. She follows Moses floating down the river; she "went forth" and inquired of his palace nursemaids: "Shall I show you one who can nurse him?" (Q 20:40; see also Q 28:12). In this instance, God enacts His purpose of returning Moses to his mother through the instinctive courage of Moses's sister (discussed as well in the previous chapter). In these cases, the command of God is manifest through communication to, and through the actions of, a woman and a girl. The girl's watchfulness of her brother is a thematic reinforcement of God's very own watchfulness over Moses. The girl helps to fulfill the prophecy that God has given to her mother.

God also acts directly to "fortify the heart" of the mother of Moses as a remedy to her intense grief at having been separated from her infant child: "But the heart of Moses's mother became empty, and she would have disclosed it, had We not fortified her heart, that she might be among the believers" (Q 28:10). Here, God not only knows the most intimate states of a woman's heart but also acts directly to alter those states. The English rendering of "heart" does not capture a subtle detail of the original Arabic: in the first instance, her heart (*fuʾād*) becomes empty (*fārigh*); in the second instance, God says, "We fortified (*rabaṭnā ʿalā*) her heart (*qalbihā*)." In order to appreciate the Qur'anic descriptions, we must probe these terms further. What does it mean for a heart to "become empty"? The term *fuʾād* in the plural form (*afʾida*) appears in the Qur'an in several instances to mean "feelings," coming from a root that means "to affect." The adjective *fārigh* has the sense of being void, vacant, exhausted, poured out, and finished.[24] In other words, Moses's mother is despondent over the loss of her child. This verse presents readers, reciters, and listeners an opportunity to empathize with the trauma of losing or being separated from a child.

The loss endured by Moses's mother happened as a result of political persecution, a phenomenon that affects contemporary peoples just as it did earlier peoples. But the verse does not leave the emotional wound of trauma completely raw, for *rabaṭa,* particularly in relation to God, means to bestow patient perseverance, but also to remain calm, not to be dismayed, and, literally, to bandage or bind up. The root word for "heart" (*qalb*) also means "turning."[25] God, the "turner of hearts" (*muqallib al-qulūb*), turned the heart of Moses's mother from despondency toward hopeful perseverance. Her intimate relationship with the presence and wisdom of God, the ultimate Fortifier, was her source of intense courage and emotional strength, and God kept His promise. Her child was returned to her through a turn of events she could not have expected.

## God Hears Women's Grievances

On several occasions, Qur'anic women triumph in difficult circumstances by listening to guidance from divinely inspired sources, or God hears the words of women who have been wronged in some way. For instance, one verse relates a case in which a husband dishonors his wife, and, in her distress, she complains to the Prophet Muḥammad. God hears and responds with a resolution for the wife: "God has indeed heard the words of her who disputes with you concerning her husband (*zawjihā*) and complains to God. And God hears your conversation. Truly God is hearing, seeing" (Q 58:1).[26] In the surah entitled *al-Mujādila* (lit., "She who disputes" or "The female disputer"), the husband's actions are condemned as being "indecent words and calumny," whereupon the surah provides options for expiation and therein a resolution between the couple (Q 58:2–7).

In another instance, God hears the complaint of the wife of Pharaoh, a wife who is wronged by her husband and who is described as "an example" for the believers: "And God sets forth as an example for those who believe the wife of Pharaoh when she said, 'My Lord, build for me a house near You in the garden, deliver me from Pharaoh and his deeds, and deliver me from the wrongdoing people' " (Q 66:11). The wife of Pharaoh turns to God, and God hears her supplication. Notably, she makes a unique request that is not made anywhere else in the Qur'an: she asks not just for salvation but for a "house" (*bayt*) in proximity to God in paradise. Here, the desire for a house readily functions as a metonym for the basic desires for safety, security, and freedom from oppression.[27] The verse has an affective potential to increase a sense of compassion for women under the control of tyrannical forces at home, and also to encourage readers, reciters, and listeners who may find themselves in such a situation to take consolation from the fact that God hears entreaties. In these senses, the wife of Pharaoh is, as the verse itself reiterates, "an example for those who believe."

This is not the only time in the Qur'an that this woman expresses strong desire. In her desire to foster Moses as a son, she says to her tyrant of a husband: "A comfort for me and for you! Slay him not; it may be that he will bring us some benefit, or that we may take him as a son" (Q 28:8). Her desire to intimately care for a dependent is not presented as a uniquely female drive; the viceroy—another Egyptian aristocrat with an overbearing spouse—also appeals to his wife when he wants to provide an enslaved youth (Joseph) with comfortable accommodation: "It may be that he will bring us some benefit, or that we may take him as a son" (Q 12:21). In both cases, the prospective foster parent uses the same appeal, and the vulnerable youth receives a foster home among Egyptian aristocracy. From an affective perspective, this verse could deeply resonate with those aspiring to foster and youth who need care.

Other verses, too, recount the speech of oppressed peoples in need of compassion and advocacy:

> And what ails you that you fight not in the way of God, and for the weak and oppressed—men, women, and children—who cry out, "Our Lord! Bring us forth from this city whose people are oppressors, and appoint for us from You a protector, and appoint for us from You a helper." (Q 4:75)

This verse does not refer to specific people in a specific polity; rather, it represents the sentiments of the weak and oppressed in general. By highlighting the urgent pleas of the oppressed—including women and children—the Qur'an gives voice to their suffering; God hears their cries, and in turn, readers, reciters, or listeners also hear their cries. From an affective perspective, the verses fortify those facing oppression and reassure them that God also hears their cries, condemns the oppressors, and urges upright people to support the weak and oppressed. In these ways, the Qur'an depicts God as knowledgeable about—and responsive to—the intimate needs of female figures.

## God Recognizes Women's Piety

Not only does God elevate the legitimate grievances of women, but God gives particular attention to women's spiritual dedication. Consider the case of the mother of Mary: "[Remember] when the wife of ʿImrān said, 'My Lord, truly I dedicate to You what is in my belly, in consecration. So accept it from me. Truly You are the Hearing, the Knowing' " (Q 3:35). In this case, the wife of ʿImrān earnestly desires to please God, and God responds to her intention with a righteous child. God's manifestation to the wife of ʿImrān as "the Hearing, the Knowing" is a fulfillment of her own supplication to God by those attributes. In the verse immediately preceding her supplication, God explicitly asserts the chosenness of certain individuals and emphasizes those very attributes: "the Hearing, the Knowing" (Q 3:34). In this context, the supplication of the wife of ʿImrān (in Q 3:35) demonstrates that she has an intimate awareness of these attributes of God. Her piety and theological acumen are captured in her supplication and reinforce her belonging to the elite group of those that are "chosen," as described in Q 3:33.

A juxtaposition is also possible between Mary's mother and Mary herself. Mary's mother makes a vow in secret, in which she dedicates Mary to God while Mary is in the womb. In contrast, just *after* Mary delivers her child (Jesus), she is instructed by an angel to take a vow to remain silent instead of attempting to justify or explain her miraculous pregnancy to those who question her piety (Q 19:26–29). In this instance, Mary's divinely mandated verbal passivity accentuates the proactiveness of her own mother's bold dedication and confident supplication; her mother's vow is born of a spirit of earnest dedication, and Mary's vow is fulfilled in a spirit of sincere acceptance. Both women are exceedingly pious, but they are pious in their own unique ways.

## God Speaks to the First Woman

On several occasions, God speaks to women directly, speaks to women through divine intermediaries, and speaks directly to male and female figures simultaneously. God, as depicted in the Qur'an, has been speaking to and with female figures since the creation of humanity. From the beginning of sacred history, Adam and his spouse speak to God in unison, and, in fact, the only time in the Qur'an that Adam prays to God, it is together with his spouse. When the pair repented from following the promptings of Satan over the command of God, "they said, 'Our Lord! We have wronged ourselves. If You do not forgive us and have mercy upon us, we shall surely be among the losers'" (Q 7:23). This is the only verse in which the speech of Adam's spouse is quoted in the Qur'an, making this supplication the entirety of her Qur'anic illocution.

Did the pair utter these exact words spontaneously in unison, or does the Qur'an quote a summary of their speech? Or is the speech perhaps the "words from his Lord" that Adam received (Q 2:37)?[28] Why does the Qur'an describe these words as being received by Adam specifically, when Adam and his spouse address God only in unison? Did Adam receive the words and teach the words to his spouse? Or were the words received by his spouse at the same time Adam received them? The Qur'an itself is not specific on these points, but we can glean insights from an intra-textual reading that takes into consideration God's other speech to the pair, as well as the approximate revelatory order of the surahs.

As shown in the following, God addresses the spouses in the dual grammatical form, and sometimes in the plural when their nemesis Satan (and potentially other figures who are present but unnamed) is included in the address. The widely accepted order of the surahs and verses in which God addresses the spouses is noted in the following, with the grammatical dual or plural identified:[29]

> *Sūrat al-Aʿrāf*, Q 7:22
> Thus he [Satan] lured them [dual] on through deception. And when they [dual] tasted of the tree, their [dual] nakedness was exposed to them [dual], and they [dual] began to sew together the leaves of the garden to cover

themselves [dual]. And their [dual] Lord called out to them [dual], "Did I not forbid you [dual] from that tree, and tell you [dual] that Satan is a manifest enemy unto you [dual]?"

*Sūrat al-Aʿrāf*, Q 7:24–25
He [God] said, "Get down [plural], each of you [plural] an enemy to the other! There will be for you [plural] on the earth a dwelling place, and enjoyment for a while."

He [God] said, "Therein you [plural] shall live, and therein you [plural] shall die, and from there shall you [plural] be brought forth."

*Sūrat Ṭā Hā*, Q 20:123
He [God] said, "Get down [dual] from it, together, each of you [plural] an enemy to the other. And if guidance should come to you [plural] from Me, then whoever follows My guidance shall not go astray, nor be wretched."

*Sūrat al-Baqara*, Q 2:36
Then Satan made them [dual] stumble therefrom, and expelled them [dual] from that wherein they [dual] were, and We [God] said, "Get you down [plural], each of you [plural] an enemy to the other. For you [plural] on the earth is a dwelling place, and enjoyment for a while."

*Sūrat al-Baqara*, Q 2:38
We [God] said, "Get down [plural] from it, all together. If guidance should come to you [plural] from Me, then whoever follows My guidance, no fear shall come upon them [plural], nor shall they [plural] grieve."

*Sūrat al-Aʿrāf*, the first surah listed in the preceding, emphasizes the spouses as a pair, as evidenced by the repetition of words containing the dual form. *Sūrat Ṭā Hā*, which follows *al-Aʿrāf*, is much more focused on Adam's disobedience, likely as a corrective to pre-Qur'anic versions of the story.[30] Verses in *Sūrat al-Baqara*, a chronologically later surah, relate this episode more specifically with a focus on Adam's words.[31]

In *Sūrat al-Aʿrāf*, God's speech is related in the third person, "He [God] said," followed by a rhetorical question to the pair in the grammatical first person: "Did I not forbid you [dual] from that tree, and tell you [dual] that Satan is a manifest enemy to you [dual]?" The emphasis here is on God's speech to the pair. *Sūrat Ṭā Hā* combines the third and first persons, moving seamlessly between the perspective of the omniscient narrator and the immediate intimacy of God's speech.[32] Finally, God's speech in *Sūrat al-Baqara* is related in the grammatical first person, "We said," making it even more immediate and emphatic. Thus, the account that specifically highlights Adam's intimate interactions with God is in the surah in which he receives the "words" from God. Arguably, this is a matter of narrative focus and does not exclude Adam's spouse from being a recipient of the words as well, particularly given that she, along with Adam, is addressed by God in other verses.

We can take this observation a step further. Notably, the verses focusing on Adam's relationship with God occur at the very beginning of the Qur'an and establish (quite emphatically for a reader or reciter who is familiar with this story from biblical iterations) that a woman was not, singularly, to blame for the "fall" of humanity. In this sense, the first mention of a woman in the Qur'an is a refutation of what is, arguably, one of the most demeaning pre-Qur'anic theological claims to arise from the Near Eastern milieu. The first appearance of Adam's spouse in *Sūrat al-Baqara* clearly refutes the pre-Qur'anic belief that women are the cause of humanity's fall.[33]

## Endemic Chauvinism and Female Speech

In a notable structural parallel, the first speech *by God* concerning a female figure (in this instance, Adam's spouse) appears in Q 2:35–36. The first speech *by a woman* concerning God appears in Q 3:35–36, exactly one surah later, in verses carrying identical verse numbers:

> *Sūrat al-Baqara*, Q 2:35–36
> We said, "O Adam, dwell with your mate in paradise, and eat thereof freely wherever you will. But approach not this tree, lest you be among the wrongdoers."
>
> Then Satan made them stumble therefrom, and expelled them from that in which they were, and We said, "Get you down, each of you an enemy to the other. On the earth a dwelling place shall be yours, and enjoyment for a while."

> *Sūrat Āl ʿImrān*, Q 3:35–36
> [Remember] when the wife of ʿImrān said, "My Lord, truly I dedicate to You what is in my belly, in consecration. So accept it from me. Truly You are the Hearing, the Knowing."
>
> And when she bore her [Mary], she [Mary's mother] said, "My Lord, I have borne a female,"—and God knows best what she bore—and the male

is not like the female, "and I have named her Mary, and I seek refuge for her in You, and for her progeny, from Satan the outcast."

In addition to this structural correspondence, other observations on the placement of verses with regard to female speech (and the topical content of that speech) are also significant.

The speech of individual female figures in the Qur'an is bracketed by passionate supplications, first on the part of the wife of ʿImrān and finally on the part of the wife of Pharaoh. The first individual female speech (excluding the joint words of the primordial couple, as elaborated earlier) is the verse wherein the wife of ʿImrān devoutly dedicates the baby in her womb to God: "My Lord, truly I dedicate to You what is in my belly, in consecration. So accept it from me. Truly You are the Hearing, the Knowing" (Q 3:35). This supplication is followed by God's affirmation of her female child (Q 3:36–37).[34] The last speech by a woman in the Qur'an is the wife of Pharaoh's supplication for "a house near You in the garden" and deliverance from her husband and the "wrongdoing people" (*al-qawm al- ẓālimīn*) (Q 66:11).[35] This verse links the ill treatment of one woman to the corruption of society more generally and is yet another occasion in which a woman experiencing a trial cries out to God for solace. The Qur'an itself contains little by way of specific information on this woman's circumstances, other than general descriptions of the excessive wrongdoing and tyrannical nature of her husband, Pharaoh. However, given the context of her speech, as that of a woman in domestic distress, the verse gives voice to this tragically common social reality. Notably, both the first and the last instances of women's speech in the Qur'an address endemic issues related to chauvinism on the microcosmic and macrocosmic levels. The first instance of female speech (Q 3:35–36) asserts the value and worth of a girl child. The last instance (Q 66:11) emphasizes the trials women experience in oppressive marital relationships.[36]

## God Addresses the Women of the Prophet Muḥammad's Family

In the Qur'an, God's direct speech to the Prophet Muḥammad and the women of his household corresponds topically to God's direct speech to the primordial pair. First, the only female figures whom God addresses directly in the Qur'an (beyond the many references to females as believing women in general) are the Prophet Muḥammad's womenfolk and the spouse of Adam, the female progenitor. These figures clearly occupy prominent stations in the arc of Qur'anic sacred history; yet in both cases, the Qur'an depicts these figures as fully capable of making mistakes. Adam's spouse and two of the Prophet's wives turn to God in repentance for specific acts of disobedience.[37] In their need for repentance, these women are no different from their respective prophetic husbands, whom God also explicitly corrects at times; even exemplary people—whether female or male—sometimes make mistakes.

The only speech delivered by an immediate female relation of the Prophet Muḥammad in the Qur'an appears in this context of a wife who has made a mistake. One of the Prophet's wives (who remains unnamed in the Qur'an but who is identified in early exegesis as Ḥafṣa bt. ʿUmar b. al-Khaṭṭāb) divulges a secret that the Prophet asked her to guard.[38] God informs the Prophet that she divulged the secret, the Prophet confronts her about it, and she retorts, "Who informed you of this?" (Q 66:3). Her first impulse was not to apologize or attempt to conceal her slip, but rather to find out who had betrayed her confidence. Her speech is concise and direct—just three words in Arabic. The Prophet responds equally directly, with three concise Arabic words that cannot be rendered quite as succinctly in English: "The Knower, the Aware informed me" (Q 66:3). The conversation between the pair, as depicted in the Qur'an, ends there; however, the Qur'an urges the wives to repent and emphasizes again the theme of God as Protector: "your hearts (dual, *qulūbukumā*) did certainly incline, and if you aid one another against him [the Prophet], then truly God, He is his Protector (*fa-inna Llāha huwa mawlāhu*)." And, if this promise of divine succor left any room for debate, the verse continues by adding, with seemingly unbridled force, "as are Gabriel and the righteous among the believers; and the angels support him withal" (Q 66:4).

The Qur'an immediately guides the wives in question, guidance that is enshrined in a scripture with a transhistorical and global reach. God knows the state of the wives' hearts, implying that God "sees" actions but also the feelings and intentions behind the actions. The essence of the message to the wives is clear: do not "aid one another against him [the Prophet]," for he is protected by God, Gabriel, the righteous believers, and all the angels. Here, there is a subtle but profound intra-textual juxtaposition. The phrase "aid one another" can be rendered more literally as "back each other" (*taẓāharā*). A verb from the same root appears in *Sūrat al-Aḥzāb* to condemn the practice of *ẓihār* by a husband against a wife. A different grammatical form of the same root appears in *Sūrat al-Taḥrīm* to condemn the actions of wives against a husband. The verbal root is repeated in the fourth verse of each surah, thus creating a structural parallel that further reinforces the topical and stylistic connections between the two surahs, *al-Aḥzāb* and *al-Taḥrīm* (surahs 33 and 66, respectively).

In *Sūrat al-Aḥzāb*, God first addresses the Prophet's spouses through the Prophet himself, "O Prophet! Say to your spouses . . ." (Q 33:28). The subsequent verses address the spouses directly. The same pattern is then repeated in *Sūrat al-Taḥrīm*. We can see the parallel structure of the addressee in *Sūrat al-Aḥzāb* and *Sūrat al-Taḥrīm*; the verses move from the Prophet Muḥammad to his spouses, then to the believers more generally, thereby reinforcing the status of his family and their role as exemplars for the wider community:

> Q 33:28–34 (*Sūrat al-Aḥzāb*)
>
> **O Prophet! Say to your spouses** (*azwājika*): "If you desire the life of this world and its ornament, then come! I shall provide for you and release you in a fair manner.
>
> But if you desire God and His Messenger and the abode of the hereafter, then truly God has prepared a great reward for the virtuous among you."
>
> **O women of the Prophet!** (*nisāʾ al-nabī*) Whoever among you commits a flagrant indecency, her punishment will be doubled; and that is easy for God.
>
> And whoever among you is devoutly obedient to God and His Messenger and works righteousness, We shall give her reward twice over, and We have prepared for her a generous provision.
>
> **O women of the Prophet!** (*nisāʾ al-nabī*) You are not like other women. If you are reverent, then be not overtly soft in speech, lest one in whose heart is a disease be moved to desire; and speak in an honorable way.
>
> Abide in your homes and flaunt not your charms as they did flaunt them in the prior age of ignorance. Perform the prayer, give alms, and obey God and His Messenger. God only desires to remove defilement from you, O family of the house (*ahl al-bayt*), and to purify you completely.
>
> And remember that which is recited to you in your homes and among the signs and wisdom of God. Truly God is Subtle, Aware.
>
> **For submitting men and submitting women**, believing men and believing women, devout men and devout women, truthful men and

truthful women, patient men and patient women, humble men and humble women, charitable men and charitable women, men who fast and women who fast, men who guard their private parts and women who guard [their private parts], men who remember God often and women who remember [God often], God has prepared forgiveness and a great reward.[39]

Q 66:1–6 (*Sūrat al-Taḥrīm*)

**O Prophet!** Why do you forbid that which God has made lawful to you, seeking the good pleasure of your spouses (*azwājika*)? And God is Forgiving, Merciful.

God has already ordained for you the absolution of your oaths. And God is your Master. He is the Knower, the Wise.

When the Prophet confided a certain matter to one of his spouses (*azwājihi*), but she divulged it, and God showed it to him, he made known part of it and held back part of it. When he informed her of it, she said, "Who informed you of this?" He replied, "The Knower, the Aware informed me."

**If you [two wives]**[40] **both repent unto God** . . . For your hearts did certainly incline, and if you aid one another against him, then truly God, He is his Protector, as are Gabriel and the righteous among the believers; and the angels support him withal.

It may be that if he divorces you, his Lord would give him spouses in your stead who are better than you, submitting, believing, devoutly obedient, penitent, worshiping, and given to fasting[41]—previously married, and virgins.

**O you who believe!** Shield yourselves and your families from a fire whose fuel is people and stones, over which are angels, stern and severe, who do not disobey God in what He commands of them and who do what they are commanded.

Not only do similar forms of address occur in both surahs, but also the vocative phrases "O Prophet!" and "O you who believe!" appear rhythmically throughout the whole of *Sūrat al-Aḥzāb* in the following alternating pattern:

| *Sūrat al-Aḥzāb* | *Addressee* |
|---|---|
| Verse 1 | O Prophet! |
| Verse 9 | O you who believe! |
| Verse 28 | O Prophet! |
| Verse 40 | O you who believe! |

| *Sūrat al-Aḥzāb* | *Addressee* |
|---|---|
| Verse 45 | O Prophet! |
| Verse 49 | O you who believe! |
| Verse 50 | O Prophet! |
| Verse 53 | O you who believe! |
| Verse 59 | O Prophet! |
| Verses 69 and 70 | O you who believe! |

The verses that address the Prophet and the believers in this pattern are regularly interspersed with verses that declare the unique status of the Prophet and/or his spouses in relation to the rest of the believers. For instance, the Qur'an addresses the women of the Prophet (*nisāʾ al-nabī*) and his wider household (*ahl al-bayt*) in a rhythmic structure of alternating addressees.

Multiple verses in this surah confer some kind of exemplary status on the Prophet and/or his spouses.[42] For instance, the Qur'an specifies that the Prophet is set apart from the rest of the believers with respect to marriage; he can lawfully take more wives (Q 33:38) than other Muslim men, and unlike other women, his wives may not remarry.[43] Later in *Sūrat al-Aḥzāb*, the Qur'an follows this pattern as well, in relation to the matter of women "draw[ing] their cloaks over themselves" to avoid being bothered: "O Prophet! Tell your spouses (*azwājika*) and your daughters (*banātika*), and the women (*nisāʾ*) of the believers to draw their cloaks over themselves. Thus it is likelier that they will be known and not be disturbed. And God is Forgiving, Merciful" (Q 33:59). In this verse, the guidance begins with the Prophet Muḥammad's spouses, then his daughters, then the "women of the believers" more generally.[44] This pattern is found throughout the surah and emphasizes the status of the Prophet and his family.

English Qur'an translations often render the phrases *azwāj al-nabī* and *nisāʾ al-nabī* both as "wives of the Prophet"; however, I question whether the Qur'anic addressees are so readily interchangeable. Arguably, the term *nisāʾ al-nabī* should be seen as including the Prophet's daughters, as the verse immediately following describes God's desire to purify the "family of the house" (*ahl al-bayt*), and a verse later in the same surah explicitly instructs the Prophet to "tell your spouses (*azwājika*) and your daughters (*banātika*) and the women of the believers (*nisā' al-mu'minīn*)," as noted earlier (Q 33:59).[45] The Prophet's daughters would be included in the terms "women of the Prophet" and "family of the house"; likewise, the phrase *nisā' al-nabī* appears in verses that address general matters of household ethics. By contrast, the Qur'an uses the term *azwāj al-nabī* in the conversations between God and the Prophet that pertain specifically to his marital relations; "spouses of the Prophet" (*azwāj al-nabī*) has a more narrowly defined meaning than "women of the Prophet" (*nisā' al-nabī*), which is arguably broader and includes his other women relatives.

Finally, we may note that in *Sūrat al-Taḥrīm*, the narrative voice of God warns the two wives of the Prophet that they may be replaced with "better" spouses who are "submitting, believing, devoutly obedient, penitent, worshiping, and given to fasting" (Q 66:5). This definition of wifely virtues resonates with the description of virtue in *Sūrat al-Aḥzāb*, where both virtuous men and virtuous women are submitting, believing, devout, truthful, patient, humble, charitable, given to fasting, guard their private parts, and remember God often (Q 33:53). The list in *Sūrat al-Taḥrīm* appears in the context of God enumerating characteristics of an ideal spouse for the Prophet. These traits of an ideal wife directly parallel those enumerated in the list in *Sūrat al-Aḥzāb* that describe both men and women; hence, the traits desirable in a wife are desirable *human* virtues, not exclusively female or feminine virtues.

In Q 66:5, the ideal spouses could be "previously married [or] virgins"; this equivalency indicates that virginity does not make a virgin superior to someone who has been previously married, even though sociocultural values often emphasize virginity as particularly desirable in prospective wives. In this respect, the verse affirms the honorable place of widows or divorcees, who are often wrongfully stigmatized or discouraged from remarrying in some cultural contexts. The Qur'an itself, it should be noted, does not make virginity one of the qualities of an ideal prospective wife.

## Damned Women

*Sūrat al-Taḥrīm* presents the wives of Noah and Lot as negative examples for the believers: "They [the spouses of Noah and Lot] were under two of Our righteous servants [Noah and Lot]; then they [the wives] betrayed them [Noah and Lot], and they [Noah and Lot] availed them [their wives] naught against God" (Q 66:10).[46] This mention of the wives of Noah and Lot is the only instance in the Qur'an in which a wife is described as being "under" (*taḥt*) a husband or male figure. Is this specific case of wives being "under" husbands meant to be prescriptive for the relationship between spouses or the relationship between men and women more generally?

In the verse in question (Q 66:10), God specifically refers to Noah and Lot as "Our righteous servants," thereby putting Noah and Lot into a specific category of "righteous servants" of God, a category to which other women and men belong, as noted in numerous other instances in the Qur'an. God declares, "They [the wives] were under two of Our righteous servants"; here, the appellation "Our righteous servants" or "Our righteous slaves" (*ʿabdayni min ʿibādinā ṣāliḥayn*) emphasizes the utter servitude of Noah and Lot, who are righteous in their humble submission to God. The wives of Noah and Lot "betrayed" their husbands, who called them to the way of God; hence, rather than being elevated in their righteousness, they are debased. These two female figures do not just evoke wretchedness on an individual level; rather, their characters parallel the widespread iniquities of their respective people. Indeed, no other peoples are so frequently condemned in the Qur'an as the peoples of Noah and Lot.[47]

*Sūrat al-Taḥrīm* begins with emphatic addresses to the Prophet and to his two noble but contriving wives and ends with God "set[ting] forth as an example for those who believe" two unrighteous wives, followed by two righteous women, one without a husband (Mary) and one (the wife of Pharaoh) whose husband is a tyrannical ruler.[48] The two wives of the Prophet Muḥammad are then implicitly positioned as having the agency to choose which of the two extremes (righteous or unrighteous) they will follow.[49] *Sūrat al-Taḥrīm* begins with a husband (the Prophet Muḥammad) in need of God's intervention, but then also references a righteous woman (the wife of Pharaoh) who seeks God's succor against her husband (Q 66:11). The surah includes a substantial threat of retaliation should the wives of the Prophet continue to conspire against him, but interestingly, it concludes by extolling a righteous woman (Mary) who has no husband.

The wives of Noah and Lot are given a divine decree in the Qur'an, but, in contrast to the women addressed by God or angels, the divine decree to the wives of Noah and Lot is in the passive voice, without a known speaker. It is as if these treacherous wives do not deserve to be addressed with an active verb: "And it was said to both, 'Enter the fire with those who enter'" (Q 66:10). The passive dismissal of these two figures underscores their detestable nature for "betraying" God's "righteous servants." The otherworldly speech directed toward these two wives on this occasion stands in contrast to the many other women who receive guidance and encouragement.

## Lying Speech from a Woman

In the first chapter, I focused on the sexual misconduct of the viceroy's wife and the ways in which the women around her initially exacerbate the situation. What remains to be observed is that the viceroy's wife is not only nefarious, but she is also quick-witted. One climactic moment highlights this characteristic:

> And they [Joseph and the wife of the viceroy] raced to the door, while she tore his shirt from behind. And they encountered her husband (*sayyidahā*) at the door. She said, "What is the recompense for one who desires ill toward your wife (*ahlika*), save that he be imprisoned, or [face] a painful punishment?" (Q 12:25)

In this example, the wife of the viceroy refers to herself using the euphemism *ahl,* a term that can mean the wife of a given figure but that can also signify the family or household more broadly. In this way, her question, "What is the recompense for one who desires ill toward your wife?" carries the significance, "What is the recompense for one who desires ill toward your family?" With these words, the speech of the viceroy's wife calls attention to the ways in which a man's social capital in a patriarchal social order is linked to his ability to protect and ensure the sexual integrity and honor of the girls and women in his charge. Thus, she not only deceitfully blames the affair on Joseph, but she does so by employing an idiom that would help achieve her purpose. She is not the only female in the Qur'an to use her quick wit, but she is the only female to use it with explicitly nefarious aims.

Her words are also the single instance where the polysemic word *sayyid* refers specifically to a husband figure.[50] The husband, we learn, is a viceroy of Egypt; his title, al-ʿAzīz ("the mighty one"), reflects his occupation as a political leader. The use of *sayyid* to mean "master, husband, or leader" occurs in a story in which the personalities are aristocrats, not in the context of verses describing human creation or telos. Hence, this use of *sayyid* can be understood to reflect a sociological dynamic, not an ontological reality.

## Affective Dimensions of Female Speech

From its discussions of mundane affairs to its cosmic assertions, the Qur'an describes itself as a book (*kitāb*) containing a "clarification of all things, and a guidance and a mercy and glad tidings for those who submit" (Q 16:89). For those listening to, reciting, or reading the Qur'an as an act of devotion, the aim of these acts may be to gain clarification, guidance, mercy, good news, or some other benefit or desired effect—even somatic and emotional benefits.[51] Thus, the listening, reciting, or reading is—for one so disposed—pregnant with sacred possibility.

In relation to women's speech, I have suggested in places how Qur'anic verses can have particular effects on readers, reciters, and listeners (such as the potential empathy generated when contemplating a narrative about the emotional struggle of a mother being forcibly separated from her child). Further studies could continue to unpack the transformative quality of such an encounter with instances of female speech in the Qur'an, where "meaning is created in the activity of reception, in the interplay of text and recipient," in "the interactive encounter of hearer/reader and text."[52] A hermeneutic that appreciates this "affective potential" does not replace philology; it simply adds another layer of potential meaning.

If we consider the Qur'an as a recitation, one that is often performed as part of ritual devotion and pious practice, we can see that the performance of gender, through the re-enactment of Qur'anic speech, adds another interpretive layer to the ways in which gender is inscribed. For instance, the verse in which Mary complains of the pains of labor, "Would that I had died before this and were a thing forgotten, utterly forgotten!" (Q 19:23), expresses the discomfort and pain women experience during childbirth.[53] Ultimately, the act of regularly revisiting such speech in the context of a devotional, ritual practice may transform a conscientious individual, and bring about an increase in empathy in that individual toward women who experience this exceptionally wondrous (but also physically and emotionally demanding) moment. The embodied experience of childbirth is necessarily and uniquely a female experience, but through the re-enactment of this distinctively female speech, even male Qur'anic reciters articulate the distressed cries of a woman in labor.[54]

This is one instance, among many in the Qur'an, in which female speech exerts a unique rhetorical influence on readers, reciters, and listeners, particularly those who experience it through a devotional episteme as speech "from the Lord of the worlds" (Q 10:47). Karen Bauer compares Mary's birth pangs and the anguish that the mother of Moses experiences when having to cast her child away to save him from Pharaoh's forces. Bauer observes how both narratives contain affective potential for the Qur'anic audience:

> God is there to relieve emotional and physical suffering, bringing these exemplary women into a state of hope, relief, and, ultimately, knowledge of God's justice and mercy. They both prove their subservience to God and willingness to put aside all worldly emotional attachments to do His bidding. The listener is brought along on the emotional journey, and is able to empathise with the comfort they receive.[55]

In these narratives, and in others, the extreme trials that pious women experience are assuaged by God's intervention. Pious women must still endure hardships, but their suffering is met with God's awareness and care; narrative functions as an illustration of God's attributes in practical circumstances and constitutes a form of assurance to individuals among the Qur'anic audience that they, too, can be privy to this care.

## The Words of Women

The Qur'an includes the speech of a number of female figures, including the young and old, oppressed and empowered, pious and corrupt, and shades in between. As we have seen, both Mary and the Queen of Sheba, two of the Qur'an's most loquacious female figures, speak in a way that is similar to—or even the same as—the speech of male figures who are designated as prophets. The Queen of Sheba ends her speech by addressing God, seeking forgiveness, and professing her submission, just as Moses does (Q 27:44). When Mary is confronted by a "well-proportioned" man, she immediately exclaims: "I seek refuge from you in the Compassionate, if you are reverent!" (Q 19:18). Similarly, when Joseph is hemmed in by the wife of the viceroy, he appeals: "God be my refuge! Truly He is my Lord, and has made beautiful my accommodation. Verily the wrongdoers will not prosper!" (Q 12:23). Similarly, the Qur'an calls Mary a "woman of truth" and Joseph a "man of truth."[56] We have also seen how Mary's speech and Zachariah's speech are juxtaposed. But neither Mary nor the Queen of Sheba preaches about God's attributes, for instance, to gatherings of people, as do prophetic figures. They teach by lived example, but they are never depicted chiding wayward peoples or publicly commanding others to worship God.

This seems to be the crucial difference between the exemplary female figures in the Qur'an and the male figures who are specifically given the title of "prophet" (*nabī*). The difference is in the specific tasks that God charges them to carry out, not in the sincerity of their worship, their conviction, or the degree of their closeness to God. More generally, many women figures speak pious words and make supplications to God, as do men figures. For another example, the wife of Pharaoh prays in the exact same idiom in Q 66:11 as does her foster son Moses upon his "fearful" and "vigilant" flight from Egypt, when he prays, "My Lord! Deliver me from the wrongdoing people!" (Q 28:21). In addition to praying for a house near God in paradise, as discussed earlier, the wife of Pharaoh prays, "My Lord . . . deliver me from the wrongdoing people!" (Q 66:11).

A significant portion of women's speech in the Qur'an—seven verses—consists of supplications to God. In fact, reading or listening to the Qur'an from the beginning, every instance in which a female figure speaks is directed to God or pertains in some way to God's blessings or benevolence, until the wife of the viceroy is mentioned more than one-quarter of the way through. Although the viceroy's wife herself never mentions God, even her women guests speak using a theologically oriented idiom: "God be praised!"[57] The Queen of Sheba and the wife of the viceroy, both aristocratic women who are depicted in their respective journeys from falsehood toward truth, are the two most loquacious female figures; their speech is a vehicle that conveys their eventual transformations of outlook and character, in accordance with the Qur'an's didactic mission. Notably, not one of the three damned female figures in the Qur'an utters a word of speech.

In general, women in the Qur'an often speak with authority, insight, and wit; on much rarer occasions, female speech has nefarious aims. The speech of the Egyptian viceroy's wife is witty, but with a disreputable goal. On the whole, speech by women does not seem to be more nor less poignant than that of men. Both male and female figures have a range of eloquence and differing degrees of forthrightness. On occasion, female figures also fumble for words when they are caught off guard. For instance, the wife of Abraham expresses her astonishment at the prospect of bearing a child in her old age with the dramatic expression "Oh, woe unto me!" (*yā waylatā*) (Q 11:72).[58] In response to receiving a divine message, the wife of Abraham not only speaks expressively, but her gestures also convey her astonishment; she smiles or laughs (Q 11:71) and cries out loud while striking her face (Q 51:29).[59] Her awkward moment of surprise at the divine message resembles the reaction of Moses when he encounters divine speech directed at him from a desert shrub; he ineloquently—almost comically—fumbles for words as he considers the various practical but rather mundane uses of his staff, including for leaning upon, for beating down leaves for sheep, and for "other uses" (Q 20:18).[60] When confronted by the Prophet Muḥammad for divulging a secret he had asked one of his wives to keep, she rejoins, "Who informed you of this?" (Q 66:3).

Several female figures articulate their thoughts clearly and effectively in difficult situations; Moses's sister, Moses's foster mother, and the Queen of Sheba all speak effectively in trying circumstances. Other women are expressive at times and contemplative at other times. Mary, who is otherwise depicted as conversing with angels and crying out with birth pangs, is silent in relation to defending her honor against charges of licentiousness; her vow of silence is a thematic echo of the silence of her guardian Zachariah. Both figures are expressive before God but must resort to gesturing before their people. Aside from public preaching, we do not, in general, find any features of female speech in the Qur'an that would distinguish it from male speech; however, a more detailed analysis of male speech—such that it could be compared systematically to female speech—could be a fruitful avenue for future study.

In Chapter 1, I addressed questions of sexual difference and sexuality in narratives involving female figures, and in Chapter 2, I examined female figures in the context of familial relationships. In this chapter, I have considered revelatory messages to women and women's speech generally. In the final chapter, I discuss Qur'anic figures according to the approximate revelatory arc.

## Notes

1. See Appendix C for a list of verses with female speech cited by order of occurrence. I also list verses containing divine and angelic speech directed toward women.

Qur'anic Arabic does not have quotation marks, so verbal cues such as "she/they said" generally signal the beginning of speech. On occasion, there are different plausible interpretations about where a direct quotation ends and/or about the identity of a speaker or addressee(s). According to my count, thirty-four verses include female speech; this does not include the laugh (or wide smile) of Abraham's wife in Q 11:71 or the speech of the ant.

2. I translate "wondering" in place of *The Study Quran*'s translation of "laughing," as the word in question can have both senses with the preposition *min*; see *AEL*, 1823–24. Laughing can imply mocking, whereas the humility expressed by Solomon's speech suggests a spirit of awe, not arrogance. For analysis of the significance of this ant figure and the interactions with the Prophet Solomon, see Jardim, *Recovering the Female Voice*, 137–38.
3. The root *w-z-ʿ* occurs in the Qur'an five times in two forms. See *AEDQ*, 1023–24. See also *AEL (Supplement)*, 3052 and *AED*, 1210.
4. The single ant is grammatically gendered as female in Arabic, but from a perspective of myrmecology, the female ant would also be the one leading the colony and issuing marching orders, as the ant does in the narrative. In a self-reflexive verse on the use of metaphor, the Qur'an highlights another insect: "Truly God is not ashamed to set forth a parable of a gnat or something smaller" (Q 2:26).
5. For verses that emphasize Solomon's power, see Q 27:36 and 27:40.
6. See Q 27:41–42. Earlier in the narrative, when told by the hoopoe of the majesty of the Queen's throne, Solomon demonstrates his righteousness by praising the majesty of God's throne. See Q 27:22–26.
7. For comparative perspectives, see Toni Tidswell, "A Clever Queen Learns the Wisdom of God: The Queen of Sheba in the Hebrew Scriptures and the Qur'an," *Hecate* 33, no. 2 (2007): 43–55. See also Jacob Lassner, *Demonizing the Queen of Sheba: Boundaries of Gender and Culture in Postbiblical Judaism and Medieval Islam* (Chicago: University of Chicago Press, 1993).
8. See Q 27:32–35. For discussion of this aspect of the Queen's persona, see Na'eem Jeenah, "Bilqis: A Qur'ānic Model for Leadership and for Islamic Feminists," *Journal for Semitic Studies* 13, no. 1 (2004): 47–58.
9. The etymology of Solomon's name, Sulaymān, could reinforce these multiple valences.
10. For an analysis of the symbolism in her conversion to Islam, see Mustansir Mir, "The Queen of Sheba's Conversion in Q. 27:44: A Problem Examined," *Journal of Qur'anic Studies* 9, no. 2 (2007): 43–56.
11. The Queen of Sheba's speech is found in eight Qur'anic verses in total, slightly more than Mary, the most oft-mentioned female figure in the Qur'an. See Appendix C for a list of the eight verses in which the Queen speaks, all of which are in *Sūrat al-Naml*.
12. For other thematic similarities between *Sūrat al-Naml* (Q 27) and *Sūrat al-Qaṣaṣ* (Q 28), see Farrin, *Structure and Qur'anic Interpretation*, 103. See also Q 21:87 for a similar supplication on the part of the prophet Jonah, who cries out, "There is no god but You! Glory be to You! Truly I have been among the wrongdoers." The extent to which prophetic figures can err is a much-debated question in Islamic intellectual history; the Qur'an does indeed depict prophetic figures making mistakes, however slight. Suffice

it to say that both male and female figures who are esteemed in the Qur'an occasionally make mistakes, and their capacity and willingness to make amends are part of what makes them exemplary.

13. See *SQ*, 953 n. 30. The *basmala* formula precedes each surah of the Qur'an with the exception of *Sūrat al-Tawba* (Q 9), whose first verse begins with a repudiation of idolaters; see *SQ*, 505 nn. 1–4 for context.
14. The "he" who speaks to Mary and offers postpartum comfort could be the baby Jesus, who miraculously spoke in a manner similar to how he is depicted speaking later in the surah. Or, it could be the angel calling out from the bottom of a hillock, as Mary gave birth in a "high place" (*rabwa*) (Q 23:50). See *SQ*, 770 n. 24. See also discussions in Gregg, *Shared Stories, Rival Tellings*, 549. For a discussion of pre-Islamic and Hellenistic birth motifs and a comparison to Hagar being given provisions for her son in the desert, see Marx, "Glimpses of a Mariology," 539. Notably, in both stories, the new mothers are nourished with a flowing spring. On the symbolism of Hagar finding water, see Osman, *Female Personalities*, 49–50. On Christian and Muslim traditions surrounding the location of the "high place" (*rabwa*) where Mary gave birth, see Mourad, "Mary in the Qur'ān," 168–72.
15. See, for instance, Q 3:47 and 19:35 for examples of God's statement "Be!" (*kun*). See also Q 3:59, "Truly the likeness of Jesus in the sight of God is that of Adam; He created him from dust, then said to him, 'Be!' and he was." See discussions of God's statement "Be!" in Gregg, *Shared Stories, Rival Tellings*, 561.
16. See Q 19:9 and 19:21 for the ease with which God's decree brings something to fruition. See also Q 30:27 for the ease with which God creates. Other words derived from this root (*h-w-n*) mean humility as a virtue (used once, in Q 25:63), as something deemed insignificant (used once, in Q 24:15, in the context of the slander of chaste women and thinking of it as a small matter and not a major sin), and finally as a condemnation of socially humiliating a woman who bears a girl child (used in Q 16:59). All seventeen other Qur'anic uses refer to the sense of God's "humiliating" punishment.
17. Here the term "human being" is often translated more specifically as "man"; the significance of the word *bashar* (among many words signifying "human being" in Arabic) is noteworthy in this case because the root *b-sh-r*, as we noted in the commentary on Q 2:187, has a semantic association with skin and sexual intercourse. See *AEDQ*, 92–94.
18. *The Study Quran* interprets the phrases "And [it is thus] that We might make him a sign to humankind, and a mercy from Us. And it is a matter decreed" as God's speech (as the Qur'anic narrator), not as God's speech as relayed to Mary by the angelic messenger. Both interpretations are plausible. For a comparative analysis of Mary in the Gospel traditions and extra-biblical literature, including reflections on Mary's speech, the figures around her, and debates about women as prophets, see Gregg, *Shared Stories, Rival Tellings*, 457–593, esp. 468. For a discussion of Mary's *miḥrāb*, see Marx, "Glimpses of a Mariology," 542, and Reynolds, *The Qur'ān and Its Biblical Subtext*, 135–37.

19. Another depiction of the scene of the angelic messages to Abraham and his wife contains a similar echo of this decree but with the different divine epithets "the Wise, the Knowing" (Q 51:30).
20. Lamptey, among others, notes the theological parallel between the Prophet Muḥammad's purity of character and Mary's virginity; see Lamptey, *Divine Voices*, 144–45. The reference to "books" in the plural may refer to the presence of Mary in pre-Qur'anic scriptures (namely, in the Gospels), which affirm her key place in sacred history, a theme I elaborate upon in the next chapter. Of the thirty-four times Mary's name is mentioned in the Qur'an, this final reference is a summary of her lofty status and import.
21. There is also a parallel between God "establishing the people in the land" in a revelation to the mother of Moses and extra-Qur'anic narratives of God's bringing Hagar, and through her the descendants of Abraham, to Mecca. See Q 2:126, 2:158, and 14:37 for discussions of Mecca and the role of the family of Abraham in establishing the sacred rites therein; see also discussions in Chapter 4.
22. For a summary of the debate on the possibility of women being prophets, see Adújar, "Feminist Readings of the Qur'an," 66. For a discussion of the Qur'anic instances in which women receive revelation, see Fierro, "Women as Prophets," 185–86.
23. For further discussion of this surah, see Michael Sells, "The Casting: A Close Hearing of Sura Ṭāhā 9–79," in *Qur'ānic Studies Today*, ed. Angelika Neuwirth and Michael A. Sells (New York: Routledge, 2016), 124–77. For further analysis, see Sayed, "Repetition in Qurʾānic *Qaṣaṣ*," 59–61.
24. The root *f-ʾ-d* occurs sixteen times in the Qur'an; its derived meanings include to affect, to be hurt, and to be burned up; see *AEL*, 2322–23. The root *f-r-gh* occurs six times in the Qur'an with meanings similar to those mentioned earlier. Some scholars note additional derived meanings that also fit this Qur'anic context (perhaps even better than the translation of "empty"); these meanings include impatient, disquieted, or disturbed; see *AEL*, 2380–82.
25. See *AEL*, 1013–15 and 2552–55 for *r-b-ṭ* and *q-l-b*, respectively. Words derived from the root *q-l-b* are particularly frequent in the Qur'an; the root appears at least 168 times in twelve grammatical forms. See *AEDQ*, 770–72.
26. The woman known as "*al-mujādila*" (lit., "the female disputer") is identified in commentary traditions as Khawla bt. Thaʿlaba, and her rebuked husband was Aws b. al-Ṣāmit. See *SQ*, 1342 nn. 1–4. See also related discussions of the Qur'an's response to women in Lamrabet, *Women in the Qur'an*, 93–98.
27. The Arabic words for "dwelling place" can also mean a place of rest, peace, and tranquility, as derived from the root *s-k-n*. See *AEDQ*, 444–46.
28. See the discussion of this and related verses in Osman, *Female Personalities*, 30–32.
29. For an analysis of the chronological ordering of these surahs, see Bodman, *The Poetics of Iblīs*, 50–54 and 245–47. In order to present a more direct, literal translation for the purposes of intra-textual analysis, I have slightly amended *The Study Quran* translations. Also, in several of the verses, who is made an enemy to whom is not entirely clear from the Qur'anic narrative alone. For different interpretations of the meaning of these references, see *SQ*, 414 nn. 24–25.

30. For a thorough discussion of the Muslim incorporation of pre-Qur'anic narratives regarding Eve, see Bronson, "Eve in the Formative Period of Islamic Exegesis."
31. For a provocative structural analysis of the depiction of the primordial couple in this surah, see Farrin, *Structure and Qur'anic Interpretation*, 74–75.
32. The use of dialogue and the frequent change of addressees (a device known as *iltifāt*) are common narrative devices in the Qur'an. See Mir, "Dialogues," *EQ*, 1:532.
33. See discussions in Hatice K. Arpagus, "The Position of Women in the Creation: A Qur'anic Perspective," in *Muslima Theology*, 115–32. For comparative perspectives, see Kristen E. Kvam, Linda S. Schearing, and Valarie H. Ziegler, eds., *Eve and Adam: Jewish, Christian, and Muslim Readings on Genesis and Gender* (Bloomington: Indiana University Press, 2009). For a formative analysis of Jewish and Christian interpretations, see Elaine Pagels, *Adam, Eve, and the Serpent* (New York: First Vintage Books, 1989). See also Barazangi, *Women's Identity and the Qur'an*, 38 and 44.
34. For analysis of this phrase, see Michael B. Schub, "'The Male Is Not like the Female' (Qur'ān 3:36): An Eponymous Passage in the Qur'ān," *Zeitschrift für Arabische Linguistik* 23 (1991): 101–4. See also the discussion in Reynolds, *The Qur'ān and Its Biblical Subtext*, 130–31. Reynolds depicts Mary's mother as being disappointed by her female child; the mother's speech could simply be expressing surprise, not necessarily disappointment. In any case, the speech of God about Mary's unique status serves to dispel any notion that a female child could be seen as unfit for service to God.
35. The exegetical literature holds that she was abused by Pharaoh for endorsing the prophetic message of her foster son Moses, and this leads to her death. See *SQ*, 1392 n. 11 for commentary.
36. This verse is not only the last in the Qur'an with female speech, but it is also widely held to be near the end of the revelatory order of the Qur'an. (See Appendix D for an approximate ordering of surahs according to the chronology of their revelation.)
37. For Adam and his spouse and two of the wives being chided, see Q 7:22 and 66:4, respectively.
38. For a concise account of the background and figures involved, see *SQ*, 1389 nn. 1–4. Many scholars hold that the secret involved the Prophet Muḥammad's Coptic concubine, Māriya (also vocalized "Māriyya"); for a critical feminist reading, see Aysha A. Hidayatullah, "Māriyya the Copt: Gender, Sex and Heritage in the Legacy of Muhammad's Umm Walad," *Islam and Christian-Muslim Relations* 21, no. 3 (2010): 221–43.
39. See Q 33:35. For a discussion of this verse, as narrated in hadith on the authority of women companions of the Prophet, see Geissinger, *Gender and Muslim Constructions*, 193–94 and 239–40.
40. In the commentary tradition, the two wives are said to be Ḥafṣa and ʿĀʾisha. See *SQ*, 1389 nn. 1–4.
41. *The Study Quran* translates the term *sāʾiḥāt* as "given to wayfaring," that is, "given to emigrating for the sake of their religion"; however, the editors also note that the meaning may be "given to fasting," which better fits the context here.
42. See Q 33:6, 21, 32, 38, 50, and 56.

43. The Prophet was, nonetheless, limited with respect to the women who were eligible spouses; on this, see Q 33:50. The matter of his wives not remarrying is discussed in Q 33:53. Such an injunction could be seen as a way of protecting his widows from a barrage of marriage proposals from piety-seeking companions and followers, as would have been the Arabian custom of the time.
44. On women's clothing, see also Q 24:31, a verse that is also addressed to the believers more generally ("O you who believe!" Q 24:27).
45. For a discussion of the term *ahl al-bayt* and other Qur'anic verses pertaining to the wives of the Prophet, as narrated in hadith on the authority of women companions of the Prophet, see Geissinger, *Gender and Muslim Constructions*, 187–89.
46. For other instances of Lot's wife's betrayal, see Q 7:83, 11:81, 15:60, 27:57, and 29:32. The verse under discussion here is the first and only instance in which Noah's wife is explicitly condemned.
47. See Kaltner and Mirza, *The Bible and the Qur'an*, 107.
48. As also pointed out by Osman, *Female Personalities*, 46.
49. As Osman observes, "the fact that precisely two women are named on either side creates a delicate balance between the good and the bad." See *Female Personalities*, 47.
50. This instance of polysemy in Q 12:25 echoes another instance in 12:23, where Joseph uses the word *rabb* to mean "lord," as in "person with authority over someone else," or possibly "Lord" as an appellation of God. For a discussion of the features of this surah, see Farrin, *Structure and Qur'anic Interpretation*, 34–43.
51. The Qur'an describes its potential to arouse somatic effects through the "most beautiful discourse" (*aḥsan al-ḥadīth*), "whereat quivers the skin of those who fear their Lord" (Q 39:23). For a range of interpretations of this verse, see *SQ*, 1124 n. 23. For a theoretical discussion of the Qur'an as God's speech and the implications of this for historical and literary studies of the Qur'an, see Neuwirth, "Two Faces of the Qur'an."
52. See McAuliffe, "Text and Textuality," 69–70.
53. As Robert Gregg astutely observes, "she has the response of a fully human woman"; *Shared Stories, Rival Tellings*, 549. For a discussion of the potential affective responses of readers/listeners to this scene, see Bauer, "Emotion in the Qur'an," 23. For discussions of Mary's birthing of Jesus and its parallels in early Christian texts, see Mustafa Akyol, *The Islamic Jesus: How the King of the Jews Became a Prophet of the Muslims* (New York: St. Martin's Press, 2017), 104–32. For further comparisons between Christian and Muslim accounts of the annunciation and birth of Jesus, see also Mourad, "Mary in the Qurʾān." In an essay that argues for valuing motherhood as a distinct category of experience, Irene Oh observes that "available information about mothers is often secondary, told through the voices of male observers, redactors, or authors, not through the voices of the mothers themselves." See Irene Oh, "Motherhood in Christianity and Islam: Critiques, Realities, and Possibilities," *Journal of Religious Ethics* 38, no. 4 (2010): 646–47. Despite exploring depictions of Mary in the Islamic tradition to some extent, Oh does not observe that in the Qur'an, Mary expresses the agony of labor pangs, a notable dimension of the embodied experience of pregnancy and motherhood.

54. For reflections on this dynamic generally, see Ali, "Destabilizing Gender, Reproducing Maternity," 90–92.
55. See Bauer, "Emotion in the Qur'an," 23. See also her subsequent analysis of grief and the ways in which God provides comfort as a key narrative trope in several stories involving prophets and their families.
56. See Q 5:75 and 12:46, respectively. For a discussion, see Gregg, *Shared Stories, Rival Tellings*, 574–75.
57. See Q 12:31 and 12:51, in which the women express, first, their astonishment at the beauty of Joseph and, second, their affirmation of his innocence in the affair involving the viceroy's wife.
58. Verse Q 11:72 in full reads: "She said, 'Oh, woe unto me! Shall I bear a child when I am an old woman, and this husband of mine is an old man? That would surely be an astounding thing.' " See also Q 51:29: "Then his wife came forward with a loud cry; she struck her face and said, 'A barren old woman!' "
59. As mentioned previously in the case of Solomon's reaction to the speech of the ant, the word in question in Q 11:71 can mean to laugh or to smile widely. See *AEL*, 1823. The Qur'an may be using a derivative sense of the word *ḍaḥikat* as, according to some exegetes, it is a euphemism for menstruation. In this case, the menstruation would be a sign of her fertility. See discussions of the laugh of Abraham's wife in Reynolds, *The Qurʾān and Its Biblical Subtext,* 87–97. See also Osman, *Female Personalities*, 47–48.
60. On this incident, Mustansir Mir comments: "An amusing situation is created by Moses's failure to appreciate a discrepancy between the profoundly significant nature of the question asked by God and the rather literal interpretation placed on it by Moses." See Mir, *Understanding the Islamic Scripture: A Study of Selected Passages of the Qurʾān* (New York: Routledge, 2016), 159.

# 4
# Women Exemplars for an Emerging Polity

In this chapter, I consider Qur'anic women in the context of the nascent Muslim polity. The chapter reprises some previously discussed narratives, but here the analysis follows the approximate revelatory progression from early Meccan verses to late Medinan verses. This heuristic (considering verses through the lens of correlated events in the nascent Muslim polity as reported in extra-Qur'anic literature) is a well-established—though not uncontroversial—technique in Qur'anic studies.[1] Much prior scholarship has been devoted to reconstructing the likely sequence of surahs, including efforts by classically trained Muslim exegetes and by Western academics alike.[2] The process entails tracking developments in Qur'anic themes and lexical styles, matching Qur'anic allusions with concurrent events in the Prophet Muḥammad's biography (*sīra*), and considering statements about the revelatory order of particular surahs and verses as passed down in early oral transmission, among other considerations.

In terms of this approximate revelatory sequence, Qur'anic verses relating to women begin with an early emphasis on the single soul and the first couple, then progress to a period in which women in shared biblical sacred history take precedence, and finally, to later verses and surahs that emphasize aspects of spousal relations and gendered social relations and that prominently feature female figures around the Prophet Muḥammad. In these later verses, the actions of women affiliated with the Prophet Muḥammad become case studies for teaching and instituting new communal precedents. This is particularly true in matters regarding female–male kinship interactions.

Using this hermeneutic, I explore how Qur'anic narratives define female virtue and vice against the background of the emerging Muslim polity. As in the preceding chapters and the study as a whole, my aim is not to establish the veracity of any particular account, nor to catalogue histories of exegetical interpretation and the disagreements therein; rather, my aim is to discern relevant tropes and themes. Paying close attention to Qur'anic structure and style, as well as thematic connections and juxtapositions, I trace the path

*Women and Gender in the Qur'an*. Celene Ibrahim, Oxford University Press (2020). © Oxford University Press.
DOI: 10.1093/oso/9780190063818.001.0001.

of women figures in sacred history along the arc of the Qur'anic revelatory sequence and highlight how episodes involving women figures function to inculcate piety and virtue. I explore how these personalities were pertinent to the self-definition of the nascent Muslim community, and I argue that certain narratives function as "case studies" that explicate new social-behavioral standards for those who look to the Qur'an as "a reminder for all the worlds" (Q 81:19). These "case studies" stand as lessons for a Qur'anic audience in any age, but for the developing Muslim polity at the time the verses were first introduced, there are additional significances.

## Early Negative Female Exemplars

The wife of Abū Lahab, an aristocratic woman who is insulted by being described in a lowly social station as a "firewood carrier" (*ḥammālat al-ḥaṭab*), is likely the first individual woman to be mentioned in the revelatory order of the Qur'an (notwithstanding the location of this surah near the end of the compiled Qur'an). Her negative example, alongside the negative example of her husband, is given special emphasis in that among the Meccans she is the first and only woman to be singled out for damnation.

The short surah with lyrical qualities is often among the first taught to students of the Qur'an, reinforcing its affective potency as a cautionary tale in devotional contexts. It reads as follows: "May the hand of Abū Lahab perish, and may he perish! / His wealth avails him not, nor what he has earned. / He shall enter a blazing fire. / And his wife, carrier of firewood, / upon her neck is a rope of palm fiber" (Q 111:1–5). The lessons in *Sūrat al-Masad* (Q 111, alternately referred to as *Sūrat al-Lahab*) are stark: wealth and social prestige avail not, wicked company corrupts, and the enemies of God do not stand a chance of victory in the long run—their status in the afterlife will be a direct manifestation of their actions and dispositions in this world. A "firewood carrier" is not only a lowly domestic epithet with respect to an aristocratic woman, but a "firewood carrier" is also the one who stirs up flames of dissent or gossip to spread animosity.[3]

Some reconstructive schemas of the revelatory sequence of the Qur'an place this surah immediately after *Sūrat al-Fātiḥa* (Q 1), the opening of the Qur'an and the most liturgically significant surah that is a mandatory component of every unit (*rakʿa*, pl. *rakaʿāt*) of ritual prayer. As set against the *Fātiḥa*, which emphasizes upright action and guidance, the negative example of Abū Lahab and his wife stands as a clear warning of the ultimate corruptibility of the human being. Together, the couple defy and mock a prophet, just as other disbelieving peoples have mocked or even attempted to assassinate their prophets in multiple other Qur'anic narratives, as we will explore again in the following.

Commentary traditions explain that the couple are closely related to the Prophet Muḥammad: Abū Lahab is a paternal uncle. This theme of treacherous kin is in fact described in multiple narratives in another early surah, *Sūrat al-Shuʿarāʾ* (Q 26), which includes instructions to the Prophet Muḥammad on how to address the familial divides that will arise from his message: "warn your nearest kin (*ʿashīrataka al-aqrabīn*) / and lower your wing to the believers who follow you. / And should they disobey you, say, 'Truly I am quit of that which you do'" (Q 26:214–16).[4] The Qur'an later speaks in more detail about the nearest kin of the Prophet and even speaks directly to the Prophet Muḥammad's wives and household, but these verses all come near the end of the revelatory sequence. This reference to the Prophet Muḥammad's kin in *Sūrat al-Shuʿarāʾ* is the only such reference given early in the revelatory order.

Other than the wife of Abū Lahab, the earliest surahs do not mention specific female personalities. *Sūrat al-Falaq* (Q 113) mentions female sorceresses, those who blow (lit., "the blowers" [f. pl.] on knots, *al-naffāthāti fī l-ʿuqad*), but there is disagreement as to when this particular surah was first revealed and whether it pertains to specific women, to sorceresses generally, or, even more generally still, to groups who engage in the practice of dark magic.[5] Another surah from the Meccan period briefly mentions a female figure, also as a negative example, in the context of a parable: "Be not like her who unravels her yarn (*allatī naqaḍat ghazlahā*), breaking it after it had been strong [by] taking your oaths to practice deception among yourselves, so that one community might be larger and wealthier than another" (Q 16:92). In some commentary literatures, though not ubiquitous, this parable is associated with a particular Meccan woman who was said to spend her days spinning yarn and then untwisting it due to an impairment in her thinking.[6]

## Persecution of Prophetic Families

The next grouping of surahs in the revelatory order includes a brief mention of the family (*ahl*) of the Arab prophet Ṣāliḥ, who was sent to the people of

Thamūd. The circumstances of the family of the Prophet Ṣāliḥ clearly parallel the circumstances of the family of the Prophet Muḥammad in this period.[7] The Qur'anic reference describes the disbelievers' plot against Ṣāliḥ's family, a plot that mirrors the trials faced by the Prophet Muḥammad's family, who were also persecuted by their kin. The attempted attack on the Prophet Ṣāliḥ and his family resonates with a well-known instance of the Prophet Muḥammad being harassed and driven out of Mecca by the powerbrokers of his own tribe, according to traditional biographical accounts.

The Qur'anic narrative of Ṣāliḥ and his family stresses that the plots of corrupt people against the prophets and their families will not succeed; instead, those who scheme are the ones harmed—in fact, destroyed—by their plotting. In the case of the people of Thamūd, only the frames of their houses are left as a testament to their annihilation:

> They [the corrupted people of Thamūd] said, "Swear by God to each other that we shall attack him and his family (*ahlahu*) by night. Then we shall surely say to his heir that we were not present at the destruction of his family (*ahlihi*) and that surely we are truthful."
>
> Then they devised a plot, and We devised a plot, while they were not aware.
>
> So behold how their plot fared in the end; truly We destroyed them and their people all together.
>
> And those are their houses, lying desolate for their having done wrong. Surely in this is a sign for a people who know. (Q 27:49–52)

Here, and in other such instances (discussed in the following), God speaks in the first person to indicate that a plot against a prophet is a direct offense against God and warrants severe retaliation. Here, the Qur'anic language evokes gutted houses, perhaps in light of the home as a metonym for family and safety. This reference to the family of Ṣāliḥ is, to the best of my knowledge, a singular example (with the exception of the Prophet Muḥammad) of a Qur'anic family that does not have corresponding biblical roots.[8]

## Women Figures Incurring God's Wrath

The narrative of the destruction of the corrupt people of Thamūd described in the preceding section is followed in *Sūrat al-Naml* by the story of the relatives of Lot (*āl/ahl Lūṭ*), a narrative in which a corrupt segment of the population torments the family of a prophet. As no fewer than seven verses reiterate, Lot's wife was not saved from destruction along with the rest of her family.[9] In the early Muslim context, such a reminder that familial affiliations alone are not sufficient to ward off the wrath of God would have been exceptionally potent, as parties from the Prophet Muḥammad's own clan, the Banū Hāshim, were forced to choose between the Prophet and his powerful detractors among his close kin. In this context, the stories of past prophets and their families clashing with kin, as recounted in particular in late Meccan verses, were directly relevant to the plight of the early Muslims and their experiences of religious persecution.[10]

Though the Qur'an does not discuss the circumstances of her treachery at length, the grim fate of the wife of Lot is mentioned multiple times, both in the Meccan and Medinan periods. The first time she is mentioned, the reference is simply to "an old woman" (*ʿajūz*). In late Meccan surahs, the family of Noah is introduced, but it is not until the Medinan period that a verse unequivocally damns the wife of Noah, along with the wife of Lot: "They [the wives] were under two of Our righteous servants [Noah and Lot]; then they [the wives] betrayed them [Noah and Lot], and they [Noah and Lot] availed them [the wives] naught against God" (Q 66:10). Again, as it relates to the context of the Prophet Muḥammad, these examples are most informative. In these verses of *Sūrat al-Taḥrīm* (Q 66), a late Medinan surah, the wife of Noah and the wife of Lot function as reminders, in an immediate sense, of two of the Prophet Muḥammad's wives whom God chides in no uncertain terms for their mischievous trickery of the Prophet (as we saw in the previous chapter).

## The Regal Proselyte

In another Meccan surah, the Queen of Sheba emerges as a commendable figure, not only for her skillful diplomacy but also, ultimately, for the power of her perception; she is a powerful aristocratic woman who nonetheless chooses to submit to the the "Lord of the worlds" (Q 27:44). In his report back to Solomon, the hoopoe bird specifically points out the Queen's gender: "I found a *woman* ruling over them" (Q 27:23, emphasis added). Neither God's voice in the Qur'an nor the prophetic voice of Solomon at any point in the narrative calls into question her status as a female sovereign. (See Chapter 3 for a detailed discussion of this narrative.)

In terms of the unfolding Qur'an, this episode is a story of the conversion of a politically powerful woman at a time when the women of the esteemed Quraysh tribe were being forced to choose between the followers of Muḥammad and the polytheists of their clans. This is a story of two sovereigns engaging in diplomacy and statecraft, and it perhaps foreshadows the Prophet Muḥammad's political ascendency, which was driven in large part by intertribal diplomacy and the backing of influential women. The narrative of the Queen of Sheba, in this context, affirms the roles of socially and politically powerful female actors in the theologically driven mission of prophets.

## An Abrahamic Polity, from Mecca to Medina

The figure of Abraham enters the Qur'anic discourse in the middle Meccan period, and stories of Abraham and his family members continue into the Medinan period of the revelation.[11] The approximate revelatory schema agreed on by early Muslim exegetes and academics alike points to an early reference to the worship of the family of Ishmael (*ahl Ismāʿīl*) in *Sūrat Maryam* (Q 19): "He [Ishmael] used to bid his family/people to prayer and almsgiving, and he was pleasing to his Lord" (Q 19:55). This reference to Ishmael is followed in the revelatory schema not long after by a reference to the "family of the house" of Abraham in *Sūrat Hūd* (Q 11).[12]

Later Medinan revelations explicitly emphasize the pious example of the family of Abraham for the Prophet Muḥammad and his followers:

> There is indeed a beautiful example for you in Abraham and those with him (*wa-lladhīna maʿahu*), when they said to their people, "Truly we are quit of you and of all that you worship apart from God. We have rejected you, and enmity and hatred have arisen between us and you forever, till you believe in God alone." (Q 60:4)

In the same surah (*Sūrat al-Mumtaḥana*, Q 60), another verse reinforces the beautifully exemplary nature of Abraham "and those with him," expanding the sense of polity to "whoever hopes for God and the last day" (Q 60:6). Although family is not mentioned specifically in this reference to "those with him," the followers of Abraham do indeed include his family members.

In the structural organization of the Qur'an, the first instance of the concept of a "beautiful example" is found in *Sūrat al-Aḥzāb* (Q 33), where the Qur'an declares the Prophet Muḥammad to be a "beautiful example" (*uswa ḥasana*) (Q 33:21), as discussed in Chapter 1. *Sūrat al-Aḥzāb* and *Sūrat al-Mumtaḥana* are regarded as late Medinan surahs, and both solidify the connection between the two prophetic households. The "beautiful example" is not limited to the prophetic persona, but also extends to the prophetic household and then to members of the polity of believers.

## Kindred Prophetic Missions

Explicit topical and more subtle structural links between the families of the prophets Moses and Muḥammad are also noteworthy. For instance, *Sūrat Ṭā Hā* (Q 20), a mid- to late Meccan surah that traces key moments of the journey of Moses, concludes with the explicit instruction to the Prophet Muḥammad to urge his family to be steadfast and devout: "And enjoin prayer upon your family (*ahlaka*) and be steadfast therein. We [God] ask no provision of you; We provide for you. And the end belongs to reverence" (Q 20:132). This lesson of God's continued provision for His prophet and the steadfast devotion of the family of Moses throughout his life is a central feature of the narratives in *Sūrat Ṭā Hā* and in narratives involving Moses more generally.

Later in the revelatory sequence, *Sūrat al-Aḥzāb*, which focuses on the proper etiquette of and with the Prophet Muḥammad and his family, concludes with an explicit reference to the prophetic mission of Moses, as if in parallel: "O you who believe! Be not as those who affronted Moses, then God declared him innocent of what they alleged, and he was honored with God" (Q 33:69). Whereas the verse at the end of *Sūrat Ṭā Hā* is directed to the Prophet Muḥammad about his family (and perhaps also to people more generally, as the word *ahl* can have both significances), the parallel verse at the end of *Sūrat al-Aḥzāb* contains guidance directed to the community of believers around the Prophet Muḥammad (his *ahl*). Such verses reinforce the connection, stylistically and typologically, not just between past prophets, but to the households of these figures and their followers as well. Notably, Q 20:132 is the fourth-to-last verse in *Sūrat Ṭā Hā*, and Q 33:69 is the fifth-to-last verse of *Sūrat al-Aḥzāb*; this structural parity in the framing of the surahs can be seen as reinforcing their thematic connection.

## "Chosenness" and Continuity

In previous chapters, we have seen the importance of Mary being "chosen above the women of the world" (Q 3:42), and we have explored stylistic elements pertaining to her words and deeds. From another angle, the importance of Mary as a figure common to multiple religious communities cannot be overstated: Mary, without a doubt the most dominant female figure in the Qur'an, was a Jewish woman initially made known to history by Christians. The power of the figure of Mary was not lost on the early Muslims; in the Meccan period, Muslim refugees to Abyssinia are said to have recited parts of *Sūrat Maryam* in an attempt to win favor and ultimately refuge with the ruling monarch. In this way, the extraordinary honor given to Mary in the Qur'anic discourse is a point of connection between distinct faith communities, even as doctrinal differences involving the nature and identity of her son remain a point of acute theological difference. In the same way that Mary both linked and differentiated Jewish and Christian civilizational paradigms, the nascent community of the Prophet Muḥammad straddled alliances and attempted to forge a renewed commitment to a larger monotheistic polity, in part by affirming a robust connection to a shared sacred past. As the most celebrated woman in Qur'anic discourse, Mary reinforces the dialogic nature of the Qur'an's relationship with preceding Semitic monotheisms.[13] No other woman in sacred history holds such a simultaneously unifying and divisive position.[14]

In this context, Mary (along with other biblical figures in the Qur'an) is a point of convergence with prior Semitic peoples. Not surprisingly, biblical figures appear in the Qur'an in a period in which the Prophet Muḥammad was in the process of forging new alliances, grounded in part in a theological—rather than strictly biological—sense of kinship.[15] Mary is introduced into the Qur'anic discourse in the later Meccan period, but she is also present in Medinan surahs. Why does her importance stretch into the later period of the revelation, unlike other female figures with biblical roots?

Mary is preeminent not merely in her status as a pious individual, but also in her unique role in bearing the Word of God. In this respect, Mary's having been divinely "chosen" and informed of this election directly by God (Q 3:42) resonates with the example of the women of the household of the Prophet Muḥammad (*nisāʾ al-nabī*), who are also specially selected to bear certain burdens and potentially earn special rewards. They are, as the narrative voice of God proclaims to them directly, "not like other women" (Q 33:32).[16]

Even in the organization of the Qur'an, a significant structural association can be seen between these influential prophetic households. *Sūrat al-Aḥzāb* contains numerous verses on the women of the Prophet Muḥammad's family, and in this surah, verse 33 contains the axiomatic Qur'anic reference to the purity of the "family of the house" (*ahl al-bayt*), that is, the Prophet Muḥammad's household: "God only desires to remove defilement from you, O family of the house, and to purify you completely" (Q 33:33). In *Sūrat Āl ʿImrān* (Q 3), verse 33 also contains an axiomatic reference to the womenfolk of earlier families of prophets, that is, the "House of Abraham" (*āl Ibrāhīm*) and the "House of ʿImrān" (*āl ʿImrān*), who were chosen by God: "Truly God chose Adam, Noah, the House of Abraham, and the House of ʿImrān above the worlds" (Q 3:33).[17] In the revelatory order of surahs, *Sūrat al-Aḥzāb* (Q 33) is widely thought to have come directly after *Sūrat Āl ʿImrān* (Q 3).[18] If we accept the premise that the Qur'an was deliberately (not haphazardly) composed, then these correspondences are significant; at the very least, they are a helpful heuristic for locating interconnected topical content.

*Sūrat al-Aḥzāb*, the main surah that defines the nature and status of the Prophet Muḥammad and his family, also contains an explicit reference to this prophetic genealogy in its opening verses—this time explicitly including the Prophet Muḥammad, Moses, and Jesus the son of Mary: "And [remember] when We made with the prophets their covenant, and with you [Muḥammad], and with Noah, Abraham, Moses, and Jesus the son of Mary; We made with them a solemn covenant" (Q 33:7).[19] This genealogy reinforces that found in Q 3:33, but Q 33:7 focuses on the taking of a specific prophetic covenant. In Q 3:33, the chronologically earlier verse, the discourse does not mention "covenant" but is more generally about God's special selection of certain individuals and households. The title "House" (*āl*) is specifically used in Q 3:33 in conjunction with Abraham and ʿImrān, but not in conjunction with Noah and Adam. This is perhaps because delinquent women are among the households of Adam and Noah (as discussed in Chapter 2).

*Sūrat Āl ʿImrān* (Q 3) also contains a verse that refers, in general, to the sons/children (*abnāʾ*) and the women (*nisāʾ*) of the Muslim community and the sons/children and women of those who dispute with the Prophet on theological matters pertaining to the nature of Jesus. Namely, the Qur'an instructs the Prophet Muḥammad to propose a mutual swearing between parties "so as to place the curse of God on those who lie" (Q 3:61). The incident is depicted in detail in early biographical sources.[20]

## Women, Law, and Polity

We have seen how connections between prophetic families in sacred history constitute one facet of the female legacy in shaping and defining a sense of transhistorical polity. Next, we see how the legacy of women—those mentioned directly and those alluded to—relates to matters of polity, law, and ethics. Often, new norms serve to distinguish the developing Muslim polity by correcting or reforming a practice or social custom that was disadvantageous to women. The Qur'an uses what contemporary law schools refer to as a "case study method" in order to achieve its didactic aims, and many of these "case studies" involve the practical needs, safety, or well-being of women. My discussion continues along the approximate revelatory arc.

## Not Your Mother's Back

I have previously discussed the Qur'an's condemnation of *ẓihār*, a form of degrading speech for which the Qur'an establishes penal implications.[21] In pre-Islamic practice, a proclamation of *ẓihār* (i.e., a husband declaring that his wife is to him like the back of his mother) would release the husband from his duties toward his wife but would not release the wife to remarry, thus leaving her in a state of limbo. In the initial verses of *Sūrat al-Aḥzāb* and the initial verses of *Sūrat al-Mujādila* (Q 58, a surah named for a wife who complained to the Prophet Muḥammad that her husband had repudiated her through the practice of *ẓihār*), the Qur'an prohibits this repudiation. According to the Qur'an, "the disputing woman" (*al-mujādila*) brought a valid claim of wrongdoing against her husband, and *ẓihār* is "indecent" and "a calumny" (Q 58:2).[22]

A Qur'anic solution was established to counter the practice; it states that if a husband wishes to resume the fullness of the marital relationship (including his financial obligations) and "before they touch one another," he must expiate his sin by freeing a slave, fasting two consecutive months, or feeding sixty indigent people (Q 58:3–4).[23] The Qur'anic verse not only seeks to establish a new normative practice, but also gives the nascent Muslim polity an immediate example of when and how to apply the new ruling.

## A Test of Loyalty: "When the Believing Women Come" (Q 60:10)

The Qur'an teaches through a case study approach in another instance: during a conflict that divided households into supporters of the Prophet Muḥammad and detractors, the issue of establishing the loyalty of women arose. What is the litmus test for accepting a woman into the Muslim polity through marriage? How should the legal apparatus deal with previously existing marriages between a monotheist and a polytheist? How should female migrants be treated? What basic criteria are incumbent on women who wish to reside among and marry Muslims? *Sūrat al-Mumtaḥana* (lit., "She who is tested") takes up these practical questions and the financial transactions involved in the dissolution of marriages.[24] This surah is of particular interest for its explicit affirmation of women's political allegiance (*bayʿa*) in Q 60:12.[25]

As we have seen in the other late Medinan surahs, *Sūrat al-Mumtaḥana* begins with the voice of God addressing the believers and the Prophet, then continues with God addressing the Prophet directly:

> **O you who believe!** When the believing women come to you as emigrants, examine them. God knows best their faith. Then if you know them to be believers, do not return them to the disbelievers. They [the women] are not lawful for them [the men], nor are they [the men] lawful for them [the women]. And give them [the disbelieving men] what they have spent. There is no blame on you if you marry them when you have given them [the women] their due compensation. And hold not the [matrimonial] ties of disbelieving women. Ask for what you have spent, and let them [the disbelieving men] ask for what they have spent. That is the judgment of God; He judges between you. And God is Knowing, Wise.
>
> And if any of your wives should go over to the disbelievers, and then you have your turn [to make amends], give those whose wives have gone the like [sum] of what they have spent. And reverence God, in whom you are believers.
>
> **O Prophet!** When believing women come to you, pledging to you that they will not associate anything with God, nor steal, nor fornicate, nor slay their children, nor bring a slanderous lie that they have fabricated between their hands and feet, nor disobey you in anything honorable, then accept

> their pledge and seek God's forgiveness for them. Truly, God is Forgiving, Merciful. (Q 60:10–12)[26]

In terms of its contemporary significance, this passage elevates issues of justice involved in the treatment of female migrants. The Qur'an calls for reimbursement on both sides of the religious divide, whether it is husbands or wives who become Muslims. Interpersonal and communal peacemaking is the ostensible aim of the mandates.

With regard to marriage eligibility in Q 60:10, the Qur'an distills these restrictions in a verse that comes later in the revelatory order. In this later verse, the instructions are simpler and marriage eligibility is expanded to "the chaste women (*muḥṣanāt*) of those who were given the Book before you, when you have given them their bridewealth as married women, not as fornicators, nor as secret lovers" (Q 5:5). In the earlier verse, the women seeking to join the new Muslim polity were to be tested with a more elaborate standard; the later verse specifies only chastity and religious identity, without the other aspects. The first set of criteria could be seen as measures to draw together the polity and deal with familial schisms that arose because of the spread of a new religious paradigm. Alternatively, the simpler criteria in Q 5:5 could be seen as reinforcing certain principles as articulated in Q 60:10, without easing the other requirements. In any case, an important takeaway is that the criteria outlined for women in the pledge of loyalty are virtues and behaviors that are also incumbent upon men; this underscores that men and women are held to similar standards of upright sexual conduct. In other words, chastity is not merely a feminine virtue.

## Punishments for Slandering Upright Women

When people in Medina began to slander a wife of the Prophet Muḥammad, the Qur'an issued an emphatic condemnation: "Truly those who brought forth the lie were a group among you" (Q 24:11).[27] This so-called affair of the lie was set in motion, according to the commentary tradition, when one of the Prophet Muḥammad's wives, ʿĀʾisha, was accidentally left behind in the desert. Her absence went unnoticed, and her caravan moved on. ʿĀʾisha was later rescued by a scout from among the Muslims, Ṣafwān b. Muʿaṭṭal, who happened to be a handsome youth of similar age. When the pair returned to the caravan together, gossip about the character of

ʿĀʾisha began to spread among the wider Medinan polity. Some speculate that Ḥamna bt. Jaḥsh spread the gossip partly in the hopes that her cousin, Zaynab bt. Jaḥsh (another wife of the Prophet and an elite woman from the Prophet's clan, the Banū Hāshim), would then become the favored wife in place of ʿĀʾisha. The Qur'an rebukes ʿĀʾisha's defamers, among them Ḥamna, who is said to have faced a corporal penalty for the unsubstantiated defamation of a chaste woman.[28] ʿĀʾisha, Ḥamna, and the affair of the lie, as enshrined in the Qur'an, serve to establish normative communal standards of justice: it is a grave sin to accuse chaste women of indecency.

## The Qur'an and the Female Presence

Considering the female figures along the approximate chronological arc of revelation, in the earliest surahs we have a treacherous and irrevocably corrupt woman, sorceresses from whom the Qur'an offers a supplication for protection, and a parable in which a woman senselessly undoes her good deeds. All are negative examples. The Qur'anic references to women personalities in chronologically early surahs are stark, but this period also includes many verses that assert female value and worth in universal terms (as described in Chapters 1 and 2).

On the whole, the Qur'an contains more flattering depictions of female figures than it does negative ones. Many other verses celebrate the qualities of pious women and exalt the status of the Prophet Muḥammad's wives and household (as in Q 33 especially). Descriptions of multiple pious women occur especially in the late Meccan and early Medinan periods. Yet, the Qur'an presents women along the whole spectrum, from moral exemplars to troublemakers. In some cases, otherwise clear-cut binaries of good and evil are complicated by a woman's own moral or theological development, as in the case of the wife of the viceroy, who eventually offers candid testimony against herself, or the Queen of Sheba, who converts to monotheism. Even otherwise pious figures, such as the wives of the Prophet Muḥammad, occasionally err but are, on the whole, exalted.[29] On one occasion, the Qur'an gives the Prophet Muḥammad's wives collectively the option of amicable divorce should they desire "the life of this world and its ornaments" (Q 33:28), but the wives seemingly all decide to remain with the Prophet.[30]

In terms of identifying where women and girls factor into the revelatory sequence of the Qur'an, we find certain noteworthy patterns. The earliest

Qur'anic revelations feature Arab figures, mid- to late Meccan revelations introduce female figures common to the biblical tradition, biblical figures continue to appear in revelations that date to the early Medinan period, and then a host of verses in later Medinan revelations take up specific issues of polity that primarily involve women contemporaries of the Prophet Muḥammad. Aside from the brief negative examples of the wife of Abū Lahab and the woman who unravels her yarn, it is not until *after* the emigration from Mecca to Medina (in 622 CE) that additional women figures from the immediate Arabian context of the Prophet Muḥammad feature regularly in the Qur'anic narratives. In this later period, there are also fewer narratives with shared biblical female figures, and no new biblical figures are introduced.

In exploring women's voices in the preceding chapter, and in demonstrating here how the experiences of individual women become Qur'anic precedents of communal behavior and norms, we see that the Qur'anic discourse is decidedly responsive to women's concerns. From the first surahs to the last, female figures and women's issues regularly constitute a Qur'anic point of concern. In early and later verses (in the approximate chronology or revelatory schema), values and virtues such as justice, equity, integrity, and sincerity are emphasized at the micro-level of the soul and at the macro-level of society.

By organizing the stories in their approximate revelatory order, I have tracked the emphasis from female figures shared with the biblical tradition in chronologically earlier verses (when the nascent Muslim community was first orienting itself vis-à-vis pre-Islamic religious movements) to a more significant emphasis on women contemporaries of the Prophet Muḥammad in chronologically later verses (which originated as the polity was taking shape in a Muslim-ruled city-state, as described extensively in the Qur'an and in extra-Qur'anic accounts). In the evolving sociopolitical context of the early Muslim polity, vignettes concerning chronologically earlier prophetic households can be seen as helping to frame the roles that the women in the household of the Prophet Muḥammad come to play in the emerging polity.

At the same time, women's demands for justice and accountability are the backdrop for social precedents and Qur'anic pronouncements that then help to define the burgeoning polity as a distinct entity. New normative rulings based on the circumstances of specific women then serve as guidance for the entire community of believers, then and now. The numerous female figures who were involved in the circumstances leading to the establishment of new Qur'anic rulings and ethical norms, most explicitly in the later years of the Qur'anic revelation, left a legacy—a female legacy—worthy of significant consideration.

## Notes

1. Though this technique is well established in scholarship on the Qur'an from both devotional and critical perspectives, it is not universally accepted in Qur'anic studies. For a skeptical perspective, see Reynolds, *The Qur'ān and Its Biblical Subtext,* 3–22. On the other side, Carl Ernst describes the "chronological approach" as a way to access the way the Qur'an "was received by its first listeners, as a fresh oral composition," whereby "the Qurʾan builds up a vocabulary and repertoire of themes and styles in dialogical communication with its audience." Ernst, *How to Read the Qurʾan,* 205–6. I employ this heuristic for literary—not historical—analysis. I am concerned with the broad contours of the providential order of verses; I do not discuss more minor differences in the schema and the views of one scholar or another.
2. In the academy, the most prevalent schema for ordering surahs remains that of Theodore Nöldeke (in *Geschichte des Qorāns,* originally published in 1860); see Farrin, *Structure and Qur'anic Interpretation,* 125–28. For a concise summary of prior scholarship, as well as a discussion of the specific sources and methods for hypothesizing about the revelatory order of surahs and verses, see Gerhard Bowering, "Chronology and the Qur'ān," *EQ* 1:316–35. See also Robinson, *Discovering the Qur'an,* chaps. 4 and 5.
3. For a discussion of the context of this surah and the personalities involved according to early biographical sources, see *SQ,* 1575–76. For instance, we read that the rope of palm fiber is thought to correspond to a valuable necklace that the wife of Abū Lahab used to flaunt and that, on one occasion, she was even so bold as to swear upon it against the Prophet Muḥammad and his message. See also Geissinger, *Gender and Muslim Constructions,* 185.
4. For a discussion of the context and personalities involved, see *SQ,* 924 n. 214.
5. See Q 113:4. Some consider this surah to be a later revelation and relate it to the daughters of a sorcerer named Labīd al-Yahūdī. For a discussion of these verses and the episodes to which they may correspond, see David Cook, "The Prophet Muḥammad, Labīd al-Yahūdī and the Commentaries to Sūra 113," *Journal of Semitic Studies* 45, no. 2 (2000): 323–45. For a perspective on sorcery in the ancient Near East, including blowing on knots, see Adam Collins Bursi, "Holy Spit and Magic Spells: Religion, Magic and the Body in Late Ancient Judaism, Christianity, and Islam" (PhD diss., Cornell University, 2015). For contemporary perspectives and debates, see Arnold Yasin Mol, "The Denial of Supernatural Sorcery in Classical and Modern Sunnī Tafsīr

of Sūrah al-Falaq (113:4): A Reflection of Underlying Construction," *Al-Bayān* 11, no. 1 (2013): 1–18.

6. For a general analysis of Qur'anic discourses on (dis)ability, see Staffan Bengtsson, "Building a Community: Disability and Identity in the Qur'an," *Scandinavian Journal of Disability Research* 20, no. 1 (2018): 210–18.
7. For brief reflections on this "topological relationship," see Lawson, "Duality," 37.
8. For a study of Arab prophets, including a discussion of the figure of Ṣāliḥ, see Brannon M. Wheeler, "Arab Prophets of the Qur'an and Bible," *Journal of Qur'anic Studies* 8, no. 2 (2006): 37–41.
9. See Q 7:83, 15:60, 26:171, 27:57, 29:32–33, 37:135.
10. See detailed arguments to this effect in Walid Saleh, "End of Hope: Suras 10–15, Despair, and a Way out of Mecca," in *Qur'ānic Studies Today*, ed. Angelika Neuwirth and Michael A. Sells (New York: Routledge, 2016), esp. 109–113. See also Nicolai Sinai, *The Qur'an: A Historical-Critical Introduction* (Edinburgh: Edinburgh University Press, 2017), 180–81.
11. See detailed discussions of the development of the Qur'anic Abraham in Angelika Neuwirth, "The House of Abraham and the House of Amran: Genealogy, Patriarchal Authority, and Exegetical Professionalism," in *The Qur'ān in Context: Historical and Literary Investigations into the Qur'ānic Milieu*, ed. Angelika Neuwirth, Nicolai Sinai, and Michael Marx (Leiden: Brill, 2010), 499–503.
12. See Q 11:73 in the context of angelic speech directed to Abraham's family generally or his wife specifically: "The mercy of God and His blessings be upon you, O people [family] of the house! Truly He is praised, glorious."
13. See Angelika Neuwirth, "Imagining Mary—Disputing Jesus: Reading *Sūrat Maryam* and Related Meccan Texts within the Qur'ānic Communication Process," in *Fremde, Feinde und Kurioses: Innen- und Außenansichten unseres muslimischen Nachbarn*, ed. Benjamin Jokisch, Ulrich Rebstock, and Lawrence I. Conrad, 383–416 (Berlin: De Gruyter, 2009). For further discussion, see Hosn Abboud, *Mary in the Qur'an: A Literary Reading* (New York: Taylor and Francis, 2014).
14. For a thorough exploration of how the biblical Abraham and a figure such as Mary come to play a distinctive role in Qur'anic sacred history, see Neuwirth, "The House of Abraham." In relation to this shared legacy in general, Travis Zadeh observes that there are "many historical communities implicated within the Qur'anic text," that there is a "profound dialectic relationship that the Quran evinces with the pre-existing textual corpora of late antiquity," and that "Quranic intertextuality and self-referentiality [are] deployed within a broader sectarian environment." Zadeh, "Quranic Studies," 338.
15. See discussions to this effect in Marx, "Glimpses of a Mariology," 535–36.
16. See Gregg, *Shared Stories, Rival Tellings*, 589; see also discussions at Gregg, 543–44.
17. For a commentary on this verse, see Reynolds, *The Qur'ān and Its Biblical Subtext*, 145–46. For analysis of this surah's narrative structure, see A. H. Mathias Zahniser, "The Word of God and the Apostleship of ʿĪsā: A Narrative Analysis of Āl ʿImrān (3):33–62," *Journal of Semitic Studies* 37 (1991): 77–112.

18. For a provocative analysis of the genealogy presented in Q 3:33 and its significance to the revelatory order of surahs, see Neuwirth, "Mary and Jesus," 245–46.
19. For an analysis of the roles of the Prophet Muḥammad in this surah as compared to earlier surahs, see Sinai, *The Qur'an*, 125.
20. See commentary in *SQ*, 147 n. 61.
21. See Q 33:4 and 58:2–3.
22. For reflections on women's "freedom of expression" in relation to these verses, see Lamrabet, *Women in the Qur'an*, 131–34.
23. Slavery is not explicitly encouraged by the Qur'an; rather, manumitting slaves is encouraged as an excellent deed and as an expiation for sins. For a critical reading of jurisprudence related to slavery and sex, see Kecia Ali, "Slavery and Sexual Ethics in Islam," in *Beyond Slavery: Overcoming Its Religious and Sexual Legacies*, ed. Bernadette J. Brooten, 108–22 (New York: Palgrave MacMillan, 2010). See also Ali, *Sexual Ethics*, 50–71, and Jonathan A. C. Brown, *Slavery and Islam* (London: Oneworld, 2019).
24. The surah is so named after the phrase in Q 60:10. For a discussion of women's oaths of political allegiance, see Lamrabet, *Women in the Qur'an*, 116–22.
25. For hadith reports relating to the context of this verse, see Geissinger, *Gender and Muslim Constructions*, 193. Geissinger notes that many exegetes elaborate "acceptable additional strictures above and beyond those given in Q 60:12, such as not traveling without a male escort, avoiding being alone with a man who is not a close relative, and especially not lamenting their dead" (Geissinger, 193). For a discussion of this verse (Q 60:12) as narrated in hadith on the authority of women companions of the Prophet, see Geissinger, *Gender and Muslim Constructions*, 187–89.
26. Some commentators take the "fabrication" in this final verse to be specifically about false claims of paternity. See *SQ*, 1362 n. 12. The general address, "O you who believe!" can be gender inclusive, while the verses that describe the exchange of compensation could be interpreted as directed exclusively to men, who are required to give compensation to their new wives. Alternatively, it could be understood that these are general communal norms that all responsible members of the polity—male and female—are expected to uphold. In other words, ensuring that adequate compensation is paid could be a responsibility of the individuals directly involved, or reimbursement could be the responsibility of the political leadership.
27. For a discussion of this episode, see *SQ*, 870–71 nn. 10–22.
28. See Q 24:4 and subsequent verses for descriptions of "chaste women" (*muḥṣanāt*) who face slander (*qadhf*); in Q 24:5, the Qur'an offers God's forgiveness and mercy for a repentant slanderer. For discussion of slander, fornication, and related punishments in the Qur'an from a gender-conscious lens, see Barazangi, *Women's Identity and Rethinking the Hadith*, 8–9.
29. See Q 66:5 for the wives being chided by God in the strongest terms for betraying the Prophet's trust, as discussed in the previous chapter. For a succinct account of the contextual details drawn from extra-Qur'anic sources, see *SQ*, 1389 nn. 1–4.

30. Despite times of discord, according to biographical traditions, no wife with whom the Prophet Muḥammad had consummated a marriage was ever permanently divorced. For a discussion of reports that one of the Prophet Muḥammad's wives gave her conjugal rights to another wife to avoid being divorced, see Barazangi, *Women's Identity and the Qur'an*, 128–34. For a comprehensive discussion of relevant hadith reports, see Scott Lucas, "Divorce, Ḥadīth-Scholar Style: From al-Dārimī to al-Tirmidhī," *Journal of Islamic Studies* 19, no. 3 (2008): 325–68, esp. 340.

# Conclusion

In this work, I have discussed the progression of female personalities in the Qur'an from the female progenitor to the female contemporaries of the Prophet Muḥammad. I have examined narratives of conquest, filial devotion, romantic attraction, and more, paying close attention to how Qur'anic rhetoric, thematic interconnectivity, linguistic structure, and other literary features reinforce core Qur'anic dictates involving sex and sexuality, gender and kinship relations, women's voices, and female virtue. I have analyzed Qur'anic figures from the central character of Mary to peripheral figures, such as the cohort of the unsuccessful wet nurses of the infant Moses and the gossiping elites who conspired to have an innocent young man imprisoned and later exonerated.

I have relied on philological methods to illuminate the artistry of Qur'anic narratives on the wide-ranging depictions of female identity, including in the context of sexual embodiment, kinship roles, and divine–human relationships. By giving attention to thematic and structural dimensions of the Qur'an, this work has raised questions about female agency and has probed the interplay between the Qur'anic prophets and the figures who are their mothers, wives, daughters, female supporters, and even, occasionally, their adversaries. I have examined female speech in the Qur'an and suggested how, as a liturgical text, the persistent repetition of narratives involving female figures attempts to inculcate piety and virtue, represents the interests of the socially marginalized, and generates particular affective responses. I have identified how the affective potential of Qur'anic narrative constructs from the past a sacred present for contemporary readers, reciters, and listeners.

I have also examined, in a preliminary way, how the trials of specific Qur'anic figures intersect poignantly with the reported experiences of the earliest Muslim polity. I have discussed how Qur'anic vignettes engineer a moral framework, often harkening back to the contexts of the Qur'an's immediate audience, this emerging polity. I have demonstrated ways in which Qur'anic sacred history delivers ethical and theological lessons through a distinct blend of narrative and poetic forms.

*Women and Gender in the Qur'an.* Celene Ibrahim, Oxford University Press (2020). © Oxford University Press.
DOI: 10.1093/oso/9780190063818.001.0001.

## Women and Girls in the Stories of Revelation

Far from being ancillary to the narrative arc of sacred history, women figures drive the action and often reinforce the message and mission of their prophetic companions. Narratives involving women figures do more than establish a sense of group identity constructed from an ethno-nationalistic past; they offer a value-based shared present wherein the Qur'anic reader, reciter, or listener is urged to consider her own virtue against the characters of sacred history. In this way, narratives—those shared with pre-Qur'anic sacred history, alongside those pertaining to the experiences of the Prophet Muḥammad and his associates—contain reinforcing moral themes that hold didactic import for Qur'anic readers, reciters, and listeners throughout the ages.

The Qur'anic stories of women and girls weave together theology and ethics to demonstrate God's ultimate wisdom, justice, and omnipotence and to reinforce the ideas of submission to God and moral accountability. As a pedagogical work, the Qur'an contains clear, oft-repeated moral themes, and upon closer examination, intra-textual subtleties and juxtapositions of themes also support and reinforce the driving Qur'anic ideas. In this context, I have highlighted overt and subtle ways in which Qur'anic narrative themes involving sex, sexuality, procreation, parenting, kinship, and female–male relations reinforce overarching Qur'anic truth claims and ethical imperatives.

Narrative vignettes offer provocative juxtapositions of corruption and piety. Moreover, we cannot identify a single archetypal female figure in the Qur'an; rather, the female figures of the Qur'an are decidedly heterogeneous, falling on a spectrum between pious and impious, insightful and ignorant, assertive and timid, old and young, famous and obscure. If there is one common element to these disparate figures, it is that the Qur'an depicts them with the agency and responsibility to shape their destinies, for better or worse. The Qur'an celebrates the aptitudes and competencies of women in the realms of spirituality and piety, in political maneuvering, and in the work of protecting family relations; yet, women also use their agency to promote corruption and treachery (as is clear from the wives of Noah, Lot, and Abū Lahab, as well as the wife of the viceroy and, to some extent, her elite companions). In the case of women figures who are irrevocably corrupt and explicitly damned, the Qur'an narrates notably little about their personas. The Qur'an presents many more examples of pious women who inspire, protect, guide, and raise prophets from among their men.

Women figures are depicted birthing prophets, saving them from calamities, and accompanying them—literally—on sacred journeys. Despite an emphasis on the trials and adventures of male prophets, women consistently play pivotal roles in narratives of sacred history and in the revelation of Qur'anic truth itself. Women figures, although never explicitly named as prophets or messengers, often function to confirm God's Word and promises, even in ways that men do not; for instance, Mary delivers the "Word" of God corporally. Men are regularly and explicitly tasked with preaching to their communities and at times conveying new scripture, but women, too, are charged with carrying, protecting, and establishing God's message, albeit in slightly different ways. In other instances, the speech or actions of women and men are similar or identical. Some women, for example, speak using the same idioms as prophets do when addressing God (as in the cases of the Queen of Sheba and Mary). Adam does not speak in the Qur'an save in unison with his spouse.

Sacred history is just one narrative genre in the Qur'an. Stories involving well-known pre-Qur'anic figures—Adam's spouse, Abraham's spouse, or Mary the mother of Jesus, for instance— represent just one type of Qur'anic story that brings the past into a new sacred present. A second type of story is the vignette that alludes to contemporaneous events unfolding in the life of the wider community of the Prophet Muḥammad, as frequently related in prose containing allusions that require explication from extra-Qur'anic sources. A third type—one that rarely involves female figures—is the parable with its archetypal figures. Whether through sacred history, vignette, or parable, narratives are a primary medium through which the Qur'an achieves its didactic purpose, and stories involving female figures reiterate core Qur'anic themes, including the agency and moral responsibility of the individual and the need to guard the self against base desires or infringement upon the rights of others.

## Qur'anic Stories in a Gendered Social World

The Qur'an narrates stories of female figures in sacred history, figures that offer affirmative perspectives on female agency and capacity—often directly from the vantage point of the Qur'an's omniscient narrator, God. In some verses, female figures are rebuked for their comportment; in other verses, they are extolled. In their breaches, however great or slight, and in their virtues and magnanimity, the wives of the Prophet Muḥammad and a handful of other early female companions offer examples of the struggles experienced by human beings generally and God-fearing believers specifically. Some of their trials are specific to girls and women, but the vast majority of their struggles are common to the human experience across time. Stories of their virtuous deeds, their mistakes, and in some cases their major moral failings have been enshrined in perpetuity in a recitation that has reached billions of people over the course of fourteen hundred years.

As a literary artifact and as a ritualized aural phenomenon, the ubiquity of the Qur'an is unparalleled in the realm of Islamicate culture. It provides a window into late Arab antiquity and insights into the theological, social, and political forces that contributed to the subsequent spread of Islam to societies throughout the world. It is a profound vessel of meaning—but also of mystery—and this is part of the Qur'an's enduring appeal in any age. I have illuminated the Qur'an's overarching aim of inculcating monotheism, teaching virtue, and demonstrating ethical action in a variety of circumstances. From the Qur'anic worldview, the physiological differences between men and women, namely, their distinct biological functions in the reproductive sphere, have implications in the gendered social world; I have made subtle suggestions about how renewed attention to Qur'anic stories involving female figures can inform contemporary Muslim conversations about sex, sexuality, and gender, including notions of sexual assault, domestic violence, marriage, parenting, and other concepts that relate to gendered social experiences.

I have also shown how depictions of female figures are, on balance, flattering, how God's voice and the speech of divine intermediaries "reveal" information to female figures, and how God regularly intervenes to remedy social situations that are unfavorable to vulnerable or oppressed women. In short, the Qur'an regularly celebrates female wit and spiritual excellence and often engages with affairs of direct importance to women in an affirming manner; just as women and girl figures are not at all ancillary in Qur'anic narratives of sacred history, so too do they factor significantly in Qur'anic moral discourse.

## Future Directions

In the course of this work, I have raised questions that I could not answer within the confines of this project. Nonetheless, it is valuable to frame and articulate questions, even if their answers remain elusive. For instance, I remain curious as to why, with the exception of Mary, all other women and girls are named only relationally and not with given personal names. At the very least, the Qur'an's special treatment of Mary among other women and girls could be seen as another aspect of God having "chosen" her "above the women of the worlds" (Q 3:42), that is, as a way to further emphasize her special nature and status.

From a different angle, attention to gendered human bodies, angelic bodies, and paradisal bodies raises questions about embodiment in the Qur'an more generally. The Qur'an offers many vivid descriptions of human bodies and body parts; it also discusses abstract topics related to embodiment, such as beauty and purity. Rhetoric and imagery about the body and its various frailties, capacities, and mysteries induce powerful affective responses and communicate—at a fundamental level—the didactic aims of the Qur'an. Whether in its depictions of pain and suffering, corporal metaphors, depictions of human (dis)abilities, discussions of embodied rituals, references to bodily functions, descriptions of bodily resurrection, or rules regarding sexual intercourse and a host of other bodily activities, the Qur'an underscores the centrality of embodied experience in communication and socio-emotional learning. In short—and as gender theorists have argued—bodies matter. I have explored specifically female bodies, sexualities, kinship networks, voices, and roles in narratives of sacred history in the Qur'an itself, but more remains to be said about embodiment generally.

This work has been focused on the Qur'an itself. I have not discussed at length pre-Qur'anic works, including Arabic poetry or biblical and post-biblical literatures, nor have I analyzed hadith narratives involving female figures and their reported contributions to the rise and spread of Islam. Further consideration of this literature holds promise for enriching scholarship on depictions of women and girls in the Qur'an. For devotionally inclined audiences, there are also many more pastoral lessons in these narratives that I hope to discuss in subsequent works. Finally, studies of masculinity in the Qur'an—particularly studies that continue to complicate claims of male normativity—could offer a promising avenue for further scholarship.

APPENDICES

APPENDIX A

# Female Figures in the Qur'an

(Listed alphabetically by Qur'anic name or title. This listing includes only those figures who are explicitly mentioned in narrative contexts.)

*banāt Lūṭ*: Lot's daughters. They are mentioned by Lot before an unruly mob from among Lot's people as a reminder of the parameters of licit sexual attraction.

*imraʾat Abī Lahab*: wife of Abū Lahab. She is made to accompany her husband into the hellfire as a firewood carrier, feeding the flames; she wears a rope of palm fiber around her neck.

*imraʾat al-ʿAzīz*: wife of the viceroy of Egypt. On two occasions, she attempts, unsuccessfully, to seduce her foster son; she lies about the affair and schemes with other women; she admits to her culpability years later when interrogated by the sovereign at Joseph's behest.

*imraʾat Ibrāhīm*: wife of Abraham. She is given news from angelic messengers that she will become pregnant despite being elderly and barren; she converses with the angelic messengers; she experiences wonder and marvels at the command of God as she receives news of her progeny, Isaac and Jacob.

*imraʾat ʿImrān*: wife of ʿImrān and mother of Mary. She dedicates her unborn infant to God; she is surprised by a girl child; she names the child Mary and seeks refuge from Satan for the child and her progeny.

*imraʾat Firʿawn*: wife of Pharaoh. She convinces her tyrannical husband to adopt an infant found in a receptacle floating on the river; she later beseeches God to save her from her husband and his iniquitous people.

*imraʾat Lūṭ*: wife of Lot. She is a treacherous old woman who is left behind and destroyed with her people while the rest of her family escapes the destruction under God's protection.

*imraʾat Yaʿqūb*: wife of Jacob and mother of Joseph. She is reunited with her son after years of separation, and she and her husband are embraced by Joseph during a joyous reunion.

*imraʾat Zakariyyā*: barren wife of Zachariah. By God's intervention, she conceives a child named John, who is described by God as dutiful, tender, and reverent.

*imraʾatāni min Madyan*: two women from Midian, daughters of a wise old man. They water the family's flocks and take an interest in a disheveled yet obliging fugitive (Moses) who appears at their watering hole; they encourage their father to hire the fugitive; one of the two marries him.

*malikat Sabaʾ*: Queen of Sheba. She is a wise leader with a magnificent throne. She rules her kingdom and vies with Solomon for political power; when she travels to visit Solomon on a diplomatic mission, she correctly identifies her disguised throne, is impressed by Solomon's architectural prowess, and converts to monotheism.

*Maryam*: Mary, an infant consecrated by her mother and placed in the care of the prophet Zachariah. She resides in the sanctuary and receives miraculous divine provisions in her chamber; she is selected by God and purified; she communes with God's messengers, is impregnated through miraculous means, and delivers her baby (Jesus) under a date palm near a spring; she is instructed by God's messengers to take a vow of silence, and, when she is ridiculed by her people, her honor is defended by her loquacious, prophetic infant.

*al-mujādila:* lit., "she who disputes." She is a woman who complains to the Prophet Muḥammad about her husband's unjust treatment and receives a favorable reply from God.

*nisāʾ al-nabī*: lit., "women of the Prophet." The female family of the Prophet Muḥammad, who are pious exemplars for the Prophet's followers. On one occasion, they are addressed by God as "family of the house" (*ahl al-bayt*). The Prophet's wives must follow supererogatory rules because of their elevated status; on one occasion, two among the group are divinely threatened for divulging an intimate secret of the Prophet. They are also referred to as "spouses of the Prophet" (*azwāj al-nabī*) and "spouses of the Messenger of God" (*azwāj rasūl Allāh*); they are given the honorific title "mothers of the believers" (*ummahāt al-muʾminīn*).

*nisāʾ Banī Isrāʾīl:* lit., "women of the Children of Israel." The Israelite women who are spared by Pharaoh and his troops when the sons of Israel are executed.

*niswatun fī l-madīna*: lit. "women in the city." Women who gossip about the affairs of the wife of the Egyptian viceroy and her adopted son; these women attend a banquet hosted by the wife of the viceroy, conspire to have an innocent youth (Prophet Joseph) imprisoned, and only later testify that the young man did no wrong.

*ukht Mūsā:* sister of Moses. She tracks her brother who is floating down a river in a small vessel; under the guise of finding the baby a wet nurse, she uses her wit to safely return her infant brother to their mother.

*umm Mūsā:* mother of Moses. She receives revelation from God to cast her infant into the river to save him from the hostile machinations of Pharaoh; her heart is fortified by God and her infant is returned to her, as God promised, when she takes the role of Moses's wet nurse for the House of Pharaoh.

*zawj Ādam:* spouse of Adam and female progenitor. She and her husband are deceived and expelled from the garden; they repent but are sent to dwell on the earth; she and her husband stitch garments of leaves to cover their newly discovered nakedness.

APPENDIX B

# Female Figures and Families in Qur'anic Narratives

Female Figures and Families in Qur'anic Narratives Listed by Approximate Order of Sacred History

| Qur'anic terms | Translation (name or title as derived from context or extra-Qur'anic sources in Arabic / English) | Verse(s) where these figures are explicitly mentioned or otherwise implied |
|---|---|---|
| *zawj (Ādam)* | Spouse (of Adam) (known as Ḥawwāʾ / Eve in commentary traditions) | 2:35–37, 7:19–25, 20:117–23 |
| *ahl (Nūḥ)* | Family (of Noah) | 11:40, 11:45–46, 21:76, 23:27 |
| *imraʾat Nūḥ* | Wife of Noah | 66:10 |
| *ahl (Ayyūb)* | Family (of Job) | 21:84, 38:43 |
| *ahl (Ṣāliḥ)* | Family (of Ṣāliḥ) | 27:49 |
| *āl Ibrāhīm* | House of Abraham | 3:33, 4:54 |
| *ahl (Ibrāhīm)* | Family (of Abraham) | 51:26 |
| *ahl bayt (Ibrāhīm)* | Family of the house (of Abraham); a likely reference to Abraham's wife, the mother of Isaac (Isḥāq) (known widely as Sāra / Sarah) | 11:73 |
| *wālidā (Ibrāhīm)* | Parents (of Abraham) | 14:41 |
| *imraʾat (Ibrāhīm)* | Wife of Abraham | 11:69–73, 51:24–30; see also 15:53 for the same episode recounted without specific mention of Abraham's wife |
| *ahl (Ismāʿīl)* | Family (of Ishmael) | 19:55 |
| *āl Lūṭ* | House of Lot | 15:59, 27:56, 54:34 |
| *ahl (Lūṭ)* | Family (of Lot) | 11:81, 15:65, 26:169–70, 27:57, 29:32–33, 37:134 |
| *imraʾat Lūṭ* | Wife of Lot | 7:83, 11:81, 15:60–61, 27:57, 29:32–33, 66:10 |
| *ʿajūz* | Old woman (i.e., wife of Lot) | 26:171, 37:135 |
| *banāt (Lūṭ)* | Daughters (of Lot) | 11:78–79, 15:71 |
| *imraʾat al-ʿAzīz* | Wife of the viceroy (known as Zulaykhā) | 12:21–35, 12:50–53 |
| *ahl (imraʾat al-ʿAzīz)* | Family (of the wife of the viceroy) | 12:26 |

| Qur'anic terms | Translation (name or title as derived from context or extra-Qur'anic sources in Arabic / English) | Verse(s) where these figures are explicitly mentioned or otherwise implied |
|---|---|---|
| *niswatun fī l-madīna* | Women in the city | 12:30–32, 12:50–51 |
| *āl Yaʿqūb* | House of Jacob | 12:6, 19:6 |
| *ahl (Yaʿqūb)* | Family (of Jacob) | 12:65, 12:88, 12:93 |
| *abawā (Yūsuf)* | Parents (of Joseph) | 12:99–100 |
| *āl Mūsā and āl Hārūn* | House of Moses and House of Aaron | 2:248 |
| *ahl (Mūsā)* | Family (of Moses) | 20:10, 20:29, 27:7, 28:29 |
| *umm Mūsā* | Mother of Moses | 20:38–40, 28:7–13 |
| *ukht (Mūsā)* | Sister (of Moses) | 20:40, 28:11–12 |
| *imraʾat Firʿawn* | Wife of Pharaoh (commonly known as Āsiyā bt. Muzāḥim) | 28:9, 66:11 |
| *āl Firʿawn* | House of Pharaoh | 2:49, 2:50, 3:11, 7:130, 7:141, 8:52, 8:54 (two mentions), 14:6, 28:8, 40:28, 40:45–46, 54:41 |
| *nisāʾ Banī Isrāʾīl* | Women of the Children of Israel (oppressed by Pharaoh) | 2:49, 7:127, 7:141, 14:6, 28:4, 40:25 |
| *al-marāḍiʿ* | Wet nurses (assigned to Moses) | 28:12 |
| *ahl Madyan* | Family of Midian (i.e., Moses's in-laws) | 20:40 |
| *imraʾatāni min Madyan* | Two women from Midian (Moses's future wife and her sister) | 28:23–29 |
| *abawā ghulām* | Parents of a boy (slain in front of Moses) | 18:80–81 |
| *āl Dāwūd* | House of David | 34:13 |
| *wālidā (Sulaymān)* | Parents (of Solomon) | 27:19; 38:21–25 may allude to the biblical figure of Bathsheba, Solomon's mother |
| *malikat Sabaʾ* | Queen of Sheba (Bilqīs) | 27:22–44 |
| *āl ʿImrān* | House of ʿImrān | 3:33 |
| *imraʾat ʿImrān* | Wife of ʿImrān and the mother of Mary (known as Ḥanna bt. Fāhūdh; commonly held to be the sister of Zachariah's wife Īshāʿ) | 3:33–37 (see also reference in 19:28) |
| *ahl (Maryam)* | Family (of Mary) | 19:16 |

| Qur'anic terms | Translation (name or title as derived from context or extra-Qur'anic sources in Arabic / English) | Verse(s) where these figures are explicitly mentioned or otherwise implied |
|---|---|---|
| *Maryam* | Mary | Mary herself is explicitly referred to as "Maryam" in ten verses: 3:36–37, 3:42–45, 4:156, 4:171, 19:16, and 19:27 |
| | as "daughter of ʿImrān" (*ibnat ʿImrān*) | 66:12 |
| | in "son of Mary" (*ibn Maryam*) | 23:50 and 43:57 |
| | in "the Messiah, son of Mary" (*al-masīḥ ibn Maryam*) | 3:45, 5:17 (mentioned twice), 5:72, 5:75, and 9:31 |
| | in "Jesus son of Mary" (*ʿĪsā ibn Maryam*) | 2:87, 2:253, 4:157, 4:171, 5:45, 5:46, 5:78, 5:110, 5:112, 5:114, 5:116, 19:34, 33:7, 57:27, 61:6, 61:14 |
| *allatī aḥṣanat farjahā* | She who fortified her pudenda (in reference to Mary) | 21:91 |
| *ahl (Muḥammad)* | Family (of Muḥammad) | 3:121, 20:132; for additional verses relating to the family of the Prophet generally, see 3:61, 24:11–26, 26:214, 33:28–62, and 66:1–6 |
| *ahl al-bayt (bayt Muḥammad)* | Family of the house (of Muḥammad) | 33:33 |
| *ummahāt* | Mothers (i.e., wives of Muḥammad) | 33:6 |
| *nisāʾ al-nabī* | Women of the Prophet | 33:30, 33:32 (see also 3:61) |
| *azwāj (rasūl Allāh)* | Spouses (of the Messenger of God) | 33:53, 33:55 |
| *azwāj al-nabī* | Spouses of the Prophet | 33:6, 33:28, 33:50, 66:1, 66:3 |
| *banāt (al-nabī)* | Daughters (of the Prophet) | 33:59 (see also 3:61) |
| *al-ashīra al-aqrabīn* | Closest kin (of the Prophet Muḥammad) | 26:214 |
| *al-mujādila* | The disputer (commonly identified as Khawla bt. Thaʿlaba) | 58:1 |
| *al-mumtaḥana* | She who is examined (commonly identified as Umm Kulthūm bt. ʿUqba) | 60:10 |
| *imraʾat Abī Lahab* | The wife of Abū Lahab (identified in commentary traditions as Arwā Umm Jamīl bt. Ḥarb) | 111:4–5 |
| *ḥammālat al-ḥaṭab* | Firewood carrier (derogatory term for the wife of Abū Lahab) | 111:4 |

| Qur'anic terms | Translation (name or title as derived from context or extra-Qur'anic sources in Arabic / English) | Verse(s) where these figures are explicitly mentioned or otherwise implied |
|---|---|---|
| *al-naffāthāti fī l-ʿuqad* | The [female] blowers on knots (i.e., sorceresses) | 113:4 |
| *allatī naqaḍat ghazlahā* | She who unraveled her yarn (used in the context of a parable; associated by some with a Meccan woman named Rayṭa bt. Saʿd) | 16:92 |
| *"ḥamalat ḥamlan khafīfan"* | "She bore a light burden" (referencing a pregnant woman in a parable or some say in reference to Eve) | 7:189–91 |
| *ḥūr ʿīn* | Rounded eyed [ones] (could also describe the whites of the eyes) | 4:54, 52:20, 56:22 |
| *qāṣirāt al-ṭarfi ʿīn* | Those (f. pl.) of restrained glances of the eye | 37:48–9 |
| *qāṣirāt al-ṭarfi atrāb* | Those (f. pl.) of restrained glances of like age | 38:52 |
| *qāṣirāt al-ṭarf* | Those (f. pl.) of restrained glances (who are described as "untouched") | 55:56 |
| *azwājun muṭahhara* | Pure spouses (in Paradise) | 2:25 |
| *khayrātun ḥisān* | Good and beautiful [ones] (f. pl.) | 55:70 |
| *ḥūrun maqṣūrātun fī l-khiyām* | The wide-eyed (or white-eyed) ones secluded (f. pl.) in the pavilions | 55: 72 |
| *abkāran* | Virgins/virginal | 56:36 |
| *ʿuruban atrāban* | Amorous peers | 56:37 |

APPENDIX C

# Qur'anic Verses with Female Speech and/or Messages from God to Women

Female Speakers, Listed by Verse Order

| **Speaker** | **Addressee** | **Verse number** |
|---|---|---|
| Wife of ʿImrān | God (Rabb) | 3:35–6 |
| Mary | Zachariah (Zakariyyā) | 3:37 |
| Mary | God (Rabb) | 3:47 |
| Adam and spouse | God (Rabb) | 7:23 |
| Expectant couple | God (Rabb) | 7:189 |
| Wife of Abraham | Angels, others present, or simply bemused speech | 11:72 |
| Wife of the Viceroy | Joseph (Yūsuf) | 12:23 |
| Wife of the Viceroy | The viceroy (al-ʿAzīz), possibly others present | 12:25 |
| Women in the city | Gossip among themselves | 12:30 |
| Wife of the Viceroy | Joseph (Yūsuf) | 12:31 |
| Women in the city | Unspecified, those assembled | 12:31 |
| Wife of the Viceroy | Women in the city (*niswatun fī l-madīna*) | 12:32 |
| Women in the city | Their king/sovereign (*al-malik*), others present | 12:51 |
| Wife of the Viceroy | The viceroy (al-ʿAzīz), possibly others present | 12:51 |
| Mary | God's spirit (*rūḥanā*) | 19:18, 19:20 |
| Mary | Exclamation | 19:23 |
| Sister of Moses | Unspecified, presumably the attendants of the wife of Pharaoh (Firʿawn) | 20:40, 28:12 |
| Queen of Sheba | Her court and those in the court of Solomon (Sulaymān) | 27:29, 27:31–32, 27:34–35, 27:42 |
| Queen of Sheba | God (Rabb) | 27:44 |
| Wife of Pharaoh | Pharaoh (Firʿawn) | 28:9 |
| Mother of Moses | Sister of Moses (*ukht Mūsā*) | 28:11 |
| Sister of Moses | Unspecified, presumably the attendants of the wife of Pharaoh (Firʿawn) | 28:12 |
| Sisters in Midian | Moses (Mūsā) | 28:23 |
| One of the two sisters in Midian | Moses (Mūsā) | 28:25 |

| Speaker | Addressee | Verse number |
|---|---|---|
| One of the two sisters in Midian | Her father ("*yā abati*") | 28:26 |
| Wife of Abraham | Angels, others present, or simply bemused speech | 51:29 |
| Wife of the Prophet | The Prophet Muḥammad | 66:3 |
| Wife of Pharaoh | God (Rabb) | 66:11 |

Female Speakers, Listed by the Frequency of Their Speech

| Female speakers | Number of verses containing their direct speech |
|---|---|
| Queen of Sheba (*malikat Sabaʾ*) | 8 |
| Wife of the viceroy (*imraʾat al-ʿAzīz*) | 6 |
| Mary (Maryam) | 5 |
| Women in the city (*niswatun fī l-madīna*) (in unison) | 3 |
| Wife of ʿImrān (*imraʾat ʿImrān*) (mother of Mary) | 2 |
| Wife of Abraham (*imraʾat Ibrāhīm*) | 2 |
| Mother of Moses (*umm Mūsā*) | 2 |
| Wife of Pharaoh (*imraʾat Firʿawn*) | 2 |
| Sister of Moses (*ukht Mūsā*) | 2 |
| One of the two sisters in Midian | 2 |
| Sisters in Midian (in unison) | 1 |
| Adam's spouse (in unison with Adam) | 1 |
| Expectant woman (in unison with partner) | 1 |
| Spouse of the Prophet Muḥammad (*zawj al-nabī*) | 1 |

Verses Containing the Speech of Women, Listed by Verse Order of the Compiled Qur'an

| Verse number | Full verse |
|---|---|
| 3:35 | [Remember] when the wife of ʿImrān said, "My Lord, truly I dedicate to You what is in my belly, in consecration. So accept it from me. Truly You are the Hearing, the Knowing." |
| 3:36 | And when she bore her [Mary], she [Mary's mother] said, "My Lord, I have borne a female,"—and God knows best what she bore—and the male is not like the female, "and I have named her Mary, and I seek refuge for her in You, and for her progeny, from Satan the outcast." |
| 3:37 | So her Lord accepted her [Mary] with a beautiful acceptance, and made her grow in a beautiful way, and placed her under the care of Zachariah. Whenever Zachariah entered upon her in the sanctuary, he found provision with her. He said, "Mary, from where does this come to you?" She said, "It is from God. Truly God provides for whomever He will without reckoning." |
| 3:47 | She [Mary] said, "My Lord, how shall I have a child while no human being has touched me?" He said, "Thus does God create whatever He will." When He decrees a thing, He only says to it, "Be!" and it is. |
| 7:23 | They [Adam and his spouse] said, "Our Lord! We have wronged ourselves. If You do not forgive us and have mercy upon us, we shall surely be among the losers." |
| 7:189 | It is He [God] who created you from a single soul, and made from her [the soul] her spouse, that he might find rest in her. Then, when he covered her [in reference to an unnamed couple], she bore a light burden, and carried it about. But when she had grown heavy, they called upon God, their Lord, "If You give us a healthy child, we shall surely be among the thankful." |
| 11:72 | She [Abraham's wife] said, "Oh, woe unto me! Shall I bear a child when I am an old woman, and this husband of mine is an old man? That would surely be an astounding thing." |
| 12:23 | But she in whose house he [Joseph] was staying sought to lure him from himself. She locked the doors and said, "Come, you!" He said, "God be my refuge! Truly He is my lord, and has made beautiful my accommodation. Verily the wrongdoers will not prosper!" |
| 12:25 | And they [Joseph and the wife of the viceroy] raced to the door, while she tore his shirt from behind. And they encountered her husband (*sayyidahā*) at the door. She said, "What is the recompense for one who desires ill toward your wife, save that he be imprisoned, or [face] a painful punishment?" |
| 12:30 | Some women in the city said, "The viceroy's wife sought to lure her slave boy from himself! He has filled her with ardent love. Truly we consider her to be in manifest error." |

| Verse number | Full verse |
|---|---|
| 12:31 | So when she [the viceroy's wife] heard of their [the women's] plotting, she sent for them, and prepared a repast for them, and gave each of them a knife. And she said [to Joseph], "Come out before them!" Then when they saw him, they so admired him that they cut their hands and said, "God be praised! This is no human being. This is naught but a noble angel!" |
| 12:32 | She [the viceroy's wife] said, "This is the one on whose account you blamed me. I indeed sought to lure him from himself, but he remained chaste. And if he does not do as I command, he shall surely be imprisoned; and he shall be among those humbled." |
| 12:51 | He [the king] said, "What was your purpose when you sought to lure Joseph from himself?" They [the women] said, "God be praised! We know no evil against him." The viceroy's wife said, "Now the truth has come to light. It was I who sought to lure him from himself, and verily he is among the truthful." |
| 19:18 | She [Mary] said, "I seek refuge from you in the Compassionate, if you are reverent!" |
| 19:20 | She [Mary] said, "How shall I have a boy when no human being has touched me, nor have I been unchaste?" |
| 19:23 | And the pangs of childbirth drove her [Mary] to the trunk of a date palm. She said, "Would that I had died before this and were a thing forgotten, utterly forgotten!" |
| 20:40 | When your sister went forth and said, "Shall I show you one who can nurse him?" Thus We returned you to your mother that she might be comforted and grieve not. And you slayed a soul, but We saved you from sorrow. And We tried you with trials. Then did you remain some years among the people of Midian. Then did you come, as determined, O Moses. |
| 27:29 | She [the Queen of Sheba] said, "O notables! Truly a noble letter has been delivered unto me." |
| 27:30 | "Verily, it is from Solomon and verily it is 'In the name of God, the Compassionate, the Merciful.'" |
| 27:31 | "Do not exalt yourselves against me, but come to me in submission." |
| 27:32 | She [the Queen of Sheba] said, "O notables! Give me your opinion in this matter of mine. I am not one to decide on any matter unless you are present." |
| 27:34 | She [the Queen of Sheba] said, "Verily, kings, when they enter a city, corrupt it, and make the most honorable of its people the most abased. They will do likewise." |
| 27:35 | "I will send a gift to them and observe what the envoys bring back." |
| 27:42 | Then when she [the Queen of Sheba] came, it was said, "Is your throne like this?" She said, "It seems the same." [Solomon said] "And we were given knowledge before her and we were submitters." |

| Verse number | Full verse |
|---|---|
| 27:44 | It was said to her [the Queen of Sheba], "Enter the pavilion." But when she saw it, she supposed it to be an expanse of water and bared her legs. He said, "Verily it is a pavilion paved with crystal." She said, "My Lord! Surely I have wronged myself, and I submit with Solomon to God, Lord of the worlds." |
| 28:9 | And the wife of Pharaoh said, "A comfort for me and for you! Slay him not; it may be that he will bring us some benefit, or that we may take him as a son." Yet they were unaware. |
| 28:11 | And she [Moses's mother] said to his sister, "Follow him." So she watched him from afar; yet they were unaware. |
| 28:12 | And We forbade him [Moses] to be suckled by foster mothers before that; so she [Moses's sister] said, "Shall I direct you to the people of a house who will take care of him for you and treat him with good will?" |
| 28:23 | And when he [Moses] arrived at the wells of Midian, he found there a community of people watering [their flocks]. And he found beside them two women holding back [their flocks]. He said, "What is your errand?" They said, "We water not [our flocks] until the shepherds have driven [theirs] away, and our father is a very old man." |
| 28:25 | Then one of the two [sisters at the watering hole in Midian] came to him [Moses], walking bashfully. She said, "Truly my father summons you, that he might render to you a reward for having watered [our flocks] for us." When he [Moses] came and recounted his story unto him [the father], he [the father] said, "Fear not. You have been saved from the wrongdoing people." |
| 28:26 | One of the two [of the sisters of Midian] said, "O my father! Hire him [Moses]. Surely the best you can hire is the strong, the trustworthy." |
| 51:29 | Then his [Abraham's] wife came forward with a loud cry; she struck her face and said, "A barren old woman!" |
| 66:3 | When the Prophet [Muḥammad] confided a certain matter to one of his wives, but she divulged it, and God showed it to him, he made known part of it and held back part of it. When he informed her of it, she said, "Who informed you of this?" He replied, "The Knower, the Aware informed me." |
| 66:11 | And God sets forth as an example for those who believe the wife of Pharaoh when she said, "My Lord, build for me a house near You in the garden, deliver me from Pharaoh and his deeds, and deliver me from the wrongdoing people." |

Divine and/or Angelic Speech to Specific Female Figures, Listed According to the Approximate Chronology of Sacred History

| Female addressee(s) | Verse number and full verse |
|---|---|
| *zawj Ādam* (spouse of Adam, in conjunction with Adam) | 2:36: Then Satan made them stumble therefrom, and expelled them from that wherein they were, and We said, "Get you down, each of you an enemy to the other. For you on the earth is a dwelling place, and enjoyment for a while."<br>2:38: We said, "Get down from it, all together. If guidance should come to you from Me, then whoever follows My guidance, no fear shall come upon them, nor shall they grieve."<br>7:22: Thus he lured them on through deception. And when they tasted of the tree, their nakedness was exposed to them, and they began to sew together the leaves of the garden to cover themselves. And their Lord called out to them, "Did I not forbid you from that tree, and tell you that Satan is a manifest enemy unto you?"<br>7:24: He [God] said, "Get down, each of you an enemy to the other! There will be for you on the earth a dwelling place, and enjoyment for a while."<br>7:25: He [God] said, "Therein you shall live, and therein you shall die, and from there shall you be brought forth."<br>20:123: He [God] said, "Get down from it, together, each of you an enemy to the other. And if guidance should come unto you from Me, then whoever follows My guidance shall not go astray, nor be wretched." |
| *imraʾat Nūḥ* and *imraʾat Lūṭ* (wife of Noah and wife of Lot) | 66:10: God sets forth as an example for those who disbelieve the wife of Noah and the wife of Lot. They were under two of Our righteous servants [Noah and Lot]; then they [the wives] betrayed them [Noah and Lot], and they [Noah and Lot] availed them [their wives] naught against God. And it was said to both [wives], "Enter the fire with those who enter." |
| *imraʾat Ibrāhīm* (wife of Abraham) | 11:71: And his wife was standing there and she laughed. Then We gave her glad tidings of Isaac, and after Isaac, of Jacob.<br>11:73: They [angelic messengers] said, "Do you marvel at the command of God? The mercy of God and His blessings be upon you, O family of the house! Truly He is praised, glorious."<br>51:28: Then he conceived a fear of them. They said, "Fear not!" and gave him glad tidings of a knowing son.<br>51:30: They said, "Thus has your Lord decreed. Truly He is the Wise, the Knowing." |
| *umm Mūsā* (mother of Moses) | 20:39: [God revealed] "Cast him into the vessel and cast it into the river. Then the river will throw him upon the bank. An enemy to Me and an enemy to him shall take him." And I cast upon you [Moses] a love from Me, that you might be formed under My eye.<br>28:7: So We revealed to the mother of Moses, "Nurse him. But if you fear for him, then cast him into the river, and fear not, nor grieve. Surely We shall bring him back to you and make him one of the messengers." |

| Female addressee(s) | Verse number and full verse |
|---|---|
| Maryam (Mary) | 3:42: And [remember] when the angels said, "O Mary, truly God has chosen you and purified you, and has chosen you above the women of the worlds.<br>3:43: O Mary! Be devoutly obedient to your Lord, prostrate, and bow with those who bow."<br>3:45: When the angels said, "O Mary, truly God gives you glad tidings of a Word from Him, whose name is the Messiah, Jesus son of Mary, honored in this world and the hereafter, one of those brought nigh.<br>3:46: He [the child] will speak to people in the cradle and in maturity, and will be among the righteous."<br>3:47: She [Mary] said, "My Lord, how shall I have a child while no human being has touched me?" He said, "Thus does God create whatever He will." When He decrees a thing, He but says to it, "Be!" and it is.<br>19:19: He said, "I am but a messenger of your Lord, to bestow upon you a pure boy."<br>19:21: He [the angel] said, "Thus shall it be. Your Lord says, 'It is easy for Me, and [it is thus] that We might make him a sign for humankind, and a mercy from Us. And it is a matter decreed.' "<br>19:24: So he [the angel] called out to her from below her, "Grieve not! Your Lord has placed a stream beneath you.<br>19:25: And shake toward yourself [Mary] the trunk of the date palm; fresh, ripe dates shall fall upon you.<br>19:26: So eat and drink and cool [your] eye[s]. And if you see any human being, say, 'Verily I have vowed a fast to the Compassionate, so I shall not speak this day to any human being.' " |
| *nisāʾ* and *azwāj al-nabī* (women and spouses of the Prophet [Muḥammad]) | 33:30: O wives of the Prophet! Whoever among you commits a flagrant indecency, her punishment will be doubled; and that is easy for God.<br>33:31: And whoever among you [wives of the Prophet] is devoutly obedient to God and His Messenger and works righteousness, We shall give her reward twice over, and We have prepared for her a generous provision.<br>33:32: O wives of the Prophet! You are not like other women. If you are reverent, then be not overtly soft in speech, lest one in whose heart is a disease be moved to desire; and speak in an honorable way.<br>33:33: Abide in your homes and flaunt not your charms as they did flaunt them in the prior age of ignorance. Perform the prayer, give the alms, and obey God and His Messenger. God only desires to remove defilement from you, O family of the house, and to purify you completely.<br>66:4: If you both [two wives of the Prophet Muḥammad] repent to God, [it is best,] for your hearts did certainly incline, and if you aid one another against him, then truly God, He is his Protector, as are Gabriel and the righteous among the believers; and the angels support him withal.<br>66:5: It may be that if he divorces you [two wives of the Prophet Muḥammad], his Lord would give him wives in your stead who are better than you, submitting, believing, devoutly obedient, penitent, worshiping, and given to fasting—previously married, and virgins. |

APPENDIX D

# Female Figures and Families in the Qur'an by Surah

Female Figures and Their Families, Listed by Approximate Revelatory Sequence of Surahs

| Surah name (number) | Approx. revelatory sequence | Female figures/families explicitly mentioned (name as given in extra-Qur'anic sources) |
|---|---|---|
| *al-Masad* (111) | 6th | *imra'at Abī Lahab* (wife of Abū Lahab, Arwā Umm Jamīl bt. Ḥarb) |
| *al-Qamar* (54) | 37th | *āl Lūṭ* (House of Lot)<br>*āl Firʿawn* (House of Pharaoh) |
| *Ṣād* (38) | 38th | *ahl Ayyūb* (family of Job) |
| *al-Aʿrāf* (7) | 39th | *zawj Ādam* (spouse of Adam, Ḥawwā', or Eve)<br>*imra'at Lūṭ* (wife of Lot)<br>*nisā' Banī Isrā'īl* (women of the Children of Israel)<br>*āl Firʿawn* (House of Pharaoh) |
| *Maryam* (19) | 44th | *imra'at Zakariyyā* (wife of Zachariah)<br>*āl Yaʿqūb* (House of Jacob)<br>Maryam (Mary; also in "Jesus, son of Mary," *ʿĪsā ibn Maryam*)<br>*ahl Maryam* (family of Mary)<br>*umm* and *abū Maryam* (mother and father of Mary)<br>*ahl Ismāʿīl* (family of Ishmael) |
| *Ṭā Hā* (20) | 45th | *ahl Mūsā* (family of Moses)<br>*zawj Ādam* (spouse of Adam, Ḥawwā', or Eve) |
| *al-Shuʿarā'* (26) | 47th | *ahl Lūṭ* (family of Lot)<br>*ʿajūz* (old woman, referring to the wife of Lot)<br>*ʿashīrataka al-aqrabīn* (your [Muḥammad's] closest kin) |
| *al-Naml* (27) | 48th | *ahl Mūsā* (family of Moses)<br>*wālidā Sulaymān* (parents of Solomon)<br>*malikat Saba'* (Queen of Sheba, Bilqīs)<br>*ahl Ṣāliḥ* (family of Ṣāliḥ)<br>*āl Lūṭ* (House of Lot)<br>*ahl Lūṭ* (family of Lot)<br>*imra'at Lūṭ* (wife of Lot) |
| *al-Qaṣaṣ* (28) | 49th | *nisā' Banī Isrā'īl* (women of the Children of Israel)<br>*āl Firʿawn* (House of Pharaoh)<br>*umm Mūsā* (mother of Moses)<br>*ukht Mūsā* (sister of Moses)<br>*al-marāḍiʿ* (the wet nurses)<br>*imra'at Firʿawn* (wife of Pharaoh, Āsiyā bt. Muzāḥim)<br>*imra'atāni min Madyan* (two women from Midian)<br>*ahl Mūsā* (family of Moses) |

| Surah name (number) | Approx. revelatory sequence | Female figures/families explicitly mentioned (name as given in extra-Qur'anic sources) |
|---|---|---|
| *Hūd* (11) | 52nd | *ahl bayt Ibrāhīm* (family of the house of Abraham)<br>*imraʾat Ibrāhīm* (wife of Abraham, Sarah)<br>*ahl Nūḥ* (family of Noah)<br>*banāt Lūṭ* (daughters of Lot) |
| *Yūsuf* (12) | 53rd | *āl Yaʿqūb* (House of Jacob)<br>*imraʾat ʿAzīz Miṣr* (wife of the viceroy of Egypt, Zulaykhā)<br>*niswatun fī l-madīna* (women in the city)<br>*ahl Yaʿqūb* (family of Jacob)<br>*abawā Yūsuf* (parents of Joseph) |
| *al-Ḥijr* (15) | 54th | *āl Lūṭ* (House of Lot)<br>*banāt Lūṭ* (daughters of Lot)<br>*imraʾat Lūṭ* (wife of Lot) |
| *al-Ṣāffāt* (37) | 56th | *ahl Lūṭ* (family of Lot)<br>*ʿajūz* (old woman, referring to the wife of Lot) |
| *Sabaʾ* (34) | 58th | *āl Dāwūd* (House of David) |
| *Ghāfir* (40) | 60th | *nisāʾ Banī Isrāʾīl* (women of the Children of Israel)<br>*āl Firʿawn* (House of Pharaoh) |
| *al-Zukhruf* (43) | 63rd | Maryam (in "son of Mary," *ibn Maryam*) |
| *al-Dhāriyāt* (51) | 67th | *ahl Ibrāhīm* (family of Abraham)<br>*imraʾat Ibrāhīm* (wife of Abraham, Sarah) |
| *Ibrāhīm* (14) | 72nd | *nisāʾ Banī Isrāʾīl* (women of the Children of Israel)<br>*āl Firʿawn* (House of Pharaoh)<br>*ahl Ibrāhīm* (family of Abraham)<br>*wālidā Ibrāhīm* (parents of Abraham) |
| *al-Anbiyāʾ* (21) | 73rd | *ahl Nūḥ* (family of Noah)<br>*ahl Ayyūb* (family of Job)<br>*imraʾat Zakariyyā* (wife of Zachariah)<br>*allatī aḥṣanat farjahā* (she who fortified her pudenda [i.e., Mary]) |
| *al-Muʾminūn* (23) | 74th | Maryam (in "son of Mary," *ibn Maryam*) |
| *al-ʿAnkabūt* (29) | 85th | *ahl Lūṭ* (family of Lot)<br>*imraʾat Lūṭ* (wife of Lot) |
| **Beginning of verses attributed to the Medinan Period** | | |
| *al-Baqara* (2) | 87th | *zawj Ādam* (spouse of Adam, Ḥawwāʾ, or Eve)<br>*ahl Ibrāhīm* (family of Abraham)<br>*nisāʾ Banī Isrāʾīl* (women of the Children of Israel)<br>*āl Firʿawn* (House of Pharaoh)<br>*āl Mūsā* (House of Moses)<br>*āl Hārūn* (House of Aaron)<br>Maryam (in "Jesus, son of Mary," *ʿĪsā ibn Maryam*) |
| *al-Anfāl* (8) | 88th | *āl Firʿawn* (House of Pharaoh) |

| Surah name (number) | Approx. revelatory sequence | Female figures/families explicitly mentioned (name as given in extra-Qur'anic sources) |
|---|---|---|
| *Āl ʿImrān* (3) | 89th | *āl Ibrāhīm* (House of Abraham)<br>*āl ʿImrān* (House of ʿImrān)<br>*imraʾat ʿImrān* (wife of ʿImrān)<br>Maryam (Mary); also occurs in *al-masīḥ ibn Maryam* (the Messiah, son of Mary)<br>*imraʾat Zakariyyā* (wife of Zachariah)<br>*āl Firʿawn* (House of Pharaoh) |
| *al-Aḥzāb* (33) | 90th | *ummahāt al-muʾminīn* (mothers of the believers, i.e., wives of the Prophet Muḥammad)<br>*azwāj al-nabī* (wives of the Prophet [Muḥammad])<br>*ahl al-bayt* (family of the house [of the Prophet Muḥammad])<br>*nisāʾ al-nabī* (women of the Prophet [i.e., Muḥammad])<br>Maryam (in "Jesus, son of Mary," *ʿĪsā ibn Maryam*) |
| *al-Mumtaḥana* (60) | 91st | Contains verses said to concern Umm Kulthūm bt. ʿUqba |
| *al-Nisāʾ* (4) | 92nd | *āl Ibrāhīm* (House of Abraham)<br>Maryam (Mary)<br>Maryam (in "Jesus, son of Mary," *ʿĪsā ibn Maryam*) |
| *al-Ḥadīd* (57) | 94th | Maryam (in "Jesus, son of Mary," *ʿĪsā ibn Maryam*) |
| *al-Ṭalāq* (65) | 99th | Discussions of divorce therein may have concerned Ḥafṣa bt. ʿUmar b. al-Khaṭṭāb or a woman from among her kin |
| *al-Nūr* (24) | 102nd | Contains verses said to concern ʿĀʾisha bt. Abī Bakr and Maymūna bt. al-Ḥārith |
| *al-Mujādila* (58) | 105th | Said to concern Khawla bt. Thaʿlaba |
| *al-Ḥujurāt* (49) | 106th | Surah named after the private apartments of the Prophet Muḥammad's wives in Medina |
| *al-Taḥrīm* (66) | 107th | *azwāj al-nabī* (verses reported to directly concern Ḥafṣa bt. ʿUmar b. al-Khaṭṭāb and ʿĀʾisha bt. Abī Bakr, and perhaps indirectly Māriya al-Qibṭiyya)<br>*imraʾat Nūḥ* (wife of Noah)<br>*imraʾat Lūṭ* (wife of Lot)<br>*imraʾat Firʿawn* (wife of Pharaoh, Āsiyā bt. Muzāḥim)<br>*ibnat ʿImrān* (daughter of ʿImrān, i.e., Mary) |
| *al-Ṣaff* (61) | 109th | Maryam (in "Jesus, son of Mary," *ʿĪsā ibn Maryam*) |
| *al-Māʾida* (5) | 112th | Maryam (in "Jesus, son of Mary," *ʿĪsā ibn Maryam*, and in "the Messiah, son of Mary," *al-masīḥ ibn Maryam*) |
| *al-Tawba* (9) | 113th | Maryam (in "the Messiah, son of Mary," *al-masīḥ ibn Maryam*) |

APPENDIX E

# Select Women Relatives of the Prophet Muḥammad

Spouses of the Prophet Muḥammad (consummated marriages, ordered by approximate date of marriage):

Khadīja bt. Khuwaylid
Sawda bt. Zamʿa
ʿĀʾisha bt. Abī Bakr
Ḥafṣa bt. ʿUmar b. al-Khaṭṭāb
Zaynab bt. Khuzayma
Umm Salama (Hind bt. Abī Umayya)
Zaynab bt. Jaḥsh
Juwayriya bt. al-Ḥārith
Umm Ḥabība (Ramla bt. Abī Sufyān)
Ṣafiyya (Zaynab bt. Ḥuyayy b. Akhṭab)
Maymūna bt. al-Ḥārith
Māriya bt. Shamʿūn, known as Māriya al-Qibṭiyya (concubine)

Daughters of the Prophet Muḥammad:

Zaynab
Ruqayya
Umm Kulthūm
Fāṭima

Additional Notable Women Relatives:

Asmāʾ bt. ʿUmays: wife of the Prophet's paternal cousin Jaʿfar b. Abī Ṭālib
Fāṭima bt. Asad: wife of the Prophet's paternal uncle Abū Ṭālib
Ḥamna bt. Jaḥsh: paternal cousin of the Prophet through his aunt Umayma bt. ʿAbd al-Muṭṭalib
Ṣafiyya bt. ʿAbd al-Muṭṭalib: paternal aunt of the Prophet, the sister of the famed martyr Ḥamza b. ʿAbd al-Muṭṭalib
Umayma bt. ʿAbd al-Muṭṭalib: paternal aunt of the Prophet, the full sister of ʿAbd Allāh, Abū Ṭālib, and Zubayr, later the Prophet's mother-in-law through his marriage to Zaynab bt. Jaḥsh
Umm al-Faḍl (Lubāba bt. al-Ḥarith): wife of ʿAbbās b. ʿAbd al-Muṭṭalib (the paternal uncle of the Prophet), and later the Prophet's sister-in-law through his marriage to her sister Maymūna bt. al-Ḥārith

# Bibliography


Abboud, Hosn. *Mary in the Qur'an: A Literary Reading*. Routledge Studies in the Qur'an. New York: Routledge, 2014.

Abboud, Hosn. "Qur'anic Mary's Story and the Motif of Palm Tree and the Rivulet." *Parole de l'Orient* 30 (2005): 261–80.

ʿAbd al-Raḥmān, ʿĀʾisha [Bint al-Shāṭiʾ]. *Banāt al-nabī*. Cairo: Dār al-Hilāl, 1956.

Abdel Haleem, Muhammad A. S. *The Qur'an: A New Translation*. Rev. ed. Oxford World Classics. New York: Oxford University Press, 2015.

Abdel Haleem, Muhammad A. S. "Quranic Paradise: How to Get to Paradise and What to Expect There." In *Roads to Paradise: Eschatology and Concepts of the Hereafter in Islam*, edited by Sebastian Günther and Todd Lawson. Vol. 1, *Foundations and Formation of a Tradition: Reflections on the Hereafter in the Quran and Islamic Thought*, edited by Sebastian Günther, Todd Lawson, and Christian Mauder, 49–66. Islamic History and Civilization. Leiden: Brill, 2017.

Abou-Bakr, Omaima. "Turning the Tables: Perspectives on the Construction of 'Muslim Manhood.'" *Hawwa: Journal of Women of the Middle East and the Islamic World* 11 (2014): 89–107.

Abugideiri, Hibba. "Hagar: A Historical Model for 'Gender Jihad.'" In *Daughters of Abraham: Feminist Thought in Judaism, Christianity, and Islam*, edited by John Esposito and Yvonne Haddad, 87–107. Gainesville: University Press of Florida, 2001.

Abu-Lughod, Lila. *Do Muslim Women Need Saving?* Cambridge, MA: Harvard University Press, 2013.

Adújar, Ndeye. "Feminist Readings of the Qur'an: Social, Political, and Religious Implications." In *Muslima Theology: The Voices of Muslim Women Theologians*, edited by Elif Medeni, Ednan Aslan, and Marcia Hermansen, 59–80. Frankfurt am Main: Peter Lang Verlag, 2013.

Afsaruddin, Asma. *The First Muslims: History and Memory*. Oxford: Oneworld Publications, 2007.

Ahmed, Leila. *A Quiet Revolution: The Veil's Resurgence, from the Middle East to America*. New Haven, CT: Yale University Press, 2011.

Ahmed, Leila. *Women and Gender in Islam: The Historical Roots of a Modern Debate*. New Haven, CT: Yale University Press, 1992.

Ahmed, Waleed. "Lot's Daughters in the Qurʾān: An Investigation through the Lens of Intertextuality." In *New Perspectives on the Qurʾān: The Qurʾān in Its Historical Context 2*, edited by Gabriel Said Reynolds, 411–24. Routledge Studies on the Qurʾān. Abingdon, UK: Routledge, 2011.

Ahmed, Waleed. "The Qurʾānic Narratives through the Lens of Intertextual Allusions: A Literary Approach." PhD dissertation, Georg-August-Universität Göttingen, 2014.

Akyol, Mustafa. *The Islamic Jesus: How the King of the Jews Became a Prophet of the Muslims*. New York: St. Martin's Press, 2017.

al-Azami, Mahmoud M. *The History of the Qur'ānic Text from Revelation to Compilation: A Comparative Study with the Old and New Testaments*. Leicester: UK Islamic Academy, 2003.

al-Azmeh, Aziz. *The Emergence of Islam in Late Antiquity*. Cambridge, MA: Harvard University Press, 2017.

Ali, Kecia. "'A Beautiful Example': The Prophet Muhammad as a Model for Muslim Husbands." *Islamic Studies* 43, no. 2 (2004): 273–91.

Ali, Kecia. "Destabilizing Gender, Reproducing Maternity: Mary in the Qur'ān." *Journal of the International Qur'anic Studies Association* 2 (2017): 89–110.

Ali, Kecia. *The Lives of Muhammad*. Cambridge, MA: Harvard University Press, 2014.

Ali, Kecia. *Marriage and Slavery in Early Islam*. Cambridge, MA: Harvard University Press, 2010.

Ali, Kecia. "Muslim Scholars, Islamic Studies, and the Gendered Academy." Annual al-Faruqi Memorial Lecture at the American Academy of Religion Annual Meeting, Boston, MA (November 19, 2017). Online: https://www.youtube.com/watch?v=ai5XF-bP3KE.

Ali, Kecia. "The Omnipresent Male Scholar." *Critical Muslim* 8 (September 2013): 61–73.

Ali, Kecia. *Sexual Ethics and Islam: Feminist Reflections on Qur'an, Hadith, and Jurisprudence*. Rev. ed. Oxford: Oneworld, 2016.

Ali, Kecia. "Slavery and Sexual Ethics in Islam." In *Beyond Slavery: Overcoming Its Religious and Sexual Legacies*, edited by Bernadette J. Brooten, with the editorial assistance of Jacqueline L. Hazelton, 108–22. New York: Palgrave MacMillan, 2010.

Alshech, Eli. "Out of Sight and Therefore Out of Mind: Early Sunnī Islamic Modesty Regulations and the Creation of Spheres of Privacy." *Journal of Near Eastern Studies* 66, no. 4 (2007): 11–24.

Alwani, Zainab, and Celene Ibrahim. "Religion, Gender, and Family Law: Critical Perspectives on Integration for European Muslims." In *Applying Sharia in the West: Facts, Fears and the Future of Islamic Rules on Family Relations in the West*, edited by Maurits S. Berger, 227–40. Debates on Islam and Society Series. Leiden: Leiden University Press, 2013.

Anthony, Sean W., and Catherine L. Bronson. "Did Ḥafṣah Edit the Qur'ān? A Response with Notes on the Codices of the Prophet's Wives." *Journal of the International Qur'anic Studies Association* 1, no. 1 (2016): 93–125.

Anwar, Etin. *Gender and Self in Islam*. New York: Routledge, 2006.

Archer, George. "A Short History of a 'Perfect Woman': The Translations of the 'Wife of Pharaoh' before, through, and beyond the Qur'ānic Milieu." *Mathal/Mashal* 3, no. 1 (2013): 1–20.

Arpagus, Hatice K. "The Position of Women in the Creation: A Qur'anic Perspective." In *Muslima Theology: The Voices of Muslim Women Theologians*, edited by Elif Medeni, Ednan Aslan, and Marcia Hermansen, 115–32. Frankfurt am Main: Peter Lang Verlag, 2013.

Ayoub, Mahmoud. *The Qur'an and Its Interpreters*. 2 vols. Albany: State University of New York Press, 1984.

Ayubi, Zahra. *Gendered Morality: Classical Islamic Ethics of the Self, Family, and Society*. New York: Columbia University Press, 2019.

Azim, Hina. *Sexual Violation in Islamic Law: Substance, Evidence, and Procedure*. Cambridge Studies in Islamic Civilization. New York: Cambridge University Press, 2015.

Badawi, Elsaid M., and Muhammad Abdel Haleem. *Arabic-English Dictionary of Qur'anic Usage*. Leiden: Brill, 2008.

Badran, Margot. *Feminism in Islam: Secular and Religious Convergences*. Oxford: Oneworld, 2009.

Badran, Margot. "Gender." In *Encyclopaedia of the Qurʾān*, edited by Jane Dammen McAuliffe, 2:288–92. Leiden: Brill, 2001–6.

Bakhtiar, Laleh. *Chronological Quran as Revealed to Prophet Muhammad*. Chicago: Kazi Publications, 2015.

Bakhtiar, Laleh. *Concordance of the Sublime Quran*. Chicago: Kazi Publications, 2011.

Bakhtiar, Laleh. *The Sublime Quran*. Chicago: Kazi Publications, 2007.

Barazangi, Nimat Hafez. *Women's Identity and Rethinking the Hadith*. New York: Routledge, 2015.

Barazangi, Nimat Hafez. *Women's Identity and the Qur'an: A New Reading*. Gainesville: University Press of Florida, 2004.

Barlas, Asma. *"Believing Women" in Islam: Unreading Patriarchal Interpretations of the Qur'an*. Austin: University of Texas Press, 2002.

Barlas, Asma. "Women's Readings of the Qurʾān." In *The Cambridge Companion to the Qurʾān*, edited by Jane Dammen McAuliffe, 255–71. Cambridge Companions to Religion. New York: Cambridge University Press, 2006.

Bauer, Karen. "Emotion in the Qur'an: An Overview." *Journal of Qur'anic Studies* 19, no. 2 (2017): 1–30.

Bauer, Karen. *Gender Hierarchy in the Qur'an: Medieval Interpretations, Modern Responses*. Cambridge Studies in Islamic Civilizations. New York: Cambridge University Press, 2015.

Bauer, Karen. "'The Male Is Not like the Female' (Q 3:36): The Question of Gender Egalitarianism in the Qur'an." *Religion Compass* 3, no. 4 (2009): 637–54.

Bengtsson, Staffan. "Building a Community: Disability and Identity in the Qur'an." *Scandinavian Journal of Disability Research* 20, no. 1 (2018): 210–18.

Berkey, Jonathan. *The Formation of Islam: Religion and Society in the Near East, 600–1800*. Cambridge: Cambridge University Press, 2003.

bin Tyeer, Sarah R. *The Qur'an and the Aesthetics of Premodern Arabic Prose*. London: Palgrave Macmillian, 2016.

Bodman, Whitney S. *The Poetics of Iblīs: Narrative Theology in the Qurʾān*. Harvard Theological Studies. Cambridge, MA: Harvard University Press, 2011.

Boullata, Issa J., ed. *Literary Structures of Religious Meaning in the Qurʾān*. Routledge Studies in the Qur'an. New York: Routledge, 2009.

Bowering, Gerhard. "Chronology and the Qurʾān." In *Encyclopaedia of the Qurʾān*, edited by Jane Dammen McAuliffe, 1:316–35. Leiden: Brill, 2001–6.

Bronson, Catherine. "Eve in the Formative Period of Islamic Exegesis: Intertextual Boundaries and Hermeneutical Demarcations." In *Tafsīr and Islamic Intellectual History: Exploring the Boundaries of a Genre*, edited by Andreas Görke and Johanna Pink, 27–61. New York: Oxford University Press and the Institute of Ismaili Studies, 2014.

Brown, Jonathan A. C. *Hadith: Muhammad's Legacy in the Medieval and Modern World*. 2nd ed. Oxford: Oneworld, 2018.

Brown, Jonathan A. C. *Misquoting Muhammad: The Challenge and Choices of Interpreting the Prophet's Legacy*. London: Oneworld, 2014.

Brown, Jonathan A. C. *Slavery and Islam*. London: Oneworld, 2019.

Bursi, Adam Collins. "Holy Spit and Magic Spells: Religion, Magic and the Body in Late Ancient Judaism, Christianity, and Islam." PhD dissertation, Cornell University, 2015.

Chaudhry, Ayesha S. *Domestic Violence and the Islamic Tradition: Ethics, Law and the Muslim Discourse on Gender*. Oxford Islamic Legal Studies. New York: Oxford University Press, 2013.

Chaudhry, Ayesha S. "Islamic Legal Studies: A Critical Historiography." In *The Oxford Handbook of Islamic Law*, edited by Anver M. Emon and Rumee Ahmed, 1–40. Oxford Handbooks Online, September 2017. http://www.oxfordhandbooks.com/view/10.1093/oxfordhb/9780199679010.001.0001/oxfordhb-9780199679010-e-1.

Chaudhry, Ayesha S. "Unlikely Motherhood in the Qurʾān: Oncofertility as Devotion." *Oncofertility: Ethical, Legal, Social, and Medical Perspectives* 156 (2010): 287–94.

Clifford, A. "Feminist Hermeneutics." In *New Catholic Encyclopedia*, edited by Catholic University of America, 674–75. Detroit: Thompson/Gale Group, 2003.

Cook, David. *Martyrdom in Islam*. Themes in Islamic History. New York: Cambridge University Press, 2012.

Cook, David. "The Prophet Muḥammad, Labīd al-Yahūdī and the Commentaries to Sūra 113." *Journal of Semitic Studies* 45, no. 2 (2000): 323–45.

Cooke, Miriam. *Women Claim Islam: Creating Islamic Feminism through Literature*. New York: Routledge, 2001.

Cuypers, Michel. *The Banquet: A Reading of the Fifth Sura of the Qurʾan*. Rhetorica Semitica. Miami: Convivium, 2009.

Cuypers, Michel. *The Composition of the Qurʾan: Rhetorical Analysis*. Translated by Jerry Ryan. London: Bloomsbury Academic, 2015.

Cuypers, Michel. "Semitic Rhetoric as a Key to the Question of the Naẓm of the Qur'anic Text." *Coherence in the Qurʾan* 13, no. 1 (2011): 1–24.

Dakake, Maria Massi. "Quranic Ethics, Human Rights, and Society." In *The Study Quran*, edited by Seyyed Hossein Nasr et al., 1785–1804. New York: HarperCollins, 2015.

Delgado, Janan, and Celene Ibrahim. "Children and Parents in the Qur'an and in Premodern Islamic Jurisprudence." In *Religious Perspectives on Reproductive Ethics*, edited by Dena Davis. New York: Oxford University Press, 2020.

De Sondy, Amanullah. *The Crisis of Islamic Masculinities*. New York: Bloomsbury, 2013.

Douglas, Mary. *Thinking in Circles: An Essay on Ring Composition*. New Haven, CT: Yale University Press, 2007.

Duderija, Adis. *Constructing a Religiously Ideal "Believer" and "Woman" in Islam: Neo-Traditional Salafi and Progressive Muslims' Methods of Interpretation*. Palgrave Series in Islamic Theology, Law, and History. New York: Palgrave Macmillan, 2011.

Dykgraaf, Christine. "The Mesopotamian Flood Epic and Its Representation in the Bible, the Quran and Other Middle Eastern Literatures." In *Sacred Tropes: Tanakh, New Testament, and Qur'an*, edited by Roberta Sterman Sabbath, 393–408. Biblical Interpretation Series. Leiden: Brill, 2009.

El-Awa, Salwa M. S. "Repetition in the Qurʾān: A Relevance Based Explanation of the Phenomenon." *Islamic Studies* 42, no. 4 (2003): 577–93.

El-Awa, Salwa M. S. *Textual Relations in the Qurʾān: Relevance, Coherence, and Structure* Routledge Studies in the Quran. New York: Routledge, 2006.

Elias, Jamal J. "Power, Prophecy, and Propriety: The Encounter of Solomon and the Queen of Sheba." *Journal of Qur'anic Studies* 11, no. 1 (2009): 57–74.

El Shamsy, Ahmed. "The Social Construction of Orthodoxy." In *The Cambridge Companion to Classical Islamic Theology*, edited by Tim Winter, 97–116. Cambridge Companions to Religion. Cambridge: Cambridge University Press, 2008.

El-Zein, Amira. *Islam, Arabs, and the Intelligent World of the Jinn*. Syracuse, NY: Syracuse University Press, 2009.

Ernst, Carl W. *How to Read the Qur'an: A New Guide with Select Translations*. Chapel Hill: University of North Carolina Press, 2011.

Esack, Farid. "Lot and His Offer: 2016 IQSA Presidential Address." *Journal of the International Quranic Studies Association* 2 (2017): 7–33.

Farrin, Raymond. *Structure and Qur'anic Interpretation: A Study of Symmetry and Coherence in Islam's Holy Text*. Ashland, OR: White Cloud Press, 2014.

Farrin, Raymond. "Surat al-Baqara: A Structural Analysis." *Muslim World* 100, no. 1 (2010): 17–32.

Farris, Sara. *In the Name of Women's Rights: The Rise of Femonationalism*. Durham, NC: Duke University Press, 2017.

Fierro, Maribel. "Women as Prophets in Islam." In *Writing the Feminine: Women in Arab Sources*, edited by Manuela Marin and Randi Deguilhem, 183–98. New York: I. B. Tauris, 2002.

Fiorenza, Elisabeth Schüssler. *Congress of Wo/men: Religion, Gender, and Kyriarchal Power*. Cambridge, MA: Feminist Studies in Religion Books, 2016.

Fitzpatrick, Coeli, and Adam Hani Walker, eds. *Muhammad in History, Thought, and Culture: An Encyclopedia of the Prophet of God*. Santa Barbara, CA: ABC-CLIO, 2014.

Fricker, Miranda. *Epistemic Injustice: Power and the Ethics of Knowing*. New York: Oxford University Press, 2007.

Galadari, Abdulla. *Qur'anic Hermeneutics: Between Science, History, and the Bible*. New York: Bloomsbury, 2018.

Galadari, Abdulla. "The Role of Intertextual Polysemy in Qur'anic Exegesis." *International Journal on Qur'anic Research* 3, no. 4 (2013): 35–56.

Geissinger, Aisha. "The Exegetical Traditions of ʿĀʾisha: Notes on their Impact and Significance." *Journal of Qur'anic Studies* 9, no. 1 (2004): 1–20.

Geissinger, Aisha. *Gender and Muslim Constructions of Exegetical Authority: A Rereading of the Classical Genre of Qurʾān Commentary*. Islamic History and Civilization: Studies and Texts. Leiden: Brill, 2015.

Geissinger, Aisha. "Mary in the Qur'an: Rereading Subversive Births." In *Sacred Tropes: Tanakh, New Testament, and Qur'an*, edited by Roberta Sterman Sabbath, 379–92. Biblical Interpretation Series. Leiden: Brill, 2009.

Giladi, Avner. "Children." In *Encyclopaedia of the Qurʾān*, edited by Jane Dammen McAuliffe, 1:301–3. Leiden: Brill, 2001–6.

Giladi, Avner. "Family." In *Encyclopaedia of the Qurʾān*, edited by Jane Dammen McAuliffe, 2:173–76. Leiden: Brill, 2001–6.

Giladi, Avner. "Parents." In *Encyclopaedia of the Qurʾān*, edited by Jane Dammen McAuliffe, 4:20–22. Leiden: Brill, 2001–6.

Gökkir, Bilal. "Form and Structure of Sura Maryam: A Study from Unity of Sura Perspective." *Süleyman Demirel Üniversitesi İlahiyat Fakültesi Dergisi* 16, no. 1 (2006): 1–16.

Goldman, Shalom. *The Wiles of Women/The Wiles of Men: Joseph and Potiphar's Wife in Ancient Near Eastern, Jewish, and Islamic Folklore*. Albany: State University of New York Press, 1995.

Gordon, Matthew, and Kathryn Hain, eds. *Concubines and Courtesans: Women and Slavery in Islamic History*. New York: Oxford University Press, 2017.

Graham, William A. *Beyond the Written Word: Oral Aspects of Scripture in the History of Religion*. Cambridge: Cambridge University Press, 1993.

Gregg, Robert C. *Shared Stories, Rival Tellings: Early Encounters of Jews, Christians, and Muslims*. New York: Oxford University Press, 2015.

Günther, Sebastian, Todd Lawson, and Christian Mauder, eds. *Roads to Paradise: Eschatology and Concepts of the Hereafter in Islam*. 2 vols. Islamic History and Civilization. Leiden: Brill, 2017.

Haj, Samira. *Reconfiguring Islamic Tradition: Reform, Rationality, and Modernity*. Cultural Memory in the Present. Palo Alto, CA: Stanford University Press, 2009.

Hallaq, Wael B. *Restating Orientalism: A Critique of Modern Knowledge*. New York: Columbia University Press, 2018.

Hammer, Juliane. *American Muslim Women, Religious Authority, and Activism: More than a Prayer*. Louann Atkins Temple Women and Culture Series. Austin: University of Texas Press, 2012.

Hammer, Juliane. "Identity, Authority and Activism: American Muslim Women's Approaches to the Qur'an." *Muslim World* 98, no. 4 (2008): 442–63.

Hammer, Juliane, Laury Silvers, and Kecia Ali, eds. *A Jihad for Justice: Honoring the Work and Life of Amina Wadud*. 2012. Online: http://www.bu.edu/religion/files/2010/03/A-Jihad-for-Justice-for-Amina-Wadud-2012-1.pdf.

Hartsock, Nancy C. M. "The Feminist Standpoint: Developing the Ground for a Specifically Feminist Historical Materialism." In *Feminism and Philosophy: Essential Readings in Theory, Reinterpretation, and Application*, edited by Nancy Tuana and Rosemarie Tong, 69–90. Boulder, CO: Westview Press, 1995.

Hawting, Gerald. "An Ascetic Vow and an Unseemly Oath?: *Īlāʾ* and *Ẓihār* in Muslim Law." *Bulletin of the School of Oriental and African Studies* 57, no. 1 (1994): 113–25.

Hermansen, Marcia. "Womb." In *Encyclopaedia of the Qurʾān*, edited by Jane Dammen McAuliffe, 5:522–23. Leiden: Brill, 2001–6.

Hidayatullah, Aysha A. *Feminist Edges of the Qur'an*. New York: Oxford University Press, 2014.

Hidayatullah, Aysha A. "Inspiration and Struggle: Muslim Feminist Theology and the Work of Elisabeth Schüssler Fiorenza." *Journal of Feminist Studies in Religion* 35, no. 1 (2009): 162–70.

Hidayatullah, Aysha A. "Māriyya the Copt: Gender, Sex and Heritage in the Legacy of Muhammad's Umm Walad." *Islam and Christian–Muslim Relations* 21, no. 3 (2010): 221–43.

Hidayatullah, Aysha A., and Judith Plaskow. "Beyond Sarah and Hagar: Jewish and Muslim Reflections on Feminist Theology." In *Muslims and Jews in America: Commonalities, Contentions, and Complexities*, edited by Reza Aslan and Aaron J. Hahn Tapper, 159–72. New York: Palgrave Macmillan, 2011.

Hooks, Bell. "Theory as Liberatory Practice." *Yale Journal of Law and Feminism* 4, no. 1 (1991): 1–12.

Ibn Hishām, Abū Muḥammad ʿAbd al-Malik. *al-Sīra al-nabawiyya*. Beirut: Dār Ibn Ḥazm, 2001.

Ibn Manẓūr, Muḥammad b. Mukarram. *Lisān al-ʿArab*. 20 vols. Būlāq: al-Maṭbaʿa al-Kubrā al-Amīriyya, 1883–90.

Ibrahim, Celene (see also Lizzio, Celene). "Family Law Reform, Spousal Relations, and the 'Intentions of Islamic Law.'" In *Women's Rights and Religious Law: Domestic and*

*International Perspectives*, edited by Fareda Banda and Lisa Fishbayn Joffe, 108–22. Law and Religion. New York: Routledge, 2016.

Ibrahim, Celene. "'The Garment of Piety Is Best': Islamic Legal and Exegetical Works on Bodily Covering." In *Claremont Journal of Religion* 4, no. 1 (2015): 19–54.

Ibrahim, Celene. "Sexual Violence and Qur'anic Resources for Healing Processes." In *Sexual Violence and Sacred Texts*, edited by Amy Kalmanofsky, 75–93. Cambridge, MA: Feminist Studies in Religion Books, 2017.

Ibrahim, Celene. "Verse 4:34: Abjure Symbolic Violence, Rebuff Feminist Partiality, or Seek Another Hermeneutic?" In *Muslim Women and Gender Justice: Concepts, Sources, and Histories*, edited by Juliane Hammer, Dina El Omari, and Mouhanad Khorchide, 170–82. Routledge Islamic Studies Series. New York: Routledge, 2019.

Izutsu, Toshihiko. *Ethico-Religious Concepts in the Qurʾān*. Montreal: McGill-Queens University Press, 2002.

Izutsu, Toshihiko. *Language and Magic: Studies in the Magical Function of Speech*. Kuala Lumpur: The Other Press, 2012.

Jalajel, David Solomon. *Women and Leadership in Islamic Law: A Critical Analysis of Classical Legal Texts*. Culture and Civilization in the Middle East. New York: Routledge, 2017.

Jamal, Amreen. "The Story of Lot and the Qurʾān's Perception of the Morality of Same-Sex Sexuality." *Journal of Homosexuality* 41, no. 1 (2001): 1–88.

Jardim, Georgina L. *Recovering the Female Voice in Islamic Scripture: Women and Silence*. Routledge New Critical Thinking in Religion, Theology, and Biblical Studies. New York: Routledge, 2016.

Jarrar, Maher. "Houris." In *Encyclopaedia of the Qurʾān*, edited by Jane Dammen McAuliffe, 2:456–58. Leiden: Brill, 2001–6.

Jarrar, Maher. "Sira." In *Muhammad in History, Thought, and Culture: An Encyclopedia of the Prophet of God*, edited by Coeli Fitzpatrick and Adam Hani Walker, 2:568–82. Santa Barbara, CA: ABC-CLIO, 2014.

Jarrar, Maher. "Strategies of Paradise: Paradise Virgins and Utopia." In *Roads to Paradise: Eschatology and Concepts of the Hereafter in Islam*. Vol 1: *Foundations and Formation of a Tradition: Reflections on the Hereafter in the Quran and Islamic Thought*, edited by Sebastian Günther, Todd Lawson, and Christian Mauder, 271–94. Islamic History and Civilization. Leiden: Brill, 2017.

Jeenah, Na'eem. "Bilqis: A Qur'ānic Model for Leadership and for Islamic Feminists." *Journal of Semitic Studies* 13, no. 1 (2004): 47–58.

Johns, A. H. "Narrative, Intertext and Allusion in the Qurʾānic Presentation of Job." *Journal of Qurʾanic Studies* 1 (1999): 1–25.

Juynboll, G. H. A. "Hadith and the Qur'an." In *Encyclopaedia of the Qurʾān*, edited by Jane Dammen McAuliffe, 2:376–97. Leiden: Brill, 2001–6.

Kahf, Mohja. "She Who Argues: A Homily on Justice and Renewal." *Muslim World* 103, no. 3 (2013): 295–304.

Kalmanofsky, Amy, ed. *Sexual Violence and Sacred Texts*. Cambridge, MA: Feminist Studies in Religion Books, 2017.

Kaltner, John, and Younus Mirza. *The Bible and the Qur'an: Biblical Figures in the Islamic Tradition*. London: Bloomsbury T&T Clark, 2018.

Kashani-Sabet, Firoozeh. "Who Is Fatima? Gender, Culture, and Representation in Islam." *Journal of Middle East Women's Studies* 1, no. 2 (2005): 1–24.

Katz, Marion Holmes. "Shame (*Ḥayāʾ*) as an Affective Disposition in Islamic Legal Thought." *Journal of Law, Religion and State* 3 (2014): 139–69.

Katz, Marion Holmes. "Gender and Law." In *Encyclopaedia of Islam, Three*, edited by Kate Fleet, Gudrun Krämer, Denis Matringe, John Nawas, and Everett Rowson. Leiden: Brill, 2017. Online: http://dx.doi.org/10.1163/1573-3912_ei3_COM_27397.

Keeler, Annabel. "Towards a Prophetology of Love: The Figure of Jacob in Sufi Commentaries on *Sūrat Yūsuf*." In *The Esoteric Interpretation of the Qurʾān*, edited by Annabel Keeler and Sajjid Rizvi, 125–54. London: Institute of Islamic Studies and Oxford University Press, 2015.

Kermani, Navid. "The Aesthetic Reception of the Qurʾān as Reflected in Early Muslim History." In *Literary Structures of Religious Meaning in the Qur'an*, edited by Issa J. Boullata, 255–76. New York: Routledge, 2000.

Khuri, Fuad. *The Body in Islamic Culture*. London: Saqi Books, 2000.

Klar, Marianna O. "Text-Critical Approaches to Sura Structure: Combining Synchronicity with Diachronicity in *Sūrat al-Baqara*. Part One." *Journal of Qur'anic Studies* 19, no. 1 (2017): 1–40.

Klar, Marianna O. "Text-Critical Approaches to Sura Structure: Combining Synchronicity with Diachronicity in *Sūrat al-Baqara*. Part Two." *Journal of Qur'anic Studies* 19, no. 2 (2017): 64–107.

Klar, Marianna O. "Through the Lens of the Adam Narrative: A Re-consideration of *Sūrat al-Baqara*." *Journal of Qur'anic Studies* 17, no. 2 (2015): 24–46.

Klemm, Verena. "Image Formation of an Islamic Legend: Fatima, the Daughter of the Prophet Muhammad." In *Ideas, Images, and Methods of Portrayal: Insights into Arabic Literature and Islam*, edited by Sebastian Günther, 181–206. Islamic History and Civilization. Leiden: Brill, 2005.

Kueny, Kathryn M. *Conceiving Identities: Maternity in Medieval Muslim Discourse and Practice*. Albany: State University of New York Press, 2013.

Kvam, Kristen E., Linda S. Schearing, and Valarie H. Ziegler, eds. *Eve and Adam: Jewish, Christian, and Muslim Readings on Genesis and Gender*. Bloomington: Indiana University Press, 2009.

Lamptey [Rhodes], Jerusha Tanner. *Divine Words, Female Voices: Muslima Explorations in Comparative Feminist Theology*. New York: Oxford University Press, 2018.

Lamptey [Rhodes], Jerusha Tanner. "From Sexual Difference to Religious Difference: Toward a Muslima Theology of Religious Pluralism." In *Muslima Theology: The Voices of Muslim Women Theologians*, edited by Elif Medeni, Ednan Aslan, and Marcia Hermansen, 231–45. Frankfurt am Main: Peter Lang Verlag, 2013.

Lamptey [Rhodes], Jerusha Tanner. *Never Wholly Other: A Muslima Theology of Religious Pluralism*. New York: Oxford University Press, 2014.

Lamptey [Rhodes], Jerusha Tanner. "Toward a Muslima Theology: Theological, Constructive, and Comparative Possibilities." *Journal of Feminist Studies in Religion* 33, no. 1 (2017): 27–44.

Lamrabet, Asma. *Women and Men in the Qur'ān*. Translated by Muneera Salem-Murdock. Cham, Switzerland: Palgrave Macmillan, 2018. [Original: *Femmes et hommes dans le Coran: quelle égalité?* Paris: Éditions Albouraq, 2012.]

Lamrabet, Asma. *Women in the Qur'an: An Emancipatory Reading*. Translated by Myriam François-Cerrah. New York: Kube, 2016. [Original: *Le Coran et les femmes: une lecture de libération*. Lyon: Éditions Tawhid, 2007.]

Lane, Edward William. *Arabic-English Lexicon*. London: Williams and Norgate, 1863.

Lange, Christian. *Paradise and Hell in Islamic Traditions*. New York: Cambridge University Press, 2016.

Lassner, Jacob. *Demonizing the Queen of Sheba: Boundaries of Gender and Culture in Postbiblical Judaism and Medieval Islam*. Chicago Studies in the History of Judaism. Chicago: University of Chicago Press, 1993.

Lawrence, Bruce B. *The Koran in English: A Biography*. Lives of Great Religious Books. Princeton, NJ: Princeton University Press, 2017.

Lawson, Todd. "Duality, Opposition and Typology in the Qur'an: The Apocalyptic Substrate." *Journal of Qur'anic Studies* 10, no. 2 (2008): 23–49.

Leaman, Oliver. "Appearance and Reality in the Qur'an: Bilqis and Zulaykha." *Islâm Araştırmaları Dergisi* 10 (2003): 23–37.

Lefkovitz, Lori Hope. *In Scripture: The First Stories of Jewish Sexual Identities*. Plymouth, UK: Rowman & Littlefield, 2010.

Lefkovitz, Lori Hope. "Not a Man: Joseph and the Character of Masculinity in Judaism and Islam." In *Gender in Judaism and Islam: Common Lives, Uncommon Heritage*, edited by Firoozeh Kashani-Sabet and Beth S. Wenger, 155–80. New York: New York University Press, 2015.

Lizzio, Celene [Ibrahim]. "Courage at the Crossroads." In *A Jihad for Justice: Honoring the Work and Life of Amina Wadud*, edited by Juliane Hammer, Laury Silvers, and Kecia Ali, 85–89 (2012). Online: https://www.bu.edu/religion/files/2010/03/A-Jihad-for-Justice-for-Amina-Wadud-2012-1.pdf.

Lizzio, Celene [Ibrahim]. "Gendering Ritual: A Muslima's Reading of the Laws of Menstrual Preclusion." In *Muslima Theology: The Voices of Muslim Women Theologians*, edited by Elif Medeni, Ednan Aslan, and Marcia Hermansen, 167–79. Frankfurt am Main: Peter Lang Verlag, 2013.

Lowin, Shari. *The Making of a Forefather: Abraham in Islamic and Jewish Exegetical Narratives*. Islamic History and Civilization. Boston: Brill, 2006.

Lucas, Scott. "Divorce, Ḥadīth-Scholar Style: From al-Dārimī to al-Tirmidhī." *Journal of Islamic Studies* 19, no. 3 (2008): 325–68.

Lumbard, Joseph E. B. "Decolonializing Qur'anic Studies." Paper presented at the Ninth Biennial Conference on the Qur'an, entitled "Text, Society & Culture," hosted by the School of Oriental and African Studies, University of London, November 11, 2016.

Lybarger, Loren. "Gender and Prophetic Authority in the Qur'anic Story of Maryam: A Literary Approach." *Journal of Religion* 80, no. 2 (2000): 240–70.

Madigan, Daniel A. "Mary and Muhammad: Bearers of the Word." *Australasian Catholic Record* 80 (2003): 417–27.

Madigan, Daniel A. *The Qur'ān's Self-Image: Writing and Authority in Islam's Scripture*. Princeton, NJ: Princeton University Press, 2001.

Madigan, Daniel A. "Reflections on Some Current Directions in Qur'anic Studies." *Muslim World* 85 (1995): 345–62.

Maghen, Ze'ev. *Virtues of the Flesh: Passion and Purity in Early Islamic Jurisprudence*. Studies in Islamic Law and Society. Leiden: Brill, 2004.

Marcotte, Roxanne D. "Muslim Women's Scholarship and the New Gender Jihad." In *Women and Islam*, edited by Zayn R. Kassam, 131–62. Women and Religion in the World. Santa Barbara, CA: Praeger, 2010.

Marx, Michael. "Glimpses of a Mariology in the Qur'an: From Hagiography to Theology via Religious-Political Debate." In *The Qur'ān in Context: Historical and Literary*

*Investigations into the Qurʾānic Milieu*, edited by Angelika Neuwirth, Nicolai Sinai, and Michael Marx, 533–63. Texts and Studies on the Qurʾān. Leiden: Brill, 2010.

Mattson, Ingrid. *The Story of the Qur'an: Its History and Place in Muslim Life*. Hoboken, NJ: Wiley-Blackwell, 2013.

McAuliffe, Jane Dammen, ed. *The Cambridge Companion to the Qurʾān*. New York: Cambridge University Press, 2006.

McAuliffe, Jane Dammen, ed. *Encyclopaedia of the Qurʾān*. 6 vols. Leiden: Brill, 2001–6.

McAuliffe, Jane Dammen. *Qur'anic Christians: An Analysis of Classical and Modern Exegesis*. Cambridge: Cambridge University Press, 1991.

McAuliffe, Jane Dammen. "Text and Textuality: Q. 3:7 as a Point of Intersection." In *Literary Structures of Religious Meaning in the Qurʾān*, edited by Issa J. Boullata, 56–76. Routledge Studies in the Qur'an. New York: Routledge, 2009.

McLarney, Ellen Anne. "Women of the Prophet: Politics of the Islamic Family." In *Soft Force: Women in Egypt's Islamic Awakening*, 45–50. Princeton, NJ: Princeton University Press, 2015.

Merguerian, Gayane Karen, and Afsaneh Najmabadi. "Zulaykha and Yusuf: Whose 'Best Story?'" *International Journal of Middle East Studies* 29, no. 4 (1997): 485–508.

Mir, Mustansir. "The Language of the Qur'an." In *The Blackwell Companion to the Qur'an*, edited by Andrew Rippin, 88–106. Blackwell Companions to Religion. Malden, MA: Blackwell, 2006.

Mir, Mustansir. "The Queen of Sheba's Conversion in Q. 27:44: A Problem Examined." *Journal of Qur'anic Studies* 9, no. 2 (2007): 43–56.

Mir, Mustansir. "The Qur'anic Story of Joseph: Plot, Themes, and Characters." *Muslim World* 1 (1986): 1–15.

Mir, Mustansir. "The Sūra as a Unity: A Twentieth-Century Development in Qur'an Exegesis." In *The Koran: Critical Concepts in Islamic Studies*, edited by Colin Turner, 4:198–209. London: Routledge, 2004.

Mir, Mustansir. *Understanding the Islamic Scripture: A Study of Selected Passages of the Qurʾān*. New York: Routledge, 2016.

Mir, Mustansir. "Unity of the Text of the Qur'an." In *Encyclopaedia of the Qurʾān*, edited by Jane Dammen McAuliffe, 5:405–6. Leiden: Brill, 2001–6.

Mir, Mustansir. *Verbal Idioms of the Qur'ān*. Michigan Series on the Middle East. Ann Arbor: Center for Near Eastern and North African Studies, University of Michigan, 1989.

Mir-Hosseini, Ziba, Mulki al-Sharmani, and Jana Rumminger, eds. *Men in Charge? Rethinking Authority in Muslim Legal Tradition*. London: Oneworld Publications, 2015.

Mirza, Younus Y. "Ibn Taymiyya as Exegete: Moses' Father-in-Law and the Messengers in *Sūrat Yā Sīn*." *Journal of Qur'anic Studies* 19, no. 1 (2017): 39–71.

Moballegh, S. Zahra. "Veiled Women Unveiling God: Understanding the Qur'an through Its Women Characters." Lecture at Harvard Divinity School (December 5, 2018). Online: https://wsrp.hds.harvard.edu/news/2018/12/05/video-veiled-women-unveiling-god.

Modarressi, Hossein. "Early Debates on the Integrity of the Qur'an." *Studia Islamica*, no. 77 (1993): 5–39.

Mohammed, Khaleel. *David in the Muslim Tradition: The Bathsheba Affair*. Lanham, MD: Lexington Books, 2014.

Mol, Arnold Yasin. "The Denial of Supernatural Sorcery in Classical and Modern Sunnī Tafsīr of Sūrah al-Falaq (113:4): A Reflection of Underlying Construction." *Al-Bayān* 11, no. 1 (2013): 1–18.

Morris, James. "Dramatizing the Sura of Joseph: An Introduction to the Islamic Humanities." *Journal of Turkish Studies* 18 (1994): 201–24.

Motzki, Harald, ed. *Hadith: Origins and Developments*. The Formation of the Classical Islamic World 28. Hampshire, UK: Ashgate, 2004.

Mourad, Suleiman A. "Mary in the Qurʾān: A Reexamination of Her Presentation." In *The Qurʾān in Its Historical Context*, ed. Gabriel Said Reynolds, 163–74. Routledge Studies in the Qur'an. London: Routledge, 2007.

Murad, Abdal Hakim. "Islam, Irigaray, and the Retrieval of Gender." April 1999. Online: http://masud.co.uk/ISLAM/ahm/gender.htm.

Murata, Sachiko. *The Tao of Islam: A Sourcebook on Gender Relationships in Islamic Thought*. Albany: State University of New York Press, 1992.

Nadwi, Mohammad Akram. *Al-Muḥaddithāt: The Women Scholars in Islam*. Oxford: Interface Publications, 2013.

Naguib, Shuruq. "Bint al-Shāṭiʾ's Approach to *Tafsīr*: An Egyptian Exegete's Journey from Hermeneutics to Humanity." *Journal of Qur'anic Studies* 17, no. 1 (2015): 45–84.

Naguib, Shuruq. "Horizons and Limitations of Muslim Feminist Hermeneutics: Reflections on the Menstruation Verse." In *New Topics in Feminist Philosophy of Religion: Contestations and Transcendence Incarnate*, edited by Pamela Sue Anderson, 33–50. Dordrecht: Springer, 2010.

Nasr, Seyyed Hossein, Caner K. Dagli, Maria Massi Dakake, Joseph E. B. Lumbard, and Mohammad Rustom, eds. *The Study Quran: A New Translation and Commentary*. San Francisco: HarperOne, 2015.

Neuwirth, Angelika. "The House of Abraham and the House of Amran: Genealogy, Patriarchal Authority, and Exegetical Professionalism." In *The Qurʾān in Context: Historical and Literary Investigations into the Qurʾānic Milieu*, edited by Angelika Neuwirth, Nicolai Sinai, and Michael Marx, 499–532. Texts and Studies on the Qurʾān. Leiden: Brill, 2010.

Neuwirth, Angelika. "Imagining Mary—Disputing Jesus: Reading *Sūrat Maryam* and Related Meccan Texts within the Qur'ānic Communication Process." In *Fremde, Feinde und Kurioses: Innen- und Außenansichten unseres muslimischen Nachbarn*, edited by Benjamin Jokisch, Ulrich Rebstock, and Lawrence I. Conrad, 383–416. Berlin: De Gruyter, 2009.

Neuwirth, Angelika. "Mary and Jesus, Counterbalancing the Biblical Patriarchs: A Re-reading of *Sūrat Maryam* in *Sūrat Āl ʿImrān* (Q 3:1–62)." *Parole de l'Orient* 30 (2005): 231–60.

Neuwirth, Angelika. "Negotiating Justice: A Pre-Canonical Reading of the Qur'anic Creation Accounts (Part I)." *Journal of Qur'anic Studies* 2, no. 1 (2000): 25–41.

Neuwirth, Angelika. "Negotiating Justice: A Pre-Canonical Reading of the Qur'anic Creation Accounts (Part II)." *Journal of Qur'anic Studies* 2, no. 2 (2000): 1–18.

Neuwirth, Angelika. "Orientalism in Oriental Studies? Qur'anic Studies as a Case in Point." *Journal of Qur'anic Studies* 9, no. 2 (2011): 115–27.

Neuwirth, Angelika. "Qur'an and History—a Disputed Relationship: Some Reflections on Qur'anic History and History in the Qur'an." *Journal of Qur'anic Studies* 5, no. 1 (2010): 1–18.

Neuwirth, Angelika. "Qurʾānic Studies and Philology: Qurʾānic Textual Politics of Staging, Penetrating, and Finally Eclipsing Biblical Tradition." In *Qur'ānic Studies Today*, edited by Angelika Neuwirth and Michael A. Sells, 178–206. Routledge Studies in the Qur'an. New York: Routledge, 2016.

Neuwirth, Angelika. *Scripture, Poetry, and the Making of a Community: Reading the Qur'an as a Literary Text*. New York: New York University Press, 2015.

Neuwirth, Angelika. "Structural, Linguistic, and Literary Features." In *The Cambridge Companion to the Qur'ān*, edited by Jane Dammen McAuliffe, 97–114. Cambridge Companion to Religion. Cambridge: Cambridge University Press, 2006.

Neuwirth, Angelika. "Two Faces of the Qur'ān: *Qur'ān* and *Muṣḥaf*." *Oral Tradition* 25, no. 1 (2010): 141–56.

Nguyen, Martin. *Modern Muslim Theology: Engaging God and the World with Faith and Imagination*. Lanham, MD: Rowman & Littlefield, 2019.

Nguyen, Martin. "Modern Scripturalism and Emergent Theological Trajectories: Moving Beyond the Qur'an as Text." *Journal of Islamic and Muslim Studies* 1, no. 2 (2016): 61–79.

Nissinen, Martti. "Prophecy as Construct, Ancient and Modern." In *"Thus Speaks Ishtar of Arbela": Prophecy in Israel, Assyria, and Egypt in the Neo-Assyrian Period*, edited by Robert P. Gordon and Hans M. Barstad, 11–35. Winona Lake, IN: Eisenbrauns, 2013.

Nöldeke, Theodore. *Geschichte des Qorāns*. Leipzig: Dieterich'sche Verlagsbuchhandlung, 1909.

Oh, Irene. "Motherhood in Christianity and Islam: Critiques, Realities, and Possibilities." *Journal of Religious Ethics* 38, no. 4 (2010): 638–53.

Ohlander, Erik. "Modern Qur'anic Hermeneutics." *Religion Compass* 3, no. 4 (2009): 620–36.

Osborne, Lauren E. "Textual and Paratextual Meaning in the Recited Qur'an: Analysis of a Performance of Surat al-Furqan by Sheikh Mishary bin Rashid al-Afasy." In *Qur'anic Studies Today*, edited by Angelika Neuwirth and Michael A. Sells, 228–46. Routledge Studies in the Qur'an. New York: Routledge, 2016.

Osman, Rawand. *Female Personalities in the Qur'an and Sunna: Examining the Major Sources of Imami Shi'i Islam*. Routledge Persian and Shi'i Studies. New York: Routledge, 2015.

Powers, David S. *Muhammad Is Not the Father of Any of Your Men*. Philadelphia: University of Pennsylvania Press, 2009.

Powers, David S. *Studies in Qur'an and Hadith: The Formation of the Islamic Law of Inheritance*. Oakland: University of California Press, 1986.

Powers, David S. *Zayd*. Philadelphia: University of Pennsylvania Press, 2014.

Qarā'ī, 'Alī Qulī, trans. *The Qur'an: With a Phrase-by-Phrase English Translation*. Elmhurst, NY: Tahrike Tarsile Qur'an, 2011.

Qureishi-Landes, Asifa. "A Meditation on *Mahr*, Modernity, and Muslim Marriage Contract Law." In *Feminism, Law, and Religion*, edited by Marie A. Failinger, Elizabeth R. Schiltz, and Susan J. Stabile, 173–95. Gender in Law, Culture, and Society. Burlington, VT: Ashgate, 2013.

Qutb, Muhammad 'Ali. *Women around the Messenger*. Translated by 'Abdur-Rafi' Adewale Imam. Riyadh: International Islamic Publishing House, 2008.

Raber, Karen. "Chains of Pearls: Gender, Property, Identity." In *Ornamentalizing the Renaissance*, edited by Bella Mirabella, 159–80. Ann Arbor: University of Michigan Press, 2011.

Ragab, Ahmed. "Epistemic Authority of Women in the Medieval Middle East." *Hawwa: Journal of Women of the Middle East and the Islamic World* 8, no. 2 (2010): 181–216.

Rahman, Fazlur. *Major Themes of the Qur'an*. Chicago: University of Chicago Press, 1980.

Reda, Nevin. "Holistic Approaches to the Qur'an: A Historical Background." *Religion Compass* 4, no. 8 (2010): 495–506.

Reda, Nevin. "The Qur'anic Talut and the Rise of the Ancient Israelite Monarchy: An Intertextual Reading." *American Journal of Islamic Social Sciences* 25, no. 3 (2008): 31–51.

Reeves, John C., ed. *Bible and Qur'an: Essays in Scriptural Intertextuality*. Leiden: Brill, 2004.

Reynolds, Gabriel Said. *The Qurʾān and Its Biblical Subtext*. Routledge Studies in the Quran. New York: Routledge, 2010.

Rhouni, Raja. *Secular and Islamic Feminist Critiques in the Work of Fatima Mernissi*. Boston: Brill, 2010.

Rippin, Andrew, ed. *Approaches to the History of the Interpretation of the Qur'an*. Oxford: Clarendon Press, 1988.

Rippin, Andrew. "The Function of 'Asbāb al-Nuzūl' in Qur' ānic Exegesis." *Bulletin of the School of Oriental and African Studies* 51, no. 1 (1998): 1–20.

Rippin, Andrew. "Occasions of Revelation." In *Encyclopaedia of the Qurʾān*, edited by Jane Dammen McAuliffe, 3:569–73. Leiden: Brill, 2001–6.

Rippin, Andrew. *The Qur'an and Its Interpretive Tradition*. Aldershot, UK: Ashgate, 2002.

Rippin, Andrew. "The Qur'an as Literature: Perils, Pitfalls and Prospects." *British Society of Middle Eastern Studies Bulletin* 10, no. 1 (1983): 38–47.

Rippin, Andrew, ed. *The Qur'an: Formative Interpretation*. Aldershot, UK: Ashgate/Variorum, 2000.

Rippin, Andrew, ed. *The Qur'an: Style and Contents*. Aldershot, UK: Ashgate, 2001.

Robinson, Neal. *Discovering the Qur'an: A Contemporary Approach to a Veiled Text*. Washington, DC: Georgetown University Press, 2004.

Robinson, Neal. "Jesus and Mary in the Qur'ān, Some Neglected Affinities." In *The Qur'an: Style and Contents*, edited by Andrew Rippin, 21–36. The Formation of the Classical Islamic World. Hampshire, UK: Ashgate, 2001.

Robinson, Neal. "The Qur'ān as the Word of God." In *Heaven and Earth: Essex Essays in Theology and Ethics*, edited by Andrew Linzey, Peter J. Wexler, and John Bach, 38–54. Worthing, UK: Churchman, 1986.

Robinson, Neal. "*Sūrat Āl ʿImrān* and Those with the Greatest Claim to Abraham." *Journal of Qur'anic Studies* 6, no. 2 (2004): 1–21.

Roded, Ruth. "Bint al-Shati's *Wives of the Prophet*: Feminist or Feminine?" *British Journal of Middle Eastern Studies* 33, no. 1 (2006): 51–66.

Roded, Ruth. *Women in Islamic Bibliographical Collections: From Ibn Saʿd to Who's Who*. Boulder, CO: Lynne Rienner, 1994.

Roded, Ruth. "Women in the Qurʾān." In *Encyclopaedia of the Qurʾān*, edited by Jane Dammen McAuliffe, 5:523–41. Leiden: Brill, 2001–6.

Rustomji, Nerina. "Are Houris Heavenly Concubines?" In *Concubines and Courtesans: Women and Slavery in Islamic History*, edited by Matthew Gordon and Kathryn Hain, 266–77. New York: Oxford University Press, 2017.

Rustomji, Nerina. "Beauty in the Garden: Aesthetics and the *Wildān, Ghilmān*, and *Ḥūr*." In *Roads to Paradise: Eschatology and Concepts of the Hereafter in Islam*, edited by Sebastian Günther and Todd Lawson. Vol. 1, *Foundations and Formation of a Tradition: Reflections on the Hereafter in the Quran and Islamic Thought*, 295–310. Islamic History and Civilization. Leiden: Brill, 2017.

Rustomji, Nerina. *The Garden and the Fire: Heaven and Hell in Islamic Culture*. New York: Columbia University Press, 2009.

Sadeghi, Behnam. "The Chronology of the Qur'ān: A Stylometric Research Program." *Arabica* 58 (2011): 210–99.

Sadeghi, Behnam. "The Codex of a Companion of the Prophet and the Qur'ān of the Prophet." *Arabica* 57 (2010): 343–436.

Sadeghi, Behnam. *The Logic of Law Making in Islam: Women and Prayer in the Legal Tradition*. Cambridge Studies in Islamic Traditions. New York: Cambridge University Press, 2013.

Salama, Mohammad. *The Qur'ān and Modern Arabic Literary Criticism: From Ṭāhā to Naṣr*. Suspensions: Contemporary Middle Eastern and Islamic Thought. New York: Bloomsbury, 2018.

Saleh, Walid. "The Arabian Context of Muhammad's Life." In *The Cambridge Companion to Muhammad*, edited by Jonathan E. Brockopp, 21–38. Cambridge Companions to Religion. New York: Cambridge University Press, 2010.

Saleh, Walid. "End of Hope: Suras 10–15, Despair, and a Way out of Mecca." In *Qur'ānic Studies Today*, ed. Angelika Neuwirth and Michael A. Sells, 105–23. Routledge Studies in the Qur'an. New York: Routledge, 2016.

Saleh, Walid. "The Etymological Fallacy and Qur'anic Studies: Muhammad, Paradise, and Late Antiquity." In *The Qur'ān in Context: Historical and Literary Investigations into the Qur'ānic Milieu*, edited by Angelika Neuwirth, Nicolai Sinai, and Michael Marx, 649–98. Texts and Studies on the Qur'ān. Leiden: Brill, 2010.

Saleh, Walid. "Quranic Commentaries." In *The Study Quran*, edited by Seyyed Hossein Nasr et al., 1645–58. New York: HarperCollins, 2015.

Sayed, Faraan Alamgir. "Repetition in Qur'ānic *Qaṣaṣ*: With Reference to Thematic and Literary Coherence in the Story of Moses." *Journal of Islamic and Muslim Studies* 2, no. 2 (2017): 53–75.

Sayeed, Asma. *Women and the Transmission of Religious Knowledge in Islam*. New York: Cambridge University Press, 2013.

Schmid, Nora K. "Lot's Wife: Late Antique Paradigms of Sense and the Qur'ān." In *Qur'ānic Studies Today*, edited by Angelika Neuwirth and Michael A. Sells, 52–81. Routledge Studies in the Qur'an. New York: Routledge, 2016.

Schub, Michael B. "'The Male Is Not like the Female' (Qur'ān 3:36): An Eponymous Passage in the Qur'ān." *Zeitschrift für Arabische Linguistik* 23 (1991): 101–4.

Seedat, Fatima. "Islam, Feminism, and Islamic Feminism: Between Inadequacy and Inevitability." *Journal of Feminist Studies in Religion* 29, no. 2 (2013): 25–45.

Seedat, Fatima. "On the Convergence of Islam, Feminism, and Qur'anic Interpretation: A Critical Review of Aysha Hidayatullah's *Feminist Edges of the Qur'an*." *Journal of the Society for Contemporary Thought and the Islamicate World* (March 24, 2016): 1–10.

Seedat, Fatima. "On Spiritual Subjects: Negotiations in Muslim Female Spirituality." *Journal of Gender and Religion in Africa* 22, no. 1 (2006): 21–37.

Seedat, Fatima. "When Islam and Feminism Converge." *Muslim World* 103, no. 3 (2013): 404–20.

Sells, Michael. *Approaching the Qur'an: The Early Revelations*. Ashland, OR: White Cloud Press, 1999.

Sells, Michael. "The Casting: A Close Hearing of Sura ṬāHā 9–79." In *Qur'ānic Studies Today*, edited by Angelika Neuwirth and Michael A. Sells, 124–77. Routledge Studies in the Qur'an. New York: Routledge, 2016.

Sells, Michael. "A Literary Approach to the Hymnic Suras of the Qur'ān: Spirit, Gender, and Aural Intertextuality." In *Literary Structures of Religious Meaning in the Qur'an*, edited by Issa J. Boullata, 3–25. London: Curzon Press, 2000.

Sells, Michael. "Sound, Spirit, and Gender in *Sūrat al-Qadr*." In *The Qur'an: Style and Contents*, edited by Andrew Rippin, 332–53. Aldershot, UK: Variorum, 2001.

Shahid, Irfan. "A Contribution to Koranic Exegesis." In *Arabic and Islamic Studies in Honor of Hamilton A. R. Gibb*, edited by George Makdisi, 563–80. Leiden: E. J. Brill, 1965.

Shaikh, Saʿdiyya. *Sufi Narratives of Intimacy: Ibn ʿArabī, Gender, and Sexuality*. Chapel Hill: University of North Carolina Press, 2012.

Shaikh, Saʿdiyya. "Transforming Feminisms: Islam, Women and Gender Justice." In *Progressive Muslims: On Justice, Gender and Pluralism*, edited by Omid Safi, 147–62. Oxford: Oneworld Publications, 2003.

Shaltūt, Maḥmūd. *The Quran and Woman: Annotated English Version with Arabic Text* (*al-Qur'ān wa-l-mar'a*). Translated by Wajihuddin Ahmed and Abdel Malik Dardir. Cairo: International Islamic Center for Population Studies and Research, 1986. [1st edition, Cairo: Academy of Islamic Research of al-Azhar, 1936.]

Sharify-Funk, Meena. *Encountering the Transnational: Women, Islam and the Politics of Interpretation*. Gender in a Global/Local World. Burlington, VT: Ashgate, 2008.

Sharify-Funk. "From Dichotomies to Dialogues: Trends in Contemporary Islamic Hermeneutics." In *Contemporary Islam: Dynamic, Not Static*, edited by Abdul Aziz Said, Mohammed Abu-Nimer, and Meena Sharify-Funk, 64–80. New York: Routledge, 2006.

Sheibani, Mariam, Amir Toft, and Ahmed El Shamsy. "The Classical Period: Scripture, Origins, and Early Development." In *The Oxford Handbook of Islamic Law*, edited by Anver M. Emon and Rumee Ahmed. Oxford Handbooks Online, April 2017. http://www.oxfordhandbooks.com/view/10.1093/oxfordhb/9780199679010.001.0001/oxfordhb-9780199679010-e-13.

Siddiqui, Mona. "Reflections on Mary." In *Christians, Muslims, and Jesus: Gaining Understanding and Building Relationships*, edited by Carl Medearis, 149–70. Bloomington, MN: Bethany House, 2008.

Sinai, Nicolai. *The Qur'an: A Historical-Critical Introduction*. The New Edinburgh Islamic Surveys. Edinburgh: Edinburgh University Press, 2017.

Smith, Jane I., and Yvonne Y. Haddad. "Eve: Islamic Image of Woman." *Women's Studies International Forum* 5, no. 2 (1982): 135–44.

Smith, Jane I., and Yvonne Y. Haddad. "The Virgin Mary in Islamic Tradition and Commentary." *Muslim World* 79 (1989): 161–87.

Spectorsky, Susan A. *Women in Classical Islamic Law: A Survey of the Sources*. Leiden: Brill, 2010.

Spellberg, Denise E. "History Then, History Now: The Role of Medieval Islamic Religio-Political Sources in Shaping the Modern Debate on Gender." In *Beyond the Exotic: Women's Histories in Islamic Societies*, edited by Amira El-Azhary Sonbol, 7–14. Gender, Culture, and Politics in the Middle East. Syracuse, NY: Syracuse University Press, 2005.

Spellberg, Denise E. "Writing the Unwritten Life of the Islamic Eve: Menstruation and the Demonization of Motherhood." *International Journal of Middle East Studies* 28, no. 3 (1996): 305–24.

Steingass, Francis Joseph. *Arabic-English Dictionary*. London: Crosby Lockwood and Son, 1884.

Stökl, Jonathan, and Corrine L. Carvalho, eds. *Prophets Male and Female: Gender and Prophecy in the Hebrew Bible, the Eastern Mediterranean, and the Ancient Near East*. Atlanta, GA: Society of Biblical Literature, 2013.

Stowasser, Barbara Freyer. "Gender Issues and Contemporary Quran Interpretation." In *Islam, Gender, and Social Change*, edited by Yvonne Yazbeck Haddad and John L. Esposito, 30–44. New York: Oxford University Press, 1998.

Stowasser, Barbara Freyer. "The Qur'an and History." In *Beyond the Exotic: Women's Histories in Islamic Societies*, edited by Amira El-Azhary Sonbol, 15–36. Gender, Culture, and Politics in the Middle East. Syracuse, NY: Syracuse University Press, 2005.

Stowasser, Barbara Freyer. "Wives of the Prophet." In *Encyclopaedia of the Qur'ān*, edited by Jane Dammen McAuliffe, 5:506–21. Leiden: Brill, 2001–6.

Stowasser, Barbara Freyer. *Women in the Qur'an, Traditions, and Interpretation*. New York: Oxford University Press, 1994.

Stratton, Kimberly B. *Naming the Witch: Magic, Ideology, and Stereotype in the Ancient World*. Gender, Theory, and Religion. New York: Columbia University Press, 2007.

Tidswell, Toni. "A Clever Queen Learns the Wisdom of God: The Queen of Sheba in the Hebrew Scriptures and the Qur'an." *Hecate* 33, no. 2 (2007): 43–55.

Toorawa, Shawkat M. "*Sūrat Maryam* (Q. 19): Lexicon, Lexical Echoes, English Translation." *Journal of Qur'anic Studies* 13, no. 1 (2011): 25–78.

Tourage, Mahdi. "Towards the Retrieval of the Feminine from the Archives of Islam." *International Journal of Zizek Studies* 6, no. 2 (2012): 1–25.

Trible, Phyllis, and Letty M. Russell, eds. *Hagar, Sarah, and Their Children: Jewish, Christian, and Muslim Perspectives*. Louisville, KY: Westminster John Knox Press, 2006.

Urban, Elizabeth. "Hagar and Mariya: Early Islamic Models of Slave Motherhood." In *Concubines and Courtesans: Women and Slavery in Islamic History*, edited by Matthew Gordon and Kathryn Hain, 225–43. New York: Oxford University Press, 2017.

Versteegh, C. H. M. *Arabic Grammar and Qur'ānic Exegesis in Early Islam*. Leiden: Brill, 1993.

Wadud, Amina. *Inside the Gender Jihad: Women's Reform in Islam*. Oxford: Oneworld Publications, 2006.

Wadud, Amina. *Qur'an and Woman: Rereading the Sacred Text from a Woman's Perspective*. New York: Oxford University Press, 1999.

Walker, Ashley Manjarrex, and Michael A. Sells. "The Wiles of Women and Performative Intertextuality: Aisha, the Hadith of the Slander, and the Surah of Yusuf." *Journal of Arabic Literature* 30, no. 1 (1999): 55–77.

Walker, Carol M. "David and the Single Ewe Lamb: Tracking Conversation between Two Texts (2 Samuel 12:3 and Q 38:23) When They Are Read in Their Canonical Contexts." In *Reading the Bible in Islamic Context: Qur'anic Conversations*, edited by Daniel J. Crowther, Shirin Shafaie, Ida Glaser, and Shabbir Akhtar, 77–87. Routledge Reading the Bible in Islamic Context Series. New York: Routledge, 2018.

Webb, Gisela. "Angels." In *Encyclopaedia of the Qur'ān*, edited by Jane Dammen McAuliffe, 1:84–92. Leiden: Brill, 2001–6.

Wheeler, Brannon M. "Arab Prophets of the Qur'an and Bible." *Journal of Qur'anic Studies* 8, no. 2 (2006): 24–57.

Wheeler, Brannon M. *Mecca and Eden: Ritual, Relics, and Territory in Islam*. Chicago: University of Chicago Press, 2006.

Wheeler, Brannon M. *Moses in the Qur'an and Islamic Exegesis*. RoutledgeCurzon Studies in the Quran. Abingdon, UK: RoutledgeCurzon, 2002.

Wild, Stefan, ed. *The Qur'an as Text*. Islamic Philosophy, Theology, and Science. Leiden: Brill, 1997.

Wright, Peter Matthews. "The Qur'anic David." In *Constructs of Prophecy in the Former and Latter Prophets and in Other Texts*, edited by Lester L. Grabbe and Martii Nissinen, 187–96. Atlanta, GA: Society of Biblical Literature, 2011.

Vaid, Mobeen. "'And the Male Is Not like the Female': Sunni Islam and Gender Nonconformity." *Muslim Matters* (July 24, 2017). Online: https://muslimmatters.org/2017/07/24/and-the-male-is-not-like-the-female-sunni-islam-and-gender-nonconformity/.

Zadeh, Travis. "Persian Qurʾanic Networks, Modernity, and the Writings of 'an Iranian Lady', Nusrat Amin Khanum (d. 1983)." In *The Qurʾan and Its Readers Worldwide: Contemporary Commentaries and Translations*, edited by Suha Taji-Farouki, 275–323. Qur'anic Studies Series. Oxford: Institute of Ismaili Studies and Oxford University Press, 2015.

Zadeh, Travis. "Quranic Studies and the Literary Turn." *Journal of the American Oriental Society* 135, no. 2 (2015): 329–43.

Zahniser, A. H. Mathias. "The Word of God and the Apostleship of ʿĪsā: A Narrative Analysis of Āl ʿImrān (3):33–62." *Journal of Semitic Studies* 37 (1991): 77–112.

Zaki, Mona. "The Depiction of Hell in Medieval Islamic Thought." PhD dissertation, Princeton University, 2015.

Zebiri, Kate. "Towards a Rhetorical Criticism of the Qur'an." *Journal of Qur'anic Studies* 5, no. 2 (2003): 95–120.

# Index of People and Places

# Index of Qur'an Citations

# Index of Subjects and Terms